SCHOOLING THE NEXT GEN...

Creating Success in Urban Eleme...

Public schools are among the most important institutions in North American communities, especially in disadvantaged urban neighbourhoods. At their best, they enable students to overcome challenges like poverty by providing vital literacy and numeracy skills. At their worst, they condemn students to failure, both economically and in terms of preparing them to be active participants in a democratic society.

In *Schooling the Next Generation*, Dan Zuberi documents the challenges facing ten East Vancouver elementary schools in diverse lower-income communities and explores the ways their principals, teachers, and parents are overcoming these challenges. Zuberi identifies the kinds of school and community programs that are making a difference and could be replicated in other jurisdictions. At the same time, he calls into question the assumptions behind a standardized test score–driven search for "successful schools." Focusing on early literacy and numeracy skills mastery, *Schooling the Next Generation* presents a slate of policy recommendations to help students in urban elementary schools achieve their full potential.

DAN ZUBERI is an associate professor and RBC Chair in the Factor-Inwentash Faculty of Social Work and the School of Public Policy and Governance at the University of Toronto.

DAN ZUBERI

Schooling the Next Generation

Creating Success in Urban Elementary Schools

UNIVERSITY OF TORONTO PRESS
Toronto   Buffalo   London

ISBN 978-1-4426-4949-1 (cloth)
ISBN 978-1-4426-2684-3 (paper)

♾

Printed on acid-free, 100% post-consumer recycled paper with vegetable-based inks.

Library and Archives Canada Cataloguing in Publication

Zuberi, Dan, author
Schooling the next generation : creating success in urban elementary
schools / Dan Zuberi.

Includes bibliographical references and index.
ISBN 978-1-4426-4949-1 (bound). – ISBN 978-1-4426-2684-3 (pbk.)

1. Education, Urban – British Columbia – Vancouver.   2. Urban
schools – British Columbia – Vancouver.   I. Title.

LC5134.3.V35Z82 2015   372.9173'20971133   C2015-901758-0

University of Toronto Press acknowledges the financial assistance to its
publishing program of the Canada Council for the Arts and the Ontario
Arts Council, an agency of the Government of Ontario.

 **Canada Council   Conseil des Arts
for the Arts   du Canada**

 ONTARIO ARTS COUNCIL
CONSEIL DES ARTS DE L'ONTARIO
an Ontario government agency
un organisme du gouvernement de l'Ontario

University of Toronto Press acknowledges the financial support of the
Government of Canada through the Canada Book Fund for its publishing
activities.

Contents

Acknowledgments   vii

1 Introduction: Urban Education in a Globalizing World   3

2 Diversity in the Classroom: Opportunities and Challenges   24

3 Coping with Challenging Students   62

4 Engaging Parents and the Community   90

5 Addressing Needs and Supporting Resiliency: Programs That Matter   117

6 Standardized Testing: Here to Stay?   150

7 Conclusion: Improving Early Literacy and Numeracy Skills Acquisition in Urban Schools in Low-Income Neighbourhoods   172

Methodology Appendix: Sitting in the Classroom: Determining School Success   193

Notes   207

References   249

Index   265

This book is dedicated to the memory of my father,
Mohammad I.H. Zuberi,
who strongly believed in the value of education.

Acknowledgments

I owe a debt of gratitude to many for their assistance, advice, and support during the research, writing, and publication of this book.

While I cannot name them in order to protect their identity, I would first like to thank the school administrators, teachers, and parents who took their valuable time to talk to members of my research team and I about their ideas and experiences in urban education. Their tireless work and advocacy are inspiring.

The late Clyde Hertzman supported this research with a CIFAR-funded postdoctoral fellowship and helped brainstorm the research design. He also introduced me to Val Overgaard, past-director of research at the Vancouver School Board, who facilitated access and ethics approval for the project.

My interest in urban educational inequality stretches back to my undergraduate studies and honours thesis at The Johns Hopkins University and my masters thesis at the University of Oxford. I thank my former advisors, Patricia Fernandez-Kelly and George Smith, for their advice and support. Professors Karl Alexander, Michael Noble, and Duncan Gallie also provided invaluable insights and resources at early stages of this research. I learned from the mentorship of Professors Katherine S. Newman, Mary C. Waters, William Julius Wilson, and Jeffrey Reitz, and I thank them for their ongoing support. I also thank Neil Guppy, Charles Hirschmann, Michèle Lamont, Christopher Jencks, David Hulchanski, Frank Furstenberg, Ito Peng, Andre Sorenson, Irene Bloemraad, Emily Paradis, John Myles, Kathryn Edin, Mario Small, Faye Mishna, and Mark Stabile. I also thank Pamela Metz and Helen Clayton.

Over the course of the research and writing, I was fortunate to have several institutional homes, including the Human Early Learning

Partnership research network and the Department of Sociology at the University of British Columbia; the Department of Sociology at the University of California, Berkeley; the Weatherhead Center for International Affairs and the Department of Sociology at Harvard University; and the Factor-Inwentash Faculty of Social Work and the School of Public Policy & Governance at the University of Toronto.

Grant funding for this research study was provided by the Social Sciences and Humanities Research Council of Canada, and I also acknowledge the support of the Canadian Institutes of Health Research New Investigator Salary Award, the University of Toronto's Connaught Foundation grant, and Royal Bank of Canada Chair for this research.

I want to thank the following research assistants who made important contributions to the fieldwork and data analysis of this book: Charlene Warrington, Siobhan Ashe, Tamara Ibrahim, and Melita Ptashnick. I also thank Tara Neufeld for her excellent transcription services. I thank the anonymous reviewers whose feedback inspired revisions that have improved the manuscript.

I thank editor Douglas Hildebrand at the University of Toronto Press for his support and guidance as well as Mary Newberry for her valuable editorial advice.

I thank the following colleagues and friends who have been a source of great conversation over the years: James R. Dunn, Phil Oreopoulos, and Arjumand Siddiqi. I also thank Wendy Roth, Ian Tietjen, Alan Jacobs, Antje Ellermann, Tamara Smyth, Tommy Babin, Jeremy Weinstein, Rachel Gibson, Shyon Baumann, Peter Moskos, Anand and Shilpa Das, Molly and Ty Sterkel, Joel Kamnitzer, Hannah Wachs, David Pinto-Duschinsky, Jeremey Ledbetter, Eliana Cuevas, and Joiwind and Amit Ronen for their friendship and support. I also thank extended family, including Cam Robinson, Michelle Robinson, Charles Lepoutre, Leslie Robinson, and Toni and David Owen.

I appreciate the support of my sisters and their families: Anita Zuberi and her husband, Steve Chase, and Sofia Thorell and her husband, Jakob Thorell.

My father, Mo Zuberi, has long believed that education is the key to success, especially for immigrants to the United States, and I appreciate this commitment throughout our lives. My mother, Lilly Zuberi, has always provided so much love and kindness.

I thank my spouse, Joanna Robinson, for her unwavering belief in me and this book, and for the wonderful life we share. I also thank my daughters, Saskia and Naomi, for being the light of my life and bringing me so much joy, inspiration, and love.

SCHOOLING THE NEXT GENERATION

Creating Success in Urban Elementary Schools

1 Introduction: Urban Education in a Globalizing World

This book and the research behind it are based on a premise that all children can learn and that strong academic achievement is possible for all schools.[1] Across advanced industrialized countries, traditional measures of academic achievement continue to correlate strongly with the income and wealth of a student's family.[2] Students from low-income families attending schools with many peers from low-income families often perform even worse academically, struggling from the early grades, falling further behind in subsequent grades, and culminating with high withdrawal and drop-out rates in later years.[3]

This book examines the unique challenges faced by urban schools in lower-income communities. While it explores challenges, it also focuses on success: the research undertaken aims to identify the kinds of school and community programs that are making a difference and could be replicated in other schools.[4] This book aims to mobilize change to improve the future opportunities of visible minority children. In addition to the more typical aggregation of statistics and quantitative program evaluations, the book draws on the perspectives of principals, teachers, parents, and community advocates, and relates stories about how programs are working on the ground.

My Determinants of School Success Study involved extensive field research at 10 East Vancouver elementary schools in a number of diverse lower-income communities. The interview data provide insights into the challenges facing urban elementary schools and their role within the broader community and social system in cities across Canada, the United States, Europe, and beyond.[5] With the growing diversity of post-industrial cities, urban education is increasingly about educating and socializing youth from a wide range of backgrounds and experiences – be they refugee children or the urban elite. Schools play a key role in promoting resiliency and in improving health outcomes among children in the urban context, helping to counteract the negative effects of a growing economic inequality.

Public schools are the most important institution in North American communities. In disadvantaged urban neighbourhoods, they play an especially central role. At their best, they construct equality of opportunity, enabling students to overcome challenges, such as poverty, by providing a foundation of critically important basic literacy and numeracy skills. At their worst, public schools condemn students to failure, not only economically but also in terms of preparing them to be active participants in a democratic society.

In his classic book *Savage Inequalities*, Jonathan Kozol presents readers with the harsh and shocking reality of poverty-stricken inner-city schools in the United States. One iconic image is of a young African American boy riding his bike on a desiccated riverbed in East St. Louis, an area so rife with pollution from a nearby factory that the friction from the boy's back tire occasionally ignites fireball trails. Elementary schools in this region are forced to close when toxic sludge periodically floods into the buildings' basements. In many cities in the United States, the public schools for the minority poor lack the basics, including decent library books and even rudimentary supplies. School buildings are often falling apart, with gaping holes in classroom walls and ceilings, and even broken windows.[6]

Kozol contrasts these urban schools with the public schools of the wealthy, who in their suburban enclaves often pay a similar or *lower* percentage rate of property taxes, yet whose children's public schools receive more than twice the amount of per-pupil resources. Some of these children attend school on "campuses" equipped with the latest computer technology and science labs. These suburban public schools attract and retain stellar teachers and graduate virtually all of their students, with most of them going on to higher education (and not a small minority to elite universities).[7] Kozol decries the inequities of the US system of school funding, which he argues is akin to breaking the legs of urban poor minority students before the starting gate in the race for society's rewards, including the opportunity for higher education, good jobs, and income.[8]

American public schools remain extremely segregated by race, even decades after the famous US Supreme Court decision in *Brown v. Board of Education*. Education professor Gary Orfield has spent his career fighting for integration, yet his research has largely shown this to be a losing battle. Indeed, with the outmigration of middle-class African Americans into suburbs after the victories of the Civil Rights era, public schools are more segregated by socio-economic class than ever before, with urban school districts primarily serving lower-income minority students.[9] Just how serious are the learning challenges in US urban elementary schools? According to leading education sociologist Karl Alexander and his co-authors of the book *On the Success of Failure*, "In many high-poverty school systems, retention rates in primary grades approach 50%."[10] While the United States represents an extreme case among advanced industrialized countries in terms of poverty, inequality, and segregation, increasing polarization is apparent in many Canadian cities and other urban metropolises in the wealthy world.[11]

Globalization has contributed to increasing income inequality and social-spatial polarization. With the well-documented decline of the central city factory and the unionized manufacturing jobs that came with it, many cities have lost their traditional means for incorporating the poor into mainstream society.[12] Instead of addressing this loss with major investments in quality education – a proven approach for improving the opportunities of the poor in a globalized economy – urban education systems continue to be underfunded relative to need, preventing the kind of improvements required to enhance employability and economic competitiveness. The failure to adequately address and improve urban education incurs substantial social and economic costs. For example, in the United States, a high proportion of prisoners had dropped out of poorly funded high schools before their arrests. While the United States spent about $5,000 per individual per year educating poor urban youth in the mid-1990s, the cost to incarcerate one person in prison per year at the time was between $60,000 and $80,000.[13]

Fundamentally, why should scholars and others interested in addressing urban poverty care about schools? Urie Bronfenbrenner's ecological framework for human development is at the root of the answer to this question and is a foundation of the research done for this book.[14] In the model that illustrates Bronfenbrenner's ecological systems theory, children are at the centre of concentric rings that represent factors that impact their future development and opportunities. The first ring is a child's family. Schools represent a meso-level ring on the multiple and interacting levels of factors that have an impact on a child's development. Public schools are one of the most important public institutions in the lives of most children. They represent a critical point of intervention where policy reforms can make a difference and help children thrive. Schools play a key role in promoting resiliency among children in the urban context, with the potential to counteract the negative effects of growing economic inequality.

Beyond the individual level, the failure of a significant percentage of the labour force to master basic literacy and math skills at an early age causes direct and residual costs to economic productivity.[15] For example, according to Robert Reich in *The Work of Nations*, US businesses spend in excess of $25 billion a year in remedial education for their employees.[16] Beyond dollars and cents, the negative consequences of the educational system's failures are lifelong and severe, impacting the economic opportunities, economic security, and well-being of wider society, as well as the vibrancy of democracy.

Too many urban elementary schools struggle to provide a strong foundation in basic literacy, numeracy, and writing skills. Jonathan Kozol argues that in the United States today, "it is the same old ballgame, with Hispanic students and now many Southeast Asian students of low-income placed in very much the same position in which black kids have been forced to play for well over 100 years, and are still forced to play."[17] New immigrants and non-white second- and third-generation immigrant youths from impoverished families have joined African Americans in being segregated into America's worst urban public schools.

The United States is not alone in facing the challenge of education in lower-income urban communities. As a result of global mass migrations, cities in Canada, Australia, New Zealand, and Europe are also experiencing growing diversity in urban schools.[18] In the past 30 years, the global flow of people into the major metropolises of these countries has transformed their urban schools during a period when their economies have also undergone a dramatic transformation away from manufacturing and towards the service sector. The children of visible minority immigrants bring challenges to many urban schools, resulting in the need for new resources.[19] This group includes the children of newcomers as well as second- and third-generation children. The new multicultural urban school is still segregated, but it is more diverse in terms of the experiences and backgrounds of visible minority students.

How does urban education research fit in with the broader debates about social inequality and urban poverty? Internationally, publicly funded urban schools are educating increasingly diverse student populations. They are the most important public institution for socializing youth, not only preparing them to enter the labour market but also imparting to them the critical skills essential for their participation in a democratic society. As sociologist Stanley Aronowitz argues, "The public school is charged with the task of preparing children and youth for their dual responsibilities to the social order: citizenship, and perhaps its primary task, learning to labour."[20]

Neoliberal ideology, technological change, and internationalization have contributed to a growing concern about educational equity, quality, and achievement. The failure to effectively educate visible minority youth is simultaneously a social justice issue and an economic issue, with individual and national level consequences.[21]

In our globalizing era – where technological advances have reorganized production and migration – basic literacy and numeracy skills provide an essential foundation for participation in economic and social life, which are the cornerstones of citizenship. As James Coleman points out in his book *Equality and Achievement in Education*, "In elementary schools, the fundamental tools of reading and arithmetic are being learned by all children."[22] Nearly all children between the ages of 5 and 16 years of age are in school across all societies, thus making schooling a universal experience. In fact, as Christopher Jencks points out in his book *Inequality*, people are mandated to spend approximately one-eighth of their lives in school.[23] Many go well beyond that, continuing on to further education. Some, like myself, never leave, turning to careers in teaching and other work within the education system.

The roles of the public school as an institution in society are diverse and often contradictory. On the one hand, public schools – at their best – create a skilled and trained population that not only fosters economic success but also train an educated and engaged citizenry, equipping them with the tools necessary for contributing to healthy and dynamic democratic societies. Ideally, public schools also foster equality of opportunity, which allows for maximizing the creative talent of the population, undermining the barriers created by economic stratification.

At worst, inequalities in public education act to reify and reproduce socio-economic inequality, entrenching class inequalities while providing an illusion of equality of opportunity but only enough training to reproduce the professionals and workers required for the capitalist system.[24] In such a system, schools play the pernicious role of translating structural inequality into lived reality for those in the lower socio-economic classes.[25] At the same time, this critique of education is somewhat limited and one-dimensional. As argued by Henry Giroux in *Schooling and the Struggle for Public Life*: "There is a strong element of truth in the Marxist critique which argues that schools contribute to the reproduction of the status quo, with all its characteristic inequalities; nevertheless, it is simply inaccurate to maintain that schools are merely agencies of domination and reproduction."[26]

As a near-universal institution, public schools educate children from all social classes and ethnicities. Except for fees for field trips and sports programs, they generally offer their services for free to all families. Public schools provide the opportunity for those who excel to be recognized and to build the credentials for upward social mobility.

Urban elementary schools play an important role in the community. According to urban sociologist and education scholar Pedro Noguera, "[Urban schools] have the potential to either contribute to the further decline of the quality of life in urban areas or to serve as a viable social asset that can further the development of positive social capital."[27] Ideally, quality education would provide urban poor youth the opportunity to learn to be creative thinkers and attain the skills to succeed in the new post-industrial economy. Successful public schools in lower-income neighbourhoods act to counter disadvantages, and thus they play a critical role in constructing a just, democratic future, especially in a post-industrial society.

Sociological debate is fierce and divided in examining the causes of educational inequality. As James Coleman astutely pointed out in his pivotal *Coleman Report* published in the United States in 1966, research into the equality of educational opportunity must include measures of student outcomes as well as educational inputs.[28] Of course, it remains difficult to compare equity of educational outcomes across schools or systems. The complexity of mediating factors makes it difficult methodologically to isolate the role of causal factors in assessing standardized test scores or graduation rates. That does not mean researchers do not attempt to make these comparisons.

While much research on educational inequality focuses on the issues of school resources, there is some research into the role of factors outside the classroom. Often even before beginning school, children from economically privileged families have already mastered many of the building blocks required for successful reading and for solving math problems. One important research finding has been that, even in the early years, students from socio-economically privileged households learn more when they are *not* in school than do their peers from less wealthy households.[29] According to Karl Alexander and his colleagues, "One particularly compelling study finds that 3-year-olds in professional families have a more extensive working vocabulary than do adults in welfare families!"[30]

Research on children between kindergarten and the first grade found that inequalities in educational achievement and learning between children from different socio-economic backgrounds increase during summer vacations – and these socio-economic effects are non-linear and highest for those in the highest and lowest quintiles.[31] That means that the wealthiest pull ahead the most, and the poorest fall the furthest behind, when these children are *not* in school.

During the school year, socio-economic factors have less of an effect on educational achievement. These findings make sense intuitively. Children from wealthier families who are enrolled in stimulating summer camps and programs, and are taken on vacations or on educational side trips during weekends to museums and plays, continue to learn even when not in school. Those less fortunate economically – whose families are unable to afford camps, trips, and vacations – are more likely to spend their days in front of the television or just hanging out. Sociologists Doris Entwistle and Karl Alexander call this phenomenon the "summer setback," by which children from poor families – black and white – in the United States lose ground educationally every summer.[32] School does indeed act as an equalizing institution, especially in the early years; when children are in classrooms together learning, they are progressing forward together, with the children from lower-income families making equal or greater progress than their more economically privileged counterparts. These scholars conclude that children from poor families benefit the most from school.[33]

While schools reduce some inequalities, certain social inequalities are replicated in the classroom. The greater the cultural capital, the more the training and the experiences of students from privileged backgrounds are rewarded by teachers and administrators.[34] According to American sociologist Annette Lareau, "upper–middle-class parents closely supervise and frequently intervene in their children's learning."[35] The active engagement of parents in their children's education and at their schools bias the educational system in the favour of children from privileged backgrounds.[36] Canadian sociologist Dorothy Smith goes further to argue that schools are a central institution in the "differential allocation of agency."[37] While some students are taught that they belong to groups with voice and power, other students learn that they lack agency.

According to Smith, along with class and ethnicity, gender inequality is also replicated in school settings, through gender groupings and the privileging of male voices and male-preferred activities.[38]

Sociological research has begun to focus on the deleterious consequences of growing inequality in North America and the growing social exclusion of low-income visible minorities. For example, recent immigrant children can experience a lack of comprehension owing to language issues, fragmented schooling, discontinuity between the home and the new country, social isolation, and loneliness. According to immigrant education expert Cristina Igoa, "More than 75 percent of the more than 100 immigrant children I have worked with in the past fifteen years have experienced gaps in their education because of travel, time needed for preparation of exit and entry documents, and moving around in search of a better home."[39] Children of newcomers are not the only ones to experience challenges in school; outcomes can be even worse for some second- and third-generation visible minority immigrant children.[40]

What are some of the root causes of these challenges? Urban schools in lower-income neighbourhoods often do not have adequate resources to successfully educate and meet the needs of their students. While adequate funding does not guarantee quality education, I argue that it remains a prerequisite. In the United States, individual states utilize a complex multi-level funding system that is based on often conflicting notions of local control and equity, and which frequently allocates inadequate funds to educate urban poor students while generously funding less-needy suburban schools attended by primarily middle-class students. As inequalities in wealth have grown among school districts' taxable property wealth per student, and the importance and cost of quality education has increased through the twentieth and early twenty-first centuries, state governments have been required to supply escalating amounts of revenue for public education. The funding systems that have emerged in most states continue to allow local property wealth per student to remain the determining factor of funding levels for schools, despite the fact that nearly half of the funding for public education now comes from state and federal revenue.[41] Indeed, much of the state and federal aid to public schools goes towards schools in wealthy districts. Drastic differences in local taxable property wealth per pupil mean that urban schools have less funding per pupil than in the wealthier surrounding suburbs. The consequences of underfunding of urban school systems in the United States are severe. The more equitable education funding regimes in Canada and the United Kingdom begin to address these fundamental inequalities in school funding, but they still fail to provide enough per-pupil resources for schools attended by disadvantaged or vulnerable students.[42]

Students in high-poverty urban areas face many barriers to advancing up the socio-economic ladder, making it hard for them to reach even the working class or middle class. The underfunding of urban schools in low-income neighbourhoods adds another layer of disadvantage. All too many students leave underfunded urban schools without hope or basic skills, disconnected from the institutions and social networks they need to make use of if they are to succeed in mainstream society. Underfunded urban schools also contribute to the social isolation of the urban poor by incentivizing those with greater resources to move to the suburbs, exacerbating residential segregation and further distancing the urban poor.

When it comes to per-pupil funding levels for education in a metropolitan context, both absolute and relative funding levels are important. Why? On the one hand, schools need a certain level of funding to provide adequate education, as determined by the needs of the students. On the other hand, relative funding levels, within a given region, determine which schools can attract and retain the best teachers – and often the students with the most motivated parents, who will relocate to gain access to strong public schools or avoid poor schools. Even in an increasingly globalized world, after completing their secondary education, students generally compete most directly with others in their own region for admission to local universities or in the labour market.

Research in the 1960s, including the famous *Coleman Report* and Christopher Jencks' *Inequality*, challenged the notion that school resources have a strong influence on student performance, as compared to family background and peer influences.[43] This finding continues to be argued forcefully by education scholar Eric Hanushek. In a 1981 article, he reviews 147 studies on education and concludes that no relationship existed between school resources and student performance because not enough studies demonstrated a significant positive association.[44] At the time, then US Secretary of Education William Bennett explicitly used Hanushek's conclusions to slash federal aid for education during the Reagan administration.[45] Since then, Hanushek's methodology and conclusion have been effectively critiqued and invalidated, due, in part, to his use of inappropriate statistical techniques for the analysis and also because of methodological problems with the underlying studies.[46] Clearly how resources are used is important.[47]

Other research supports the argument that increasing expenditures on education can result in improved outcomes, thereby providing a clear link between educational funding and student achievement.[48] In a study of 2.4 million students in Texas, Harvard education researcher Ronald Ferguson found that school inputs, or funding levels, predict student test scores on reading and math achievement tests, when controlling for a student's individual, family, and community demographics.[49] David Card and Alan Krueger, both economists, also found a systematic positive relationship between school funding and student outcomes.[50] Economists Richard Murnane and Randall Olsen found that higher salaries were important for retaining better teachers.[51]

The consequences of underfunding urban public schools can be severe.[52] In the United States, many schools lack adequate numbers of certified teachers as well as the resources needed to maintain the school's physical infrastructure. Jonathan Kozol describes children in Chicago sitting in classrooms without teachers, and students in the South Bronx attempting to learn to read in the washroom of a closed factory.[53]

Underfunded urban schools educate disproportionate numbers of children who are hungry or ill. They lack the basics: adequate resources, supplies, and staff. Evidence of decaying or decrepit physical infrastructure is rampant: faulty heating and cooling systems, broken toilets, insect and rodent infestations, leaks and mould, and collapsing ceilings and roofs. Underfunded urban schools are unable to create programs to meet the special needs of many of their students, nor are they able to research and experiment with more effective ways of teaching, inspire students to embrace their education, or create positive environments to counter students' family and community disadvantages.

Schools that teach many disadvantaged students (be they economically disadvantaged; disabled; struggling with trauma, addiction, or violence; or lacking native language fluency) require more financial resources to meet students' needs and create conditions in which they can thrive.[54] There is typically a much higher percentage of students with special needs in urban schools than there is in wealthier urban and suburban schools. One extreme illustration is Baltimore city schools, where according to a front-page article in the *Baltimore Sun*, in 1989–90 one out of every six children was diagnosed as hearing-impaired, deaf, speech-impaired, visually handicapped, emotionally disturbed, learning-disabled, or having multiple disabilities.[55] Even more students required special attention as a result of learning challenges caused by their environment. Some children were HIV-positive, while others suffered from the effects of prenatal exposure to malnutrition, stress and/or alcohol and drugs. Many suffered from poverty-related disabilities: undernourishment, lack of proper medical care, poor oral and physical hygiene, neglect, and even exposure to toxins.[56] Children in the Baltimore city school system tested for lead exposure had five times the levels of lead in their blood compared to children in the surrounding Baltimore County school system. Exposure to lead has been found to limit children's brain development and attention span.[57] Many urban poor students also suffer from difficult-to-measure stresses of living in a high-poverty or extreme-high-poverty neighbourhood. These include social isolation, negative peer influences, diminished social and cultural capital, and increased exposure to violence.[58] Although the degree of deprivation is generally less severe, children in low-income neighbourhoods in Canadian cities are more likely to grow up in crowded and/or substandard housing, and with greater exposure to social disorder, violence, and environmental hazards than their more privileged counterparts.[59]

The Importance of Early Academic Achievement

Studies have shown that early academic achievement correlates to positive development outcomes into adulthood. The research literature points to the critical importance of literacy as well as numeracy for social-emotional competence. Both are risk-reducing and protective factors for children. Learning to read by the third grade has been shown to be a critical benchmark of future success, as shown in several US studies.[60] Research suggests that reading at grade level in the first grade is a strong predictor of school and life success.[61] According to education researcher Pauline Lipman, "Acquisition of the knowledge, skills, and forms of literacy that are highly valued in the new economy is critical if students are to have access to higher education and job opportunities that offer a degree of economic security and well-being."[62] Investments made in early childhood education pay large dividends in the long run.[63] The early acquisition of literacy and numeracy skills creates an essential foundation for future learning and achievement.

Given the importance of early literacy and numeracy skills for a student's long-term success, the question then becomes how to teach and foster these skills. Education research has found that having high expectations for educational attainment by all students is important, and these expectations must be supported and sustained by teachers and institutions through students' demonstrable development of new competencies.[64] For politicians, school boards, administrators, and even teachers, the pressing question is, how do you create the conditions, through institutions and policies, to help schools succeed in this critically important task?

Where to Begin?

Urban schools in North America and in many European countries are educating increasingly diverse student populations. Overall, 20% of youth in the United States have parents who were born abroad, and that percentage is rapidly increasing.[65] These populations are mostly concentrated in certain regions, and particularly in cities. According to Statistics Canada data, the immigrant population in 2006 comprised 40% of the general population of metropolitan Vancouver – up from 29% in 1986.[66] That compares to 45.7% in Toronto, 34.7% in Los Angeles, 31.7% in Sydney, and 27.9% in New York City.[67] In New York City public schools, approximately 50% of the children have immigrant parents, with nearly 10% belonging to families who just recently arrived in the United States (within three years).[68] In some cities, such as London, England, the range of student backgrounds comprises what University of Oxford professor Steven Vertovec calls "super-diversity."[69] Not only are immigrants coming from a wider mix of countries of origin, they also differ in terms of immigration status, age, gender, and labour market experience. While immigrants are settling across metropolises, they generally concentrate in specific urban areas and neighbourhoods.[70] In recent years, many suburbs and traditionally non-receiving cities are also attracting new immigrants and refugees.

In developed countries, cities remain the economic drivers in our post-industrialized era. Urban diversity is not only reflected in terms of a mix of immigrants and native-born residents but also in terms of socio-economic status and class. Cities are where the creative class, corporate executives, and "symbolic analysts" live side by side with cleaners, servers, and the homeless.[71] Cities are also the site of interaction between the wealthiest and the poorest members of society, and where their children – the next generation – prepare to inherit and earn their futures. The health and vitality of these democracies is inextricably tied to the health and success of these new citizens.

As we have seen, the research literature suggests that school success is related to a number of factors including availability of resources, curriculum-related factors, parental and community involvement, teacher skills-training opportunities, and leadership from the principal.[72] The literature also points, in particular, to the vital importance of early literacy as well as numeracy and social-emotional competence, as both risk-reducing and resiliency-promoting factors for children.[73]

My research began with the goal of addressing the following questions: First, how are public elementary schools in Vancouver meeting the challenge of educating increasingly diverse student populations, including large percentages of students from immigrant families? Second, what are the policies and programs that could be replicated within other urban schools across other districts to improve the early academic achievement of visible minority children? While the preliminary findings pointed to certain trends, troubling new questions were raised as the study progressed, and I was forced to confront a broader range of issues. The research questions began to evolve over the course of the fieldwork as I found that the original "high-performing/poor-performing school" dichotomy at the heart of my initial research design was deeply problematic. Instead, the research revealed that there are common challenges, opportunities, and responses experienced by urban elementary schools resulting from increasing diversity, resource challenges, and growing economic inequality.

My research involved interviews and observations at 10 elementary schools with statistically similar student populations, according to demographic data and provincial standardized test outcomes.[74] The student populations in these schools have extremely high percentages of children from newcomer families, and a majority of the students are visible minorities. Approximately 20% come from families who are living below the poverty line, and many more are from *near poor* households; these are families who are only one missed paycheque away from serious financial hardship.[75] The schools studied are typical of many urban public schools across Canada and in cities across the United Kingdom, Australia, and the United States. At each elementary school involved in the research, the fieldwork included digitally recorded interviews with principals, teachers, parents, and community liaisons working with the school. With the help of some graduate research assistants, the research at each school also included taking guided tours of the school facilities, observing classrooms in session, sitting in on Parent Advisory Council meetings, and attending other school and neighbourhood events.[76]

Several school-specific factors initially appeared to help explain school outcome differences. In some cases, the presence of special "magnet" type curricular programs – such as specialized art or drama programs – at some schools appeared to make a difference in standardized test score passing rates. For example, Centennial Elementary has a program that provides a specialized curriculum that attracts a more privileged student demographic than that of the surrounding neighbourhood. While the school benefits from hosting this specialized magnet program, the students in the program are segregated from other students within the school for all of their classes. They even hold their own separate annual holiday concert. The existence of a special program and a mainstream program under the same roof creates administrative and other challenges. It also raises the question of whether the local children who are not enrolled in the magnet program acquire any benefit from its presence in their school.

In the cases of the other elementary schools studied, it also initially appeared that the depth and severity of the poverty in the neighbourhood surrounding the school mattered as much as the overall poverty rate. Take Lakeview Elementary, for example. It is located near a public housing project in Vancouver, and although the overall neighbourhood is gentrifying and becoming wealthier, 90 of the 300 students at the school came from this housing project. Many of these students face multiple risk factors – including growing up in extremely low-income households and the associated deprivation caused by very meagre public assistance benefits. Many of the children living in the housing project are also recently arrived refugees struggling with experiences of loss and trauma. Hence the student population at this school appeared to be different in important ways – with a higher percentage of children from very low-income and refugee families – than those of other elementary schools studied.[77] The interviews and observation data revealed that beyond the basic statistics, unique characteristics helped shape the actual demographics of the student populations in ways that seemed associated with the overall test score outcomes for each school studied. At the same time, it also quickly became apparent in the interviews that resources also clearly matter.

Lakeview Elementary is a particularly interesting case as it has recently experienced a change in leadership and received an "Inner City" designation, which dramatically increased the school's financial resources. Through Vancouver's innovative Inner City Schools Project, schools in British Columbia that have a certain percentage of low-income families in their catchment area are identified as an Inner City school. The program then provides extra resources, such as funding for resource teachers who assist in classrooms or work one-on-one with at-risk students.

Before her school's designation as an Inner City school, first-grade teacher Sarah Williams described the resource crunch at Lakeview Elementary as such: "It was awful the last couple years, not having money for anything. I mean, we didn't really go on fieldtrips ... We ran out of photocopying paper ... That and glue sticks. I mean, you don't think anything of it, but if you are teaching kindergarten or grade 1, you want glue sticks, right? ... If anyone would do a favour for you, we'd say, 'I'll give you a glue stick' [*laughs*] ... So [we didn't have] even just your very, very basic things. You can imagine: books; paper; glue sticks." When the school received extra resources as a result of its designation as an Inner City school, it was able to hire additional staff, including a "projects teacher."

In the following year, the standardized test score results of Lakeview Elementary showed a dramatic improvement.[78] But the improvements in the school also coincided with the increasing gentrification of the neighbourhoods surrounding the school and with the leadership from a new principal who came from one of the "best" public elementary schools in the region.

At that early stage in my fieldwork, it appeared that the top-performing schools being studied seemed to have only a little extra – computers in all the classrooms and a staffed computer lab, for example – as was the case at Centennial Elementary. Leadership and an atmosphere of success also emerged as important factors. Yet, over the course of the study, the top-performing schools did not always maintain their preeminence when it came to the standardized test score rankings. Dramatic gains suddenly reversed. Other schools caught up; others went up dramatically in reading but not numeracy. A more careful examination of the year-to-year testing data revealed fluctuations in participation rates and, more disturbingly, indicated that the small sample sizes and non-random variations undermined the usefulness and accuracy of the standardized test scores.

Going beyond the scores and into the schools revealed that the standardized test scores were often telling us more about the socio-economic status of the students enrolled in the school than about a school's performance. Although each school faced a unique constellation of issues determined by local conditions, history, and politics, the basic elements or challenges were similar; and many schools were trying similar approaches to meet these challenges. Over time I realized that the similarities between the schools – the approaches that each used to meet the challenges – were more interesting and more important than the differences. It became apparent that administrators, teachers, and parents in all the schools recognized that certain programs and policies were critically important for advancing the mastery of literacy and numeracy skills in elementary schools serving diverse student populations.

The first type of program identified was that which is aimed at satisfying students' *basic needs*. One is the hot lunch program. Teacher Sarah Williams at Lakeview Elementary said: "The hot lunch program is really important ... When I first started teaching ... there wasn't a hot lunch program and it was really hard. I had a grade 1 class ... and I had people stealing kids' lunches. You just can't teach when the kids are hungry, and I've gone through that before. I've had kids come up to me and say, "my tummy's sore," because they are hungry. I think [this program] is really important." This type of program can also include breakfast programs and before- and after-school care. While these programs set the stage for learning, other programs identified in our research were improving academic achievement. These included programs that focused on promoting literacy, providing extra resources for struggling individual students, implementing early childhood development programs and teacher training opportunities, and encouraging community collaboration and engagement. Another important factor was the availability of extra resource teachers to focus on helping children falling behind in reading or math on a one-on-one basis or within small groups. This kind of extra support is also ideal for students learning English as a second language (ESL) and those who are lagging in their social-emotional development.

Early childhood development programs help enable children to start school ready to learn. One example is the Parent-Child Mother Goose Program that is provided nationwide in Canada. In British Columbia the program is part of the larger Ready, Set, Learn program, which reaches out to parents of toddlers in the neighbourhood and provides them with child development insights on topics such as nutrition, creative play, and early learning.

Another kind of initiative that we identified as being beneficial in many schools was the adoption of programs that help schools create a pro-learning environment. Social-emotional competence programs such as these foster tolerance and pro-social behaviour in highly diverse environments. According to the principal of Arthur Lang Elementary, Jeffrey McAdam, these kinds of programs make an important difference: "The tone of the school, as you can notice once you walk in, is a very positive one. The children walk in and say hello. So, in [overall] terms, I've never been a part of a school that is any better than this. It is head and shoulders above a lot of situations. This is as good as it gets in a school. This is a wonderful school." Roots of Empathy is one remarkable example of a social-emotional competence program whereby a classroom of early elementary school students "adopt" a newborn baby from their community. Over the course of the school year, students get to observe and become engaged around infant development in real time. In this way the program holds their attention and imparts to them valuable lessons.[79] This successful Canadian program has now gone global and is being used in classrooms in many countries.

In the end, my research did not uncover a magic formula or silver bullet that can be used to promote early literacy and numeracy skill acquisition for all students in all urban schools. But I did discover important preconditions (such as resources), programs, and policies that make a difference. My research also makes it clear that there are many different trajectories to success – and to failure.[80] Some of the most important findings have to do with the complexity of influences affecting each school, which becomes evident when one enters the schoolhouse door and looks beyond statistics. As many teachers, administrators, and education scholars know, each school has its own history and politics and is impacted by many factors outside of its control, from government-mandated curriculum and funding levels to the state of the larger economy and the nature of the school's community.[81] The world does not stop at the schoolhouse door; every day, a school is involved in an intricate dance with the community in which it is embedded.

Overview

The next chapter presents a discussion of the trends and dynamics of diversity in the 10 East Vancouver elementary schools studied. It uses the experiences of these schools as a lens to examine the complexity and reality of new challenges facing urban public schools across North America and Europe. The chapter goes beyond positive rhetoric around multiculturalism and diversity to describe some of the specific associated challenges for urban schools in terms of poverty, crime, high turnover, and high percentages of ESL students.

Chapter 3 describes one of the most difficult issues facing urban public schools: how to cope with challenging students. In my research many teachers, administrators, and parents described the disproportionately large amount of energy required to handle such students. These students usually face several interrelated obstacles to learning, and also unfortunately tend to disrupt the learning of other students. These are the students whom many private and experimental charter schools tend to exclude or expel. Yet like all children, these children can learn if schools are given the resources to identify and address the underlying issues and are allowed to adopt the right balance of individual support and integration into mainstream classrooms. The category of "challenging students" used here is intentionally broad. It includes students who come to school hungry; those with behavioural, attention-related, and absenteeism issues; those with medical conditions that make it more difficult for them to learn; as well as those with a lack of English-language fluency.

Chapter 4 describes how these urban elementary schools engage parents and the broader community in the school. Education researchers have increasingly recognized the value of engaging parents in their children's education and in the school. Though parental involvement is the norm in most public schools serving wealthier student populations, urban public schools in lower-income communities face greater challenges with getting parents involved. There are language and cultural barriers as well as misconceptions and mistrust. There are social class issues at play. Working-poor parents frequently lack the time to visit the school, attend parent-teacher conferences, or take part in Parent Advisory Council meetings. At times cultural differences can create tensions between parents and school staff.

Administrators and teachers at the urban elementary schools studied report relying on a small number of enthusiastic parents who act as volunteers and contribute a great deal of time and energy to the school. These volunteers, while small in number, contribute valuable resources and services. Administrators and teachers acknowledge they have a long way to go in terms of building from these core groups of volunteers to create broader engagement and connections to other parents. They describe facing serious challenges in engaging parents in their children's education and schools. Some have turned to creative solutions, such as coffee clubs, to better reach out to and engage parents.

Given the challenges facing many of the students, the schools cannot alone meet such needs. They are greatly helped by the existence of partnerships with local community institutions, such as community centres. These institutions help provide important before- and after-school care, as well as affordable programming for students during the summer months.

Chapter 5 outlines some of the programs that teachers, administrators, and parents describe as critically important for early learning at their schools. Many of these programs involve providing resources to meet the needs of students. One of the most important programs is Vancouver's Inner City Schools Project, which provides extra staff and other resources to schools in poor neighbourhoods. These schools also receive additional support and resources from the broader Vancouver community, sometimes even from other elementary schools on the wealthier west side of the city. Most importantly, these kinds of programs allow for schools to have resource teachers who can work one-on-one or in small groups with children who are falling behind or have behavioural issues.

Unfortunately, as gentrification has changed the statistics in some of these neighbourhoods, some schools have recently lost their Inner City designation and therefore the critical resources the program provides, even though they are still facing many of the same challenges. Also, the amount of extra funding for Inner City–designated schools has declined, reducing the effectiveness of the program. Budget and resource cuts have also affected other essential programs at many of these schools. Shockingly, school libraries are only open a few days a week or part-time at some of them, and in some cases art and music programs have been cut. Some school district level programs that provided critical resources for ESL students were cut, although thankfully they've since been restored.

Resources matter a great deal in terms of these schools being able to deal effectively with the challenges that act as barriers to learning for these students. In some cases, corporate or private programs have helped address some of these needs, from providing much-needed free breakfast programs to mentoring students. In other cases, partnerships with non-profits and community organizations have made a difference by providing exciting learning engagement opportunities and child-care programs during non-school hours.

Other kinds of programs were identified as very important. For example, teacher development resources are essential, as they address the need for a greater focus on teaching to diverse classrooms in schools, allowing more resources and time for teachers to learn and develop teaching methods that are effective in helping students achieve early mastery of literacy and numeracy skills. Social and emotional development programs were also extolled as being extremely important for creating fertile learning environments in diverse classrooms and schools. Programs that help students begin school ready to learn were also identified as important. These include some based at the school, including full-day kindergarten and the Parent-Child Mother Goose Program, which address the need for more early childhood education programs. Chapter 5 also describes the mixed effects of magnet-type special programs, from French immersion to the Arts, at some elementary schools.

Standardized testing has emerged as an important and hotly contested issue, and Chapter 6 looks at a number of the discussions surrounding it. How effective is standardized testing in reflecting actual early academic achievement, and what exactly are the tests measuring? Do they reflect the student population, or do teachers, students, and parents learn to work around the tests in ways that have nothing to do with students' success? This chapter ends with a discussion of some of the problems with the current standardized testing regime, both in general and specifically in the province of British Columbia. It provides recommendations for reforming the current testing regime with the goal of working collaboratively with educators to generate and use data to actually improve student learning and outcomes.

Chapter 7, the final chapter, continues with a broader discussion of policy recommendations for improving early education in urban public elementary schools. The chapter provides a series of recommended reforms to improve educational outcomes and greater equality of opportunity, such as providing more resources for urban public schools from governments at all levels. The policy discussion concludes with a description of some non–education-specific policies that would improve urban education, including policies to reduce poverty, inequality, and hardship among the urban poor. These are policies that would help improve the quality of life of families, which would effectively reduce the challenges facing these schools so that teachers could focus on effectively teaching children to read, write, and do math while also imparting a love of learning.

The book concludes by summarizing the main findings of my research and explaining its applicability to broader theories and debates, including segmented assimilation of immigrant communities and social inequality. It examines the school as an institution that both challenges and reifies equality of opportunity.

In the appendix, I describe in detail the methodological design of the research, and I reflect on processes and the evolution of the research and data analysis used over the course of the study.

The importance of public schools in a globalizing world is hard to exaggerate. New immigrants are arriving to post-industrial cities in North America and Europe, where the economies are now dominated by the service sector. Some challenges facing urban public schools emerge from increasing diversity. Others emerge from growing poverty, as many countries experience increases in inequality and social exclusion. Many urban neighbourhoods are undergoing transformations such as gentrification and decline. At the same time, urban public schools located in lower-income communities play a more important role than ever before in shaping the future of the children they educate.

There are far fewer living-wage, secure jobs available to those without strong basic literacy and numeracy skills. We know that those students who do not complete high school have been the most hurt by deindustrialization. This group is facing enormous challenges securing decent employment, and in the United States they also experienced an astronomical rise in incarceration rates over the past several decades.[82] Many high school graduates are finding that their diploma is no longer enough. These macro-economic trends are projected to continue with the accelerated decline of manufacturing. More than ever, inequalities in public education undermine equality of opportunity. How many potential geniuses who could make a valuable contribution to humanity are lost? What are the consequences of educational inequality for a vibrant democracy and healthy economy?

2 Diversity in the Classroom: Opportunities and Challenges

When we hear about "diverse schools," our thoughts might turn to a playground scene: a picture of glee-filled young children from different backgrounds running around and playing together on hopscotch courts, swings, and slides. Or perhaps we envision a sun-drenched classroom – with students from India, Africa, Asia, Eastern Europe, and Canada – working studiously side-by-side in neat rows of desks. For many of us, these images of diverse schools are imbued with hope and promise.

Yet what does diversity really mean in urban schools, beyond the superficial images and statistics? What does it really look and feel like? What does diversity actually mean for the principals, the teachers in the classrooms, the students? In terms of practice, approaches, issues? What kinds of diversity matter, and what kinds create opportunities or require special resources? We often think about ethnicity; yet the greater opportunities and challenges may emerge from diversity of social class and even English language fluency.

The student populations of the urban elementary schools in East Vancouver are all highly diverse. The students at these schools come from a diverse mix of families, many of which are working class and lower middle class. Kerry Reynolds, a project teacher and literacy coach at Wellington Elementary described the student body as: "Ethnically diverse. The students come from all sorts of backgrounds. We've got students living in poverty, we have First Nation students. We have children who have just come from war-torn countries. We have students from all over the world. I think we have 32 different languages spoken at our school." Like many of the workplaces in post-industrial cities, the students at these schools include a mix of backgrounds and ethnicities.

Some are recent immigrants. Others are second- or third-generation Canadians, many of whose families still celebrate and maintain ties to their countries of origin or are tightly embedded in Vancouver's ethnic communities and institutions. Others are recently arrived refugees.

As in most cities in North America and Europe – perhaps with the exception of a few super-diverse metropolises such as London – several "sending" countries comprise the largest groups, reflecting the immigration patterns of nearby neighbourhoods and the city as a whole. This combination of high diversity with certain groups being predominant was common. Many people discussed the student populations of their urban schools in these terms. Amy Peterson, a teacher at Ashfield Elementary, described the student body as including children from countries around the world: "Most of our students are from Asian populations. We get lots from China, Taiwan, Hong Kong, the Philippines; most of them are from there. We do have some African children, and some from Central America, so we have Spanish-speaking [children] as well, and some [are] from different parts of India." Majority minority schools are now common in urban centres across Canada, the United States, and even in some European countries. At Wellington Elementary, teacher Kerry Reynolds shared that at her school, the three largest groups of students come from Vietnam, the Philippines, and China. She said, "Most students come from those countries. But also Romania, Afghanistan, Iran. And we have children from Bangladesh, and all over."

Rather than being dominated by one ethnic enclave or group, schools in East Vancouver host a diverse mix of immigrant, refugee, second-generation, and native-born Canadian students. According to Principal Tim Richards, the Great Forest Elementary student body is: "Hugely diverse. There's not one predominant ethnic background. There isn't one large group. We have quite a few Indo-Canadian families, quite a few Filipino families, quite a few Chinese and a wide variety of ethnic backgrounds outside of those. But we're not predominantly Chinese, Indo-Canadian, Vietnamese, or any other. It's a good mix of kids. It's fairly low with Caucasian kids, probably only 10% to 12%." Each of the schools studied shared a similar mix of students from around the world, with larger representations of certain groups in specific schools, reflecting geographical patterns of settlement.

In these schools, visible minority students comprise the majority of the student populations. Some schools had more students from the Philippines and others, a greater number from Vietnam or China. It is important to keep in mind that each of these groups feature not only internal variation, but also group-level differences in immigration experiences, reception, and resources. For example, the Chinese have a long history of migration to Vancouver and North America generally, stretching back to the late 1800s.[1] Within the ethnic Chinese population in Vancouver, however, there are systemic differences in terms of wealth and socio-economic class, from the wealthy Hong Kong expatriates to mainland Chinese immigrants from rural and rapidly industrializing regions of their home country. And many people who immigrated to Vancouver from China in the 1980s and 1990s have now managed to find a secure foothold in middle-class Canadian life and own single-family homes, which have enjoyed tremendous growth in property values in East Vancouver and other parts of the region.

Due to this same rapid inflation of real estate prices, newcomers arriving in Vancouver today face much greater challenges in terms of saving up to purchase homes as compared to immigrants who arrived a few decades ago. The history of immigration by the Vietnamese, overall, is shorter than that of the Chinese population. Most came to Vancouver as refugees or as "boat people" in the 1980s. Before arriving, many Vietnamese children spent time in refugee camps and, as a result, face greater challenges; some are traumatized and many live in households that struggle to make ends meet, and/or they live in social housing projects.

There are also differences between recent immigrant and refugee families as compared to more settled families who migrated in the 1980s and 1990s, and the second- and third-generation children of immigrants to Canada. Principal Jennifer Newcastle of East Harcourt Elementary pointed to this diversity in her description of her school's demographics: "We've got many different cultural groups represented here. Certainly some from India, Fiji; the Philippines would be our third largest group. But Chinese is certainly our first. Many of those children were born here. But even though they were born here, they come to school not speaking English because their families speak to them in Mandarin at home, wanting them to continue to learn and understand their first language, which we think is a very good thing and we support that completely." So even though some of these schools are teaching second- and third-generation immigrants, some students have grown up in ethnic enclaves within the city and begin formal schooling without strong English language fluency.

In some ways, East Vancouver elementary schools appear to be approaching super-diversity.[2] Denise Wallace, a mother of a New Lake Elementary student, reported, "I'd say we're 50% to 60% Asian with a high Vietnamese population. We are maybe 30% Indo-Canadian and the rest is just a melting pot. My son is one of three Caucasians. I mean, my son is not even full Caucasian, but he looks Caucasian. My son's one of three Caucasians of 29." She explained that while some of the ethnic minority students were born in Canada, many still struggled with English language fluency: "There are some second- and third-generation Indo-Canadians or Asians, but most of them are from other countries. I think we have an ESL percentage of 76% or 79%. Now, part of that is from people who are born here, but they are raised by grandparents and they're grandparents that don't speak English. So it's not that they weren't born here; it's just that they are not used to the English language." In some schools, the majority of students spoke a language other than English at home with parents and grandparents. Of course, children can easily be bilingual and master both English and another language, even more than two languages; yet many of these students begin school without a strong grasp of the English language.[3] Jennifer Newcastle, Principal of East Harcourt Elementary, said: "We have mostly Chinese and Vietnamese here. When the children come in to school at East Harcourt [Elementary], they come in for the most part with English as their second language. So, they're mostly non-English speakers in kindergarten. We have maybe two or three children that are Caucasian, or speak English, and the rest of them *do not* speak English when they arrive." Most of the elementary schools studied had extremely high percentages of ESL students as part of their student population.

In addition to high proportions of immigrant and visible minority students, these elementary schools also teach many students of Aboriginal origin. Helen Welsh, a parent of students at Great Forest Elementary, estimated that: "We have over 500 [students] total. I'd say a minimum of 30 to 40 have some Aboriginal descent, so it's fairly high. We actually have an Aboriginal worker at our school, and he does work with them separately … not on ESL, but just [on an] extra help level. But he also works throughout the school promoting Aboriginal art, music; he gives little concerts. So it's there. It's more inclusive learning rather than singling them out." The families of many Aboriginal students in East Vancouver continue to struggle with multigenerational poverty, social exclusion, discrimination, and the legacy of colonization.[4]

Economic Diversity: Students from Low-Income Families

Ethnic and language diversity are not the only common features of East Vancouver elementary school student populations. Many students come from families that are struggling financially. Principal Katherine Drucker of Ashfield Elementary said this her students' families: "I would describe most of them as working poor. A lot of the families have two jobs. Many of the women work in factories and, consequently, on the school grounds you will see grandparents here picking up the children."

Every school studied had a substantial proportion of students from families whose earnings were below that of Canada's poverty line, and many more are earning close to the poverty line.[5] Principal Harriet Drake described the student body at Lakeview Elementary: "It's a mixed cultural/economic/social group. There are some students who come from very low socio-economic groupings, and then some who are middle class." She considered that approximately 40% of the students at the school came from low-income families, saying, "I would say a lot of that is social assistance. There are certainly some working-poor families."

Principal Tim Richards of Great Forest Elementary had this to say about his school's student body demographics: "I know we have a high vulnerability rating relative to all of the measurements. And I would say, working class – many who I might describe as working poor. Then there's sort of a small middle-class component. It's not a wide scale. There [aren't] a lot of people with a lot of money, or even in the upper-end of the spectrum; there [aren't] a lot of people there. There's a group who have fairly nice homes, and their incomes are pretty comfortable, but not very many. Most [are] at the lower end."

Helen Welsh, a parent of two students at Great Forest Elementary, described the student body at her children's school: "We have the kids who are [from] low-income families. Mom and Dad are always at work, [so they] are latchkey kids. They're home alone, and they're not getting the extra help. They're not getting help with their homework, so they're at the low end."

Another parent, Michael Johnson, was even more specific. He has three children currently attending Wellington Elementary and a fourth who recently moved on to secondary school. He says that most of the parents of his children's school friends work "primarily in the service industries. Whether it be hospital workers or janitors. A lot of Filipino home-care or hotel workers." While some schools had a higher percentage of children living in families surviving on public assistance benefits – and these schools tended to be located near larger social housing developments – others had more students from working-poor families, where at least one parent was formally employed but the income earned was not enough to lift the household out of poverty.

Children from low-income families face unique educational challenges due to their family's lack of financial resources. Administrators, teachers, and parents from the schools studied all recognized the effect that poverty has on children and the tremendous burdens placed, particularly, on working-poor families, as both parents often have to work long hours and even multiple jobs simply to make ends meet. Many described the challenges facing working-poor parents. Claire Winslow, an outreach coordinator who works with New Lake Elementary, said,

> Both parents may be working, but that doesn't mean that they are earning wages that are reflective of how many hours they're putting into their jobs. It can be entry-level jobs that they're working that are minimum wage. And so, even [with] two parents working a minimum wage job, when all is said and done – when rent is paid, house bills are paid, their children [have been] fed and clothed, schools supplies and field trips [have been paid for], etcetera – what do they have left in the end? Not much.

According to Winslow, many of her students' families find it a challenge to make ends meet as a result of low incomes: "So these are parents who struggle and are literally [living] paycheque to paycheque. There isn't room for them [financially] to have their children join community programs [or] go on fancy vacations. They're getting by and they're maintaining. Their kids are healthy, their kids are here [in school] and they have food, but they struggle." While some families dealing with scarcity may not be experiencing serious hardships, they don't have the financial resources for extra educational spending and therefore can't buy the kinds of materials and programs that foster early learning. In some households where the parents have trouble making ends meet, the children do not receive adequate food at home, And even when they do, it is generally not the nutritious (and often more expensive) fresh food that promotes healthy child development. Teacher Frank Wallace at New Lake Elementary said,

> The breakfast program and the hot lunch [are] very important because a lot of these kids wouldn't be getting any food otherwise in the morning [or] at lunch. Or they'd be getting really crappy food. You should see

what some kids bring in for snacks, just terrible. Chips. One of the popular things is Ichiban soup, [you know] the noodle soup that's dry? They eat it dry, sprinkle the packet on. It makes me ill. You're supposed to add stuff to it, that's supposed to be the base and you add your vegetables and make a big pot of soup. You don't take it to school, open the package and eat it dry, but they do.

The vacancy rate has declined in Vancouver, which has led to escalating house prices and increasing rents. As a result, some families are reduced to living in basement suites, sometimes illegally. Others are sharing accommodation, which can create learning barriers for children by making it difficult for them to get a good night's sleep or find a quiet place to complete their homework.

Claire Winslow, Outreach Coordinator at New Lake Elementary, described the challenges that rising housing costs have created for the parents of students at her school:

I'm amazed at the exorbitant rent here. There are families [living in] a two-bedroom basement [suite] here that are paying over $900 [per month], just [for] rent. I had a single father with two children [living in] a tiny two-bedroom basement paying $900. I don't how he did it to this day, but that's just a few blocks away from here. There's the facade of the external view of the neighbourhood that's shifting and looking a little nicer. But internally, inside that home, it's still a rental home, and you may have [multiple] families that are renting inside: two sets of families, two or three sets of families in one household. We're finding more and more that two or three families that are related [are] living in one home in order to afford the rent. You have situations where kids are sleeping on mats in the hallway because there aren't enough bedrooms, and/or the living room becomes a bedroom in the evening as well. And so you look beyond the facade of a nice looking house, and you look inside, and what the situation is. It's very different and that's just so they can afford to remain in this area.

Amy Peterson has over 35 years' teaching experience and currently teaches at Ashfield Elementary. She describes the students there as "friendly, outgoing. They're eager to learn, [although] some [are] a little bit more hesitant. They speak English fairly well now. It's changed over the years, but they still have large language gaps. They're just really fun kids to work with." Although based on aggregate Statistics Canada census data, Ashfield Elementary's catchment area appears to have similar levels of poverty as the other schools studied in East Vancouver, it turns out that within the school's geographical area, pockets of very high-poverty neighbourhoods send disproportionate numbers of children to the school. As Peterson explains, "We have two sort of low-income catchment [areas] that feed our school, and one of them has a lot more [drugs and violence] happening. Generally I think the neighbourhood is changing a lot, but there [are] still break-ins, still thefts from cars in the parking lot." As the neighbourhood around the school is gentrifying with wealthier residents moving in, there have been improvements in the area. In Peterson's opinion: "I think it's becoming more of a *real* sort of neighbourhood. People are starting to get to know each other a little bit more, and I think the Grant Williams Neighbourhood House is fantastic at welcoming the families in now. And I think the school's been trying to do that same kind of thing. And, well, the building that's happening; it's all condos now that are worth $500,000 dollars. I mean, it's a different clientele that you're dealing with."

This process of gentrification is occurring across East Vancouver as property values have increased and young families looking for more space have begun purchasing homes in these communities. It's not surprising then, that most elementary schools in the area are not only educating students from low-income households but also those who come from other kinds of economic backgrounds. Parent Helen Welsh, whose children attend Great Forest Elementary, said, "Economically we do have a high percentage of low-income families, but because of the way the real estate market is going and has been in the last, say, three to five years, we also have dentists and lawyers and doctors and [the like]. We kind of [run the gamut], from the lady who cleans at the Hilton to the dental surgeon."

The consequences of gentrification in these communities are complex. Rapidly increasing prices are pushing lower-income families out of the city. The high turnover of households in East Vancouver might not be driven as much by evictions as it is by the phenomenon of lower-income families saving up money to purchase homes in the suburbs, where they can afford larger homes than in the city. Helen Welsh explained, "We do have a high turnover in students, just because there are a lot of rentals in the area. People will start out renting here [to] save up the money and buy. But they can't afford to buy here, so they are buying in Burnaby or Pitt Meadows or Surrey [suburbs of Vancouver] ... In the last few years, we have seen a quick turnaround in students; as well, our numbers go up and down quickly." So while many families can afford to rent in the city, they cannot afford to purchase real estate in the city, and thus they move to the suburbs where homes are more affordable.

Some Challenges of Diversity

The East Vancouver neighbourhoods surrounding the elementary schools studied reflect the diversity and dynamism that is typical of many urban communities across North America and increasingly in Europe. The diversity is exciting, but what does it mean for educating children in these schools? While diversity is cherished and celebrated, it also creates challenges.

Teacher Kerry Reynolds of Wellington Elementary feels that the diversity of her school is a strength. "Our student body is amazing. I learn so much from these kids every day. They are a powerful, strong-willed, challenging at times, bunch of children ... Every different day is something new, it's hard to describe them in one breath, it's almost impossible." She relates a story about a favourite student of hers who started at the school as a recent immigrant:

> We definitely have lots of first-generation [students]. We have children that arrive here who don't speak a word of English. A girl in grade 7 this year came to us last February from Romania, and did not have a word of English. And she is now getting A's in Language Arts. Pretty amazing! And she won some awards this year. She won what we call the Wellington Elementary 'Reach for the Top' award for her excellence in achievement in striving to become better. She was one of my peer leaders. She was involved in everything, and she's just a lovely girl and she didn't speak a word of English a year ago.

Reynolds is proud of Wellington Elementary's success in helping ESL students thrive in reading and math. How did this student achieve such success? According to Reynolds, the credit goes to, "The very, very strong resource team that we have [at Wellington Elementary]. It's composed of four teachers, a couple of them are part-time, but they work directly with the classroom teacher. So instead of having an ESL teacher and an LAC [Learning Assistance Centre] teacher and a resource teacher, [the teacher] has one person. And that one very qualified person supports the classroom however the classroom needs support. So that person is in there every single day and is modifying the curriculum with the teacher. They work very closely like partners to make it work for these kids." Supplemental instructional resources exist at many of the schools studied. They are invaluable in diverse classrooms, as they help to meet the needs of students with special needs while keeping those students included in the mainstream classroom. In addition to the resource team that helped her Romanian student, Reynolds gives credit to the extracurricular activities offered by the school: "Wellington Elementary has so many opportunities for kids to get involved, so she was doing things at lunch hour, she was doing things before school, she was doing things after school – programs and clubs and all sorts of things. It gave her that many more opportunities to practice her language skills." The achievements of these star students during the school year bring great joy and pride to teachers and administrators alike. In addition to the extracurricular activities Reynolds also gives credit to the student herself for her own initiative and to the family for providing a supportive home environment, which Reynolds feels really helps a student overcome learning barriers at school. "She came here with her mother and she has a very supportive extended family. Her mother came on a field trip with us, and things like that."

The story of the Romanian student's success exemplifies some of the many factors that can help ESL children thrive at school by mastering reading and math skills in early elementary education: specialized and trained resource teachers who can provide extra help to students who need it; extracurricular activities that provide the students with opportunities to practice their English with their peers; initiative on the part of the students, so that they seize the available opportunities; and a supportive home environment where parents engage with their children's education and get involved in the school.

It's clear how these things combined can result in a child's success, but in a diverse school all of the factors typically aren't in place for every student. Some kids come from households that are struggling financially, where the parents are too busy working to make ends meet to get involved in the school. Other children are shy or have difficult dispositions that prevent them from fully engaging in the opportunities available. Worse, some children are traumatized from being abused, or they face unacceptably difficult environments at home that interfere with their capacity to learn.

The differing home environments can range from supportive to devastating, and where a child's home falls on this spectrum has a big effect on his or her ability to learn at school. Kerry Reynolds described issues related to home environments as the number one challenge facing Wellington Elementary:

> I think that a challenge for a lot of teachers is that the home lives [of children] can be so chaotic that they bring that "baggage," let's call it, to school. It may just be one family's bad day or bad experience or bad fight or whatever is going on that infiltrates through the classroom. So that kid comes in and he's just "Arrgh! My dad's freaking out on me this morning or we can't pay our rent or –" It's just going to spread through the class, and the teacher has to take so much time to diffuse that situation, which often has affected so many other children just on the way to school or whatever ... So I think that's one of the biggest stumbling blocks for teachers, because that behaviour gets in the way of the learning.

Another teacher at Wellington Elementary, Natalie Courso, spoke about how a lack of family support affects students' success at school, emphasizing the problems of poverty and marginal parenting skills: "From the staff I know in other Inner City schools, it sounds pretty much the same. If you go [to the] home, the parents couldn't care less whether their children are at school or whether they attend school. They're not taught any discipline. If they want to sleep in, sure, no problem. They're not taught to value school or to be on time ... Some of them belong to families [that are] doing "dial a dope," and their dad is dealing in the car every night. When [kids] get to a certain age, they're working in the gang. That's the kind of thing I see that gets in the way."

Courso's insights were echoed by many other teachers and administrators at other schools studied. According to Principal Harriet Drake of Lakeview Elementary, "Another challenge is just some of the behaviours. Sometimes there are kids who come from homes where there's instability, and they bring some of that into the school." While behavioural problems often originate at home, they must be dealt with at school where they interfere with learning in the classroom. For example, an important tool that is used to facilitate reading achievement is an approach called ability grouping, but it requires putting children together from different ages, and that is problematic when some children in the group have behavioural issues. As Wellington Elementary teacher Kerry Reynolds explains:

> As a literacy coach in the school, I meet with the teachers regularly. At the very beginning of the year [I ask them] "Where do you want to go with

your class?" We talk about what teachers had success with in the past, and where they want to go in the future. And I'll say to them, "So what's getting in your way?" "Why do you feel like you weren't able to do that last year?" Nine times out of the ten, [the answer is] behaviour. They say, "Well, I want to do small groups and put kids into ability-level groupings so that I can get the higher kids working together and the lower kids can have more time with me, but I struggle to do that because of behaviour." Or, "I can't work with a small group because the rest of the class cannot work independently." And I think that is because of our inner-city families, these families that are struggling to survive.

When children are left home alone after school at an early age because both parents are working and can't afford after-school childcare expenses, it can lead to a host of negative behaviours and outcomes. The lack of appropriate adult supervision is especially problematic when kids as young as 8, 9 and 10 are left home alone or in the care of siblings, or they are expect to care for the younger children. Statistics reveal high rates of accidents and injuries in these after-school hours before parents get home from work.[6]

More seriously, some children are neglected and socially isolated. Principal Mark Brown of Wellington Elementary stressed that in these cases it's not so much a matter of not caring about being a good parent as it is that many parents do not have a lot of education and/or were themselves victims of violence and marginalized families. These factors can affect children's focus, behaviour, and performance in the classroom. Schools must cope with and address these students' needs in order to create the conditions for them to thrive academically.

Coping with the Street: Creating Safe Spaces for Learning

Urban public schools, particularly those in lower-income neighbourhoods, have unique challenges because of where they are located, requiring the principals and other school staff to work harder to make schools safe oases of learning. Principal Mark Brown described how at Wellington Elementary he periodically must remove vagrants and less desirable people from the halls as they, unsurprisingly, "frighten the children." Removal of vagrants from school hallways is not usually part of the job description for principals at schools in wealthier parts of town. According to Principal Brown, many of the people removed from the school grounds suffer from mental health issues and/or drug and alcohol abuse. He also spoke of having to regularly sweep nearby Applegate Park for needles and used condoms, as sex workers and drug addicts often congregate behind the portable classrooms adjacent to the park and school.

Other principals and school staff noted the encroachment of social problems in the area surrounding their schools. Some of the schools studied were more protected from the spillover of social problems to the school grounds than others. Principal Tim Richards of Great Forest Elementary said this when describing the area around his school:

> I don't know about theft. Drugs and prostitution are an issue up on Key Lane and East Water Street and farther south. There is some prostitution at night along East Water Street. That has not spilled over to the school grounds, as of yet. There have been lots of issues with the people in the neighbourhood that go to this school, farther towards the south, and they've had a lot of drug dealers in there. But it is not translating onto the school grounds. We don't have any evidence of drug paraphernalia or, I guess for want of a better word, sex paraphernalia. There's no evidence. We've had maybe three condoms in five years, and two needles in that same amount of time. We have the odd group of young adults smoking up, smoking what we presume is marijuana. I think we've had two incidents of people coming on [school grounds] to probably do something heavier than that, that I've noticed, but that's in the [last] five years.

Some administrators acknowledged problems in the neighbourhoods or areas near their school but felt that they did not generally affect the school community. For example, Principal Jennifer Newcastle of East Harcourt Elementary said: "We are aware that there have been some drug busts in our community. We know that there are some unsavoury characters around and so on. But we haven't been hugely affected by that in the school. We don't [find] needles or condoms or anything on our playgrounds ... Even though we have quite a protected courtyard and so on, we get partiers on the weekend, but we don't get that activity nightly." Administrators certainly are not the only ones aware of what's going on in the areas around the schools we studied, many parents have concerns too. Based on the feedback we received, there are mixed view of the schools' neighbourhoods. While overall most parents felt safe and many liked where they lived, many had concerns about particular "hot spots" or parts of their community where they felt less safe. One concerned parent is Maria Gomez, who at the time of our study had two children at Wellington Elementary, one in kindergarten and another in grade 5. When asked if she felt safe in their neighbourhood, she said, "No, not really, no." She worries about her kids' safety in school, especially because of nearby Applegate Park. "Yeah it's not very safe," she says, "because very often we see the police here in the next block."

Wellington Elementary parent Michael Johnson also described the school's community as having social problems, including drugs and prostitution: "[There are] a tremendous number of grow ops run by Vietnamese people [who] are just as much victims as anything else. I used to work with NIST, the Neighbourhood Integrated Service Team, and when we had a policing office in the Wellington area. We used to talk about all the different houses. And there were Vietnamese people in some, and they were getting free rent for doing this sort of thing. The gangs aren't really active in that area. They are there, but it's mostly [for the] drug distribution sort of thing and that's about it. And the grow ops."

Johnson describes some of the challenges of raising kids in this neighbourhood: "I can tell you examples that just scare me: [There have been] kids that my children were playing with [who] didn't have a caregiver at home. Or the [caregiver] was Vietnamese and didn't speak English. And the boyfriend of the mother, who was Filipino, and there was horrendous stuff going on. They were going out stealing stuff in stores, and [the kids] just didn't have a person at home who would take care of them properly."

Certain streets or corners near the elementary schools studied are known to be locations where transactions are carried out that have to do with the underground economy, or street trade, which are not typically visible near schools located in wealthier parts of the city.[7] This includes street solicitations for prostitution and drug dealing. Although there is less activity during the day as compared to after dark, the social disorder and crime in these areas does impact the quality of the learning environment for children. Parent Helen Welsh described the area near Great Forest Elementary:

It is really diverse; I mean, on East Water Street we do have problems with drug dealers and drugs, and within three blocks of the school at any time, we do have problems with prostitution. But in the daytime, it's not so bleak. I think we have a really good neighbourhood. We have families who look out for their children out on the street. Just because they're not their own [children] doesn't mean they won't come out if something [is] happening, and make sure everything's ok. On the whole, I'd say it's a really good neighbourhood. But definitely when the lights go dim, it definitely does turn into something different. But during school hours, I don't have any problem with my son being outside on the playground or anything like that.

She added that, generally, "violence is minimal, maybe a few high school fights" and, "Drugs, I wouldn't say during the day. Not during school hours. But definitely in the evenings." Overall, though, she feels, "it is really a safe place for the children, definitely."

While many parents expressed concerns about urban disorder and safety issues, a few spoke of other kinds of problems. For instance, Laura Truelle, a parent of a child at Wellington Elementary, described experiencing some racism in the community: "It's a good community, but it's not healthy ... Yeah, [there are] people that are not, how can I say it? They are sometimes, there's [an attitude] that pertains to your nationality like: "Why are you here?" "You should go back to your country." "You are having too many kids." "You're not working." And they don't know you!"

Other elementary schools are disadvantaged as a result of their location near certain kinds of institutions. Outreach Coordinator Claire Winslow at New Lake Elementary reported that there were several halfway houses near the school, but she was quick to qualify that none contained high-risk pedophiles: "We have a number of transition homes [nearby] for offenders who are being released. There are three transition homes – three second-stage probation homes. [The residents] are considered high-risk offenders but don't carry the so-called determined risk of pedophilia and that sort of thing, although we've had issues. There are three just within this corner block. There's one here on Mountain Avenue and [one on] Chestnut Street, which are probably within, I would say, a three-block radius of the school." Transitions homes, group homes, and social housing tend to be located in lower-income urban neighbourhoods, not in wealthy areas, where residents organize to prevent them from being located in their communities. Occasionally these kinds of institutions can cause serious challenges for nearby public schools, as Claire Winslow went on to explain: "There's Deer Pointe Park down here, which has a known complex for housing pedophiles, one of whom was in the news just a year and a half ago because he continued to breach his probation. And he's still maintaining a place on and off here at Deer Pointe Park, and it's close to this school [New Lake Elementary], Vancouver Elementary, and Wellington Elementary – exceptionally close to Wellington Elementary. So there are huge concerns … We've got these, you know, offenders being released into the school community." Unfortunately the close proximity of these types of institutes to the elementary schools have a negative effect on children even when they're not on school grounds, and sometimes the consequences are extremely serious, as Winslow went on to say: "We have issues with our local parks, where we have a lot of transient people around. Kids have talked to me numerous times, [telling me how], especially after school and on evenings and weekends, they've been exposed … exposed to men [who are] exposing themselves to [children] in the park." How does the school play a role in dealing with such incidents? In Winslow's case, "Some [kids] tell their parents, and I would say predominately they'll report it to us [even if they have fear]. And that's when we [engage] with our community police and our police liaison officers, and look into ensuring that the kids know what to do, that they're safe." Dealing with community social problems provides a unique set of challenges for those involved in these school communities, necessitating the use of innovative approaches to create safe learning environments for students.

Communities Creating a Safe Place to Learn

"When you start to get to know people around here, there is a good sense of community," says Jane Haswell, a parent of a kindergarten student at Wellington Elementary. "One of my son's best friends, he lives in our building, and his mom's out there and she's networked with so many people in the community. There really is a good sense of community. It's just unfortunate that there's sort of an underlying downside to this neighbourhood that comes out every now and then." According to Haswell, this sense of community has evolved in the face of serious problems in the neighbourhood. She explained the downside: "Yeah, there's violence. There's a lot of drugs. Well, not a lot, but they work on it. There's drugs, there's drinking, and there's that sort of stuff in the neighbourhood, which does make it difficult."

While these problems are cause for concern, they do not make Haswell feel unsafe: "No actually, I've never felt unsafe. But I think I just know this neighbourhood well [enough] that I don't feel that way. Everyone's always been really nice, even people that may have been drinking a lot. They've always really good to [my family], so I don't even think about it." Knowing the people in the area, or the "eyes on the street" as Jane Jacobs would put it, certainly helps residents cope with life in higher-poverty neighbourhoods.[8]

At the same time, the ideal location for a school is not near an area where people congregate to drink alcohol or do drugs, and this represents a challenge for many schools. A research assistant observing at Soaring Eagle Elementary noted, "The adult males on the streets [near the school] appear as if they have little else to do." She also reported, "I noticed a sign on a boarded up house, 'East Side Eye Sore'."

To address some of these problems, Vancouver has pioneered Neighbourhood Integrated Service Teams (NISTs), a program that has been recognized with an award from the United Nations. According to Thomas Frank, Community Recreation Coordinator at the New River Community Centre, "One of the committees that I work with in this neighbourhood is NIST. [It] stands for the Neighbourhood Integrated Services Team, and it's a city initiative that brings together [employees from] all of the city's services – police, fire, health, parks, libraries, engineering – to talk about and problem solve around community issues. We all get together on a regular basis and we hear from the community certainly about what the issues are. So, [for example], if someone in the neighbourhood has got an issue around their neighbour using their yard as a garbage dump, then they'll typically come to us." These innovative groups provide a forum for community problems to be discussed and for a stakeholder to address these issues. When asked if he felt his work with NIST was making a difference, Frank replied: "Typically, people don't come to the community centre and say, 'I have a problem with a neighbour who I think is a drug dealer. He gets traffic in and out of his house all day and all night, and [he is a] shady kind of character.' They don't typically [do that]. But we certainly hear [about things like this] at the NIST table. And the police liaisons who we have on this team, in particular, have been great about keeping us informed about where the "hot spots" are and what their programs currently are. And if we have certain problems, how can we get more help. So, those types of issues."

Judy Wang is a parent of two children who attend High Point Elementary. When describing her neighbours, she said, "Many of them are from the Philippines, [or they are] Vietnamese or Chinese." She said that in the neighbourhood, "I just walk past the back lane of most houses, and oh I can smell the marijuana smell. Yes, in the houses around here that's the problem: marijuana grow ops. So many houses around here ... Because I walk I know the smell; I hate the smell." Yet she still feels like it is a good neighbourhood. She really likes the New River Community Centre: "I always go to [the] neighbourhood house when there are problems; I go [to] talk and drop by and say hello to the people who work there. And sometimes they have programs there; my son goes to the after-school program for computers and karate and stuff like that."

Of the schools studied, some had fewer issues with the surrounding neighbourhood than others. Across the street from Lakeview Elementary, for example, is a boarded up franchise store and several small non-chain, run-down shops. There are a few second-hand clothing stores, a dollar store, and a Filipino video store. To the south, the area becomes exclusively residential. Walking north, it begins to change, becoming wealthier very quickly. Only 10 blocks north, there are several major chain stores, including a bank, fast food restaurant and a yuppie café as well as some upscale chains and restaurants.

Teacher Amy Peterson describes the area around Ashfield Elementary: "I think the neighbourhood is great; lots of great restaurants, lots of great shopping. I mean, we do have prostitutes along Gates Boulevard [*laughs*]. And there are, when we come [in the mornings], there are homeless people sleeping around the school. But generally I think it's a really nice area." A recent immigrant from the Philippines, Lucia Oracio, has two children attending High Point Elementary. She has this to say about the area: "The neighbourhood? Oh, [it's] great. [My family] have good neighbours because we live in a [vertically stacked apartment building]. We are staying in the lower ground and the upstairs they are also Filipino. And then nearby there is Chinese ... I think Korean or Chinese; they are okay and the others are white ... As of now I don't experience any violence in our neighbourhood."

Parent Rochelle Grant lives near Wellington Elementary, where her child is enrolled. Like many other parents interviewed, she has heard that there are problems in her neighbourhood but has not been personally affected by them, and at the time we spoke to her she said she feels safe living in the area: "I [did] not in the beginning. I was scared about all these things. People were telling me there are some junkie, some people are drunk so ... Still, I don't have any trouble." Overall, "still they are safe; I am safe. I am living alone with three kids." This was typical of the responses we most commonly heard from parents and teachers at the schools studied. They seemed to feel that the areas around the school and where they live are safe, although there are problems, some of which are concerning or need addressing, or both. The situation clearly contrasts with that of children from predominantly wealthier families, where they don't have sex workers working the street near their school or drug addicts congregating near the schoolhouse gates.

As is clear from the data, elevated rates of alcohol and drug addiction are a big part of the problem, contributing to disorder in the low-income urban environments surrounding the schools studied. Anna Sanchez is a parent of a kindergarten student at Wellington Elementary, and she said: "This neighbourhood is good; it's just that it's very close to the liquor store and a bar ... I talk to my son [and tell him] don't go to the stranger." While she warns her son to be careful, Anna Sanchez did not report witnessing any problems with drugs or violence first-hand. She said that in the park, "Sometimes they are drunk," but she feels safe. "I always tell my husband, don't go to the stranger."

Wellington Elementary parent Laura Truelle spoke about the problem with substance abuse in the nearby park: "[The neighbourhood] is very accessible to everything, but usually in summertime it's quiet. I'm concerned a little bit because when we go to the park there are usually people who are drunk in the park, and that's not good for my kids to see. But we can't do anything about it. That's about it ... Yeah, kids are there, and people who are drunk are there. That's the only thing I'm concerned about."

This contributes to a major issue: in some lower-income urban neighbourhoods, residents lack the power, resources, and/or collective efficacy to mobilize to address the challenges related to substance abuse. At the same time, it's in these neighbourhoods where more physical spaces exist for marginalized people to survive, from abandoned buildings to neglected alcoves. With all too many people experiencing homelessness and housing insecurity in British Columbia, and Vancouver in particular, the consequences of a lack of adequate social services and housing land disproportionately on those living in low-income urban communities.

What this means for the schools located in these areas is that they must dedicate more resources to protect their students from perceived risks. This requires time, energy and financial resources that often must be diverted from other tasks, such as teaching literacy and numeracy skills. The challenges are heightened for schools located near areas where drugs are sold or prostitutes solicit.[9] The consequences of a vibrant drug trade, prostitution, and street crime contribute to a climate of insecurity in the areas around the school and on the children's paths to and from school.

Certain schools that were studied have more serious issues than most of the other elementary schools in East Vancouver. At New Lake Elementary, for example, alcohol and drugs are being consumed on school grounds at night, and even the school maintenance staff report not feeling safe going out on school grounds after dark. Administrators worry about broken glass or even used needles on the school grounds in the morning. Sometimes youth will spray paint graffiti on school walls or dispose of bags of clippings from marijuana plants onto the school grounds.[10]

Schools and the children who attend them are going to be affected to some degree by the surrounding neighbourhood, this cannot be avoided. Unfortunately, as can be seen in the case of New Lake Elementary and some of the other schools studied, the problems of low-income urban neighbourhoods frequently end up in schoolyards despite the best efforts of administrators and teachers to keep them out. Yet many people decide to stay and raise their children in these economically disadvantaged communities. While some choose to stay because they want to, others stay because they have no choice due to the limited options for affordable housing. People's social networks and ties also play a role, as these are often critically important for low-income people to make ends meet or survive.[11] Having roots makes people want to stay in their community, despite the problems; however, gentrification is beginning to push more low-income families out of many East Vancouver neighbourhoods whether they want to go or not.[12]

Rapid Changes: Gentrification and New Student Populations

The gentrification that is happening throughout East Vancouver is having a profound effect on the neighbourhoods that make up this region. It's a familiar urban phenomenon, similar to when hippie-like artist communities become "yuppified," when a new group displaces the existing one. With housing prices at record-high levels across the city of Vancouver, many formerly low-income neighbourhoods are experiencing dramatic transformations as "pioneer" yuppies move into the large heritage homes or other houses and begin renovations. New condo towers are also being constructed throughout East Vancouver and units are being sold, flipped, and resold – branded as part of the "urban lifestyle" package.[13]

In East Vancouver, the class element is crucial. The increasing existence of wealthier families is changing neighbourhood demographics
and the student composition of schools. William Coleman, the principal of Pearson Elementary, said, "In 1996–7, around that time it was
probably 80% English as a second language; now I think we're down to
about 55%." Similarly, there is now a smaller percentage of the student
body who come from low-income families, which resulted in the school
losing its Inner City designation and the resources that came along with
it. Principal Coleman explained,

> We used to receive money from the Ministry of Children and Family
> Development for programs for youth, and [we'd get] family workers for
> all that kind of extra support. [The Ministry] does a study every year and
> they look at the demographics of the neighbourhood. They look at the
> crime rate; they look at the [number of] people on assistance; they look at
> education numbers, all that kind of stuff. In the late 1990s, they took our
> Inner City status away from us because the demographics of the neigh-
> bourhood had changed. So from then till now, it's an even more marked
> difference. Now we don't have nearly as many kids [who] live in low-
> income [households]. We have a few. I would say there are nearly 500
> kids in this school, and I would say we have 20 who are on [social] assis-
> tance now. And the reason for this, I think, is because the neighbourhood
> used to have a lot of basement suites and things in the houses. [But] those
> houses have now been sold. People can now no longer afford to stay in the
> city, so they're moving out. And the houses that have been bought now,
> [the owners] are using their suites for their own purposes. They are not
> renting them. So it's mostly homeowners [now], with few rental proper-
> ties in the neighbourhood.

While in the past, Pearson Elementary struggled with high student
turnover, the increasing socio-economic wealth of the student population has brought with it greater stability, thereby shifting the kinds
of associated challenges facing the school. Principal William Coleman
explained:

> [The student population] used to be very transient. We used to have kids
> who would be here for a month or two, or six months, or whatever, and
> then they would go. But now the population is fairly stable. If there was
> a challenge, I guess [it] is around our First Nation people ... A lot of chal-
> lenges getting them to school on time, getting follow-through at home,
> that kind of stuff. The Vietnamese community around the school we think

is one that really needs some looking at in terms of support services and stuff, because they also are not as willing [to access them], and maybe it's because they haven't been here as long. But [for] the Chinese people there is MOSAIC [Multilingual Orientation Service Association for Immigrant Communities] and S.U.C.C.E.S.S. [United Chinese Community Enrichment Services Society]. There are all those things for them to tap into, and they're not so afraid to go and ask for help. But the Vietnamese people are very close within their families. They don't like to go out and ask for help. They want their kids to do well, but they don't really want to participate. So that, I think, is a challenge for us – to bring the Vietnamese folks in and to try to get them on board with what we are doing, but also with the youth support and various community agencies to say it's OK to go and ask for help. That's [been] a little tough.

Near Pearson Elementary, some parents from the gentrified group have taken an active interest in improving their children's school. These parents mobilized with community groups to clean up their neighbourhood streets, and they encouraged the school administrators to join the coalition in improving the areas around the school. Improving the quality of the streets in this way has furthered the trend of neighbourhood improvement. Principal Coleman explained:

In the past, [around] 1996–7, there was a lot of bad stuff going on. There was drugs and all kinds of horrendous abuse. Gates Boulevard here used to be called the Vietnamese Corridor. There were shootings there, there was gang-related stuff going on. Sohan Singh's brother was murdered here at the corner of Gates Boulevard and McArthur Street [just across from the school]. Yeah, so the neighbourhood has really, really changed since then. We've got a group called the All Together community group, and it's a group of neighbourhood people and parents from the school who have kind of taken over the neighbourhood. They moved out all the hookers and all that street trade stuff. They do walking patrols at night, they do bike patrol, they do driving patrols; they do community events to bring people in the school and stuff together.

Pearson Elementary has played a central role in this community mobilization, including hosting the group meetings. Principal Coleman said:

Well, James Donavan, one of the fellows out here, he's sort of the head leader [of the All Together group]. They have their regular meetings and stuff, and they have their teams and captains and they work closely with the community police. They hold their annual meeting here in October, and we have anywhere from three to 300 people attend. They're [all] really concerned about their community and want to make sure that it is safe and clean, that they get what's coming to them from the city; you know, all that kind of stuff. So actually, [the group] just received an award from the Vancouver School Board in recognition for [their] work for the school and for the community, [which has] now become a neighbourhood stronghold. You [have] that strip along there that's [also] kind of seedy, so the [parents in another East Vancouver community] are taking some stuff from these folks and trying to institute the same kind of program down in their neighbourhood. I don't know if it'll work or not, but [the All Together members] are quite well known for the work they've done.

While gentrification can bring improvements such as these to a neighbourhood and, in doing so, benefit the lower-income residents who can afford to continue living there, it also brings with it the potential to undermine the residential security of the community's most vulnerable people. Some of these areas appear to be at an earlier stage of gentrification, which may stall or even reverse in the current unstable economic climate.

In some of the schools studied, the lower-income families are increasingly being segregated into specific areas within the broader neighbourhood. For example, many of the children at Lakeview Elementary live in the Frank Nichols housing projects. While these projects do not feature the levels of disorder associated with US urban housing projects, they are clearly distinctive from the surrounding gentrifying neighbourhood. As sociologist Mario Small demonstrates in his book *Villa Victoria* – an ethnographic study of a housing project in a Puerto Rican enclave in Boston – physical isolation is not necessary for residents living in government housing projects to be socially isolated.[14] Similar to the Boston projects in Small's book, the Frank Nichols housing project features design cues or signifiers that distinguish it from the surrounding housing – including the style of construction, the landscaping (or rather, the lack of it), and even the doors and numbers make it clear to an outsider that it is social housing. The buildings appear barren and run-down, standing out in sharp contrast to the lovely renovated heritage homes with beautiful landscaping and even to the other private rental buildings on the surrounding streets.

Although the overall neighbourhood around Lakeview Elementary is gentrifying and becoming wealthier, 90 of the 350 students come from the Frank Nichols social housing project – and these students face multiple risk factors. Many are recently arrived immigrants or refugees, and a high percentage live in low-income households and/or survive on meagre public assistance benefits. Lakeview teacher Sarah Williams described it in this way: "The kids who come from social housing are mostly immigrant, maybe they live in poverty. But the kids are really nice. I really like those kids, and I like the parents too. So don't get me wrong, but [where they live] does make a difference. They don't have as much money; they don't have as many resources; they don't travel as much, although some do travel. Like, they might have to go back to their home country or whatever. So it's kind of different. It's kind of a fifty-fifty kind of school: 50% in poverty and 50% not."

Michael Johnson, a parent of children at Wellington Elementary, described how the gentrification was changing the character of the school's Parent Advisory Council (PAC):

These are affluent people, a lot of them. If they have kids, it's only one child, and many don't [have any]. These are executive-type people who are coming in with higher positions or [they're] business owners and just taking advantage that there is a piece of property that they can acquire in Vancouver that is maybe not too much more than half a million dollars. The developers are doing very creative jobs at creating very attractive spaces for them to live in. And the area itself is overall changing its tone as far as the type of people that you are seeing now. It's evident, really, even on our PAC committee, and that's what I noticed immediately this year.

It is interesting. It's also exciting. It's nice to see the level of the community start to be improved, and with people who are interested in the community. They're not just there to acquire a piece of property and ignore what's going on in the community. They realize that Wellington is a community that's very diverse, culturally speaking, and that [if] they want to make it better they need to be involved in that community. And so that's another thing that I am noticing. But again, property values increase. You talk about gentrification, the housing stock is depleted, from apartments to high-end condominiums, and so it does make it more challenging for others.

There is no doubt gentrification will continue to be a major factor in East Vancouver, and more broadly in cities internationally. High fuel prices, a backlash against suburbia, and the growing popularity of urban living will result in more families choosing to raise their children in cities across Canada, parts of the United States, and Europe. The costs and benefits for low-income urban residents are mixed. While those who manage to stay in these neighbourhoods and schools will benefit from the influx of wealthier residents, others will be uprooted and forced into more economically deprived neighbourhoods.

Diverse Schools, Loved Schools

One of the conundrums in school research is that, while many people despair about the state of the education system or about schools in general, they often love their child's own school and teachers. The parents from the schools that I studied in East Vancouver were no different. Even schools experiencing serious challenges are loved by teachers, students, and parents alike. Principal Jennifer Newcastle of East Harcourt Elementary said, "I think it's very rich for children to learn about other cultures, to be able to mix with other children of other races. I think that's a very positive thing." And Principal Katherine Drucker of Ashfield Elementary celebrates the diversity: "The first word that I always use for the kids at this school is appreciative. They're the most appreciative group of children that I've ever worked with. We have a huge range in cultures. Mainly Asian, [it's a] very [big] Chinese and Vietnamese community. I think there are probably 30 different languages that are spoken in our school." The diversity of the students was frequently singled out and extolled as a virtue by administrators, teachers and parents.

Concurring with Principal Drucker, teacher Amy Peterson at Ashfield Elementary said this about her school: "I think I'd give it an A. I mean to say I love it. I think the teachers here are really concerned about these children; [they] push for them to get services that they need to have. I think it's a really good school and they're very professional staff, very social staff. We attend lots of conferences, lots of workshops. We're forever trying something [new]. [If] something [is] not quite right, [we] try to fix it. So I think it's a really good school … And we've got lots of children who have moved to Richmond [a Vancouver suburb south of the city] and the parents still drive them here because the kids don't want to leave."

These positive views of the elementary schools studied were shared by many parents. Maria Gomez, a parent of two children at Wellington Elementary, said that she would recommend the school to other parents because "the teachers are very nice and they teach them very nicely." She said: "My daughter, she really likes to [go to] school. Sometimes she is sick and she says 'No, I want to go, because I want to learn more,' and yeah, it's very important because they learn more." Her son is involved in a new program at Wellington Elementary: "He is so happy too because he says he is learning more. And I wish they can have more programs to teach the kids because like I see my son, he is very happy ... when he is included in a new program."

Michael Johnson is a parent of four Wellington Elementary students, three of whom are currently enrolled. Overall, he thinks that Wellington Elementary is a great school. He lives near the school and describes the community in this way: "I would say it is extremely culturally diverse, lower income, and with white being the minority for sure." He described the student body as "a rich blend of cultures, [which] is handled very well by the school administration ... culturally speaking, it's a potpourri of cultures and ethnic backgrounds, but that's what makes it so rich. That's what makes it exciting and vibrant, and they do a really good job there." He likes the approach that the school adopts in terms of working with students from diverse backgrounds, which he characterizes as emphasizing the positive benefits of diversity over the challenges. As he explained,

> [They have] dinners [to which] people bring a dish from [their] own country. They celebrate different ethnic days, enriching the value of each other's cultures and sharing that with the rest of the community. They embrace it, and all of these initiatives work. They encourage volunteering by the students, so there's great interaction with the students in a very positive way. Within the community [they are] doing different things and helping fundraise with the Lions Club and the different organizations, [and] raising awareness in their neighbourhood – the local Drake Shopping Centre – where they set up booths. They do a lot of activities; a lot of education around enrichment of the different cultures. Sharing that with the students, giving them insights and [highlighting] the value of what that brings to the community as opposed to the challenges. Just really positive.

Johnson says the school is also adopting a great approach in terms of overcoming literacy challenges:

> So we read all the time, and it's something that's stressed constantly at the school. And they have buddies to help them at the school. The teachers work very closely [with the children] so that if a child is having some

identifiable problems or challenges, they get the support for them right away. Sometimes it can be just simply a vision problem, they need eyeglasses or something. With our area, the school has so many cultures that [English] is not [always perfectly understood], and [the kids] really have some genuine struggles. So they get the support they need, and I'm really happy with that.

Teacher Jane Sorrento of Centennial Elementary also reports having a positive impression of her school: "What makes this school different? I think very caring teachers, very respectful teachers, and a community that is fairly involved with the school." She felt that "the children are generally very well behaved here and [there are] not as many emotional problems – they are few and far between compared to other schools where I've taught."

Administrators and teachers expressed great pride in succeeding with student populations that begin school without strong English language fluency. Principal Jennifer Newcastle of East Harcourt Elementary said, "We feel that we have done a fabulous job of teaching our children to read and write when you think of them all starting, for the most part, with no English at all. And they've managed to be very successful by the end of grade 7."

Certain teachers were singled out with praise for going beyond the call of duty. For example, active parent Helen Welsh raves about a teacher at Great Forest Elementary, Angela Hargrove:

She is one [example of an excellent teacher]. She puts in 180%. She's married, but she has no kids. She is in there early, she stays late; she takes so much work home, it's not even funny. Like, she is doing … every minute of the day she is busy in that classroom with those kids and it's crazy. Everybody wants her.

If you ask my daughter right now "Who impacted you the most in your work studies, your work habits, who shaped you the most?" [She and] all the kids would say Angela Hargrove. Yes, she's phenomenal, [although] she's hard. Some of them for the first two months hate her, because she's hard. She gives a lot of homework. She's tough, fair, but in the end, when they get into grade 5 [Great Forest Elementary has multi-year classrooms], they're like, this is nothing.

Great teachers inspire children and often also parents. Parent Lucinda Oratio is a mother of a kindergarten student at High Point Elementary.

She says, "Every time when my daughter comes back from school seems like she was too excited, happy. And I'm happy also because of that environment, there are a lot of changes. She has started socializing with some other people here, and we love the school, the teacher, everything."

Even if their children are struggling, parents speak highly of the school and the school community. Jane Haswell, whose child is a student at Ashfield Elementary, said: "One my sons had a bit of a hard time in school. He's made some good friends [and] they seem like wonderful children, but he's also, conversely, had some trouble because he's very big for his age, so he isn't fitting in very well. But they do seem like wonderful kids, and I've met some of the parents and they seem really nice."

Vietnamese parent Lucy Van Tran works in one of Vancouver's many nail salons. Her workspace is unventilated and cramped. She is constantly exposed to chemicals from haircare products and acrylic nail applicators as well as high-speed polishers that send particles of white dust into the air. She is a small woman, with red-tinged eyes and blotchy skin. Through a translator, she described having positive feelings about Arthur Lang Elementary, where her two sons are enrolled. As the translator said on her behalf, "She likes the school. She just thinks its good overall. Her kids like it; they love the school. Her husband does help. She doesn't, because she works most of the time." Yet, as the translator went on to explain, the language barriers prevent the husband from becoming more involved in the school. Because of his limited English fluency, he cannot talk to the teacher about the children.

Most of the people interviewed felt positively about the school at which they worked or their children attended, even as they were forthright about challenges. This is a critically important insight for those interested in improving educational outcomes at urban schools facing serious challenges. Characterizing schools as second-rate or as "failing" often creates a lot of defensiveness, which generally does not create the conditions necessary for the kind of productive change desired. Using test scores to adversely label schools or to place them in a hierarchy where they inevitably will be poorly ranked is discordant with the emotional attachment that administrators, teachers, and parents feel about their own school.

Most of the classrooms I observed were warm and inviting, making for fertile learning environments. For example, the wonderful second grade room at Lakeview Elementary had high ceilings and bright yellow walls, one of which featured large windows that were covered by white pull-down shades. Covering most of the green-tiled floor was a mismatch of carpets held together with a thin strip of tape. While not luxurious, you could tell the room was cared for: the tiles were clean and unchipped, the carpets were neat, and the walls were recently painted. Student art hung from strings across the room. There were plenty of books, and two modern computers sat in one corner. There was a pile of student calendars and I learned that, periodically, the calendars were sent home to parents with (generally positive) notes from the teacher about the student's performance, and the parents were required to initial the comments.

Practically every inch of space was used to its maximum benefit in this classroom, with each object's presence serving to enhance or facilitate the students' learning. In addition to a large map, large posters containing a variety of information hung everywhere. On one appeared the lyrics to "Canada in My Pocket," a song about the country's history and icons printed on our coins; on another appeared the lyrics to "Oh, Canada." Other posters detailed numbers, colours, and the months of the year. Spanning one of the walls was a large strip of paper printed with the letters of the alphabet in capital and lower-case form. There were games and dolls in cubbyholes along the back of the room, streamers were hanging off the ceiling, and art supplies were peeking out of the top of a closet. Classroom atmospheres like this facilitate student interest in learning and, therefore, academic achievement; they reflect the importance that society and teachers place on children's potential to learn and succeed.

The ESL Challenge – Students

At the same time that diversity is valued and celebrated at the schools studied, many of the administrators, teachers, and parents who were interviewed acknowledged the tremendous challenge they face teaching classrooms of children who each have different levels of fluency in the English language. Principal Teresa McDonald of Soaring Eagle Elementary said this about her school:

> We have 653 students. About 60% of them have another language at home, another first language. That doesn't mean that they're still receiving ESL support, [as it is] cut off after five years. So by grade 4, including kindergarten, most children do not have access to ESL – extra ESL support.

Approximately 60% of the school population has another language as their home language, and by far it's Cantonese. We have a sprinkling of virtually every language in the world, but by far the majority of that is Cantonese.

We have a lower-middle-class, low-middle-class to middle-class socio-economic background. We have a number of new families within that ESL. We have a number of new families to the country. So I certainly have witnessed the challenges that they go through.

Michele Ramos is a parent of children at Soaring Eagle Elementary. She said that the prevalence of inadequate English fluency among the students is a noticeable challenge for teachers, noting that these students require extra time and resources, often at the expense of the other children:

> I really feel sorry here for our staff, I really do. I think one of the challenges is working with ESL kids. They have kids who speak not one word of English [and] kids who can put sentences together but don't fully understand you when [you talk to them]. And the problem that goes unnoticed is that kids who do speak English aren't being challenged because the teachers are spending so much time on the kids who don't. They don't have time to work on these other kids, and they are making it through. They're getting A grades, they are able to work on their own. And [the teachers are] just happy to be able to do what they can do because there's nine more kids that [they] don't have to worry about, because [they've] got to worry about these 21 that don't know what the heck they're doing.

For many teachers, it would be challenging to have even a few ESL students in their classroom. It is a whole other story when there are many students – from a variety of backgrounds and with various levels of proficiency – learning English while in the early elementary classroom. Often it can be difficult determining how much ESL support each student might need. Jane Sorrento, a teacher at Centennial Elementary said:

> One of the challenges, for instance, [is] in literacy education language and literacy education: Some of the students at this level are very good at decoding/reading but not necessarily so good with meaning/comprehension/response. So there's a little bit of disparity there. So we, of course, have ESL help at the school, but sometimes [it's] a little bit tricky, sort of

thinking, "Okay, does this child still need ESL resource help?" Because on the face of things the child seems to be reading very well, is writing not too badly. But when you go to analyse it, you think, "Yeah, okay, [there are] idioms that sometimes are missed when it comes to discussing the story." There are gaps there. That's sort of one of the challenges.

The first step in providing appropriate educational resources is identifying and evaluating students who lack English language mastery.[15] The fact that there are high percentages of ESL students in many East Vancouver elementary classrooms presents unique challenges, and some teachers at these schools lack the necessary experience and training to effectively teach the ESL students. Supplemental resource and part-time teachers help, but some students still fall through the cracks.

The unique individual and group-level characteristics of ESL students can also present challenges. Angela Myers, a consultant for the Vancouver School Board, said:

The biggest challenges [arise because] Vancouver has gotten to the point of having so many ESL learners that teachers are beginning to assume [of themselves that] they understand and they know what to do. And so new groups come in and we say, "These groups are different, they have these kinds of needs." The teachers say, "Oh yeah, yeah, yeah I know all about ESL. You don't need to tell me." And it's not really true. They knew about ESL the way it was when it was three kids out of 30. Now ESL is 20 kids out of 30 and the whole dynamic has changed, and I think people have lost sight of that, and that's the struggle.

According to Myers, one of the biggest challenges is getting appropriate resources to teach these high-needs classrooms:

It's a struggle for the classroom teacher. It's a struggle for the support teacher. The support teacher may or may not have appropriate training to even understand some of [the] differences, which is another big issue we have in Vancouver.

Because of the financial constraints, our elementary support teachers tend to be people who are in entry-level positions. They are part-time because most people who have some seniority don't want part-time. Therefore, who gets part-time positions? The brand new teacher whose only classroom experience is their practicum and who doesn't have any specialist training. I mean, the odd one does, but they just finished completing their bachelor's [degree]. They are not quite ready to specialize and add other things yet, unless they chose to take a diploma in ESL or Learning Assistance or Special Needs, and that's the other part of the issue.

In our elementary system, in most cases the resource teacher has to be all those things. You have to deal with ESL learners; you have to deal with language needs, learning needs, minimal learning needs, and severe learning needs. And [these kids] are all on your caseload, and they're [all in] various grade levels, and that's a huge challenge for anybody, even with well-prepared teachers who have some specialist training in at least one area.

As a trained resource teacher, Myers feels that having a group of specialists in different areas is the best approach for creating a comprehensive team of teachers with diverse skills and training who can effectively address the multitude of challenges.

Part of the problem is resource cutbacks in the face of growing challenges. Collaboration could help, but the large number of part-time support teachers in a school makes it extremely difficult for them to coordinate their schedules to meet and consult with each other.[16] If teachers can interact and discuss cases, they can prevent children falling between the cracks; collaboration allows teachers to share notes and help at-risk students.[17] (Exploring ways for teachers and resource teachers to develop greater specialist skills and collaboration skills is discussed in chapter 8.)

Specialists are not the only ones who are concerned about the lack of resources when it comes to effectively teaching students with limited English language fluency; parents also have concerns. Jane Haswell, for example, worries that the teachers at Ashfield Elementary do not have the resources to address the challenges presented by the extremely high percentage of ESL students in many classrooms. When asked about the challenges associated with the school having such a diverse student body, she said: "I think one issue with us, at least, is just sort of with the majority of the children in my son's class, English not being their first language. I think it's an issue because he's so much further ahead. Sometimes I feel in a way it's holding him back a little bit. While he's very kind and will help other kids out, at the same time, he's doing first grade work right now. So I think in some ways it kinds of holds him back a little bit."

While Haswell is concerned that her son's classmates are holding him back, she also feels that the teacher has adapted to the situation and is succeeding. She went on to say, "In this instance she has because I didn't know until she told me that she had him doing first grade work already. So I think she does realize where the children are at and what she can do to help them."

Overcoming Language Barriers – Parents

Many of the parents of children in East Vancouver schools are not fully proficient in English themselves, which requires schools to also accommodate their needs. In order to more effectively engage parents in their children's education, some of the schools translate information and notices. For example, the Vancouver School Board called for schools to send home report cards translated into several languages. According to consultant Angela Myers, "We have report cards to go home to parents [translated] in the major languages. There is sort of a checklist [that] gives [them] the bare ideas, which is good. A great effort. It was an expensive effort, but a great effort to improve communication with parents about what's going on at school."

The need to translate report cards is only the tip of the iceberg in terms of communication issues between parents and teachers at diverse schools. Parent Michael Johnson feels that, at Wellington Elementary, the school staff has a hard time communicating with some of the parents due to language barriers. He said,

> When you're talking about the interaction between school and the household, there's a real breakdown. I think when you find these challenges [it's because] people aren't home, or you're sending messages with kids that you may as well not even send them. Especially if it's a notice to meet with the teacher, because the child is not going to pass that on if they're going to get in trouble; that's just human nature, and it's a challenge. We talked at the last PAC [Parent Advisory Council] meeting about interacting with parents via computer. Well, these people can't read or write English, never mind understand how to use a computer!

Diverse schools bring people together with a range of experiences, resources, and traditions, and the school is often the most important Canadian institution these immigrant families engage with. It's unsurprising then, that so many of the stakeholders interviewed focused on cultural issues and concerns. These concerns include the need to create more effective atmospheres for learning and focus more on building respect, trust, and good behaviour in the classroom. Others argued that it is the job of the school to acclimatize students to Canadian culture and traditions.

At Ashfield Elementary, teacher Justine Kirkpatrick's kindergarten class is composed primarily of visible minority children, many of whose parents are immigrants to Canada. In her class, students celebrate birthdays based on the Chinese calendar. One mother referred to her child's age differently than how it was reported in the official school record and on the teacher's "Birthday Wall." With Thanksgiving approaching, Kirkpatrick lamented that few of her students will celebrate it. She thinks Thanksgiving is an important Canadian tradition and one that her students should appreciate as part of their new culture.

Often multiculturalism and diversity is celebrated as an ideal. In schools, however, it can create tension and the occasional clash as teachers and children enter the classroom with very different backgrounds and outlooks. Parent Jane Haswell describes a situation that arose from a conversation her son had with a classmate of his at Ashfield Elementary:

> We had an interesting incident [happen] yesterday. We've allowed our son to make his own choices about religion, about anything like that. His Nana just passed away a little while ago, so he'd said "I want to make a Valentine for Nana because I want her to have it" and his dad was like, "Okay." But a great conversation of angels and God came up [subsequently], and then he turns to his dad and says, "Did you know that God sets people on fire?" and Michael was like, "What do you mean?" And my son replied, "Amit said God lights people on fire." So then Michael had to try and have a discussion [about] people in different cultures believing in different gods, and that was really interesting. I guess in other cultures they would have completely different perceptions of things, and it was an interesting conversation to have with him.

Haswell feels that her son is more tolerant of differences than some other students. She said, "I guess because of us being unconventional parents and him being so open-minded and being in with so many different cultures, he doesn't even think about it. He just kind of goes 'okay'." Yet she also understands how this cultural diversity could be problematic in classrooms: "I could see it being a challenge because of

having to incorporate all these different cultures and different backgrounds into it, and making sure everyone understands and accepts
it." But all in all, she feels the school does a good job managing diversity issues, saying, "I think the school actually does quite well with it
because if you think of the variety of cultures in this school and the area
that it's in, it's faced with lots of different issues. I think they do quite
well with it." For example, she added, "I've noticed there's sort of a lot
of emphasis to appreciate different holidays."

School staff must occasionally deal with difficult situations aris-
ing from tension between different groups. For example, one Chinese
immigrant parent of children who attend Ashfield Elementary, Wei
Chang, said, "[There are] too many Vietnamese around this neighbourhood; it's not good for kids." Stereotyping; prejudice; discrimination.
These kinds of tensions can unfortunately result in bullying or erupt
into fights during and after school.

Another unfortunate consequence of racism and discrimination is
that it can create barriers for visible minorities to secure housing and
employment. Youth worker Thi Vu is a parent of two children who go
to Arthur Lang Elementary. She said one of the main challenges facing
new immigrants from Vietnam is "… not being able to secure housing. Some families are constantly moving." She went on to explain,
"There's a lot of news coverage about the Vietnamese community being
involved in marijuana grow operations. So a lot of Vietnamese families
and a lot of the youth that I'm working with, their families are having a
really hard time renting. Because they'll go to a landlord and they'll see
on your form that your last name is Nguyen, Wang, Tran, [or] Lee and
that you're Vietnamese. 'Are you going to grow in my place?' [they'll
immediately wonder]. 'I don't think I can rent to you.'"

Poverty and discrimination are not the only challenges facing Vietnamese students. Vu feels that Vietnamese children are struggling in
literacy in Vancouver schools:

Vietnamese youth really struggle with the subject [of] English, regardless
of whether or not they are new immigrants or if they're Canadian-born
[and have] been here their whole life. And it was really interesting what
some of the multicultural workers have said to me: they were saying that
the teachers are calling them in to translate for the parents [to tell them]
"Your child has a lot of difficulty with reading and writing, and in terms
of creative writing." [In class] the teacher will just ask, "Tell me, what have

you done over the weekend?" and the kids can't seem to write that. It become[s] more of a social issue, and the multicultural workers have identified that the kids, or this specific group of youth or children that they have worked with, haven't been exposed to anything else other than TV over the weekend. So they had nothing to write. And they weren't stimulated in that sense.

It starts very young and it carries on to grade 12, where you have these Vietnamese youth who excel at math, science, chemistry, [but] when it comes to English it's their weakest subject because it starts from a very young age, and they can't grasp the grammar aspect even though they were born here. A lot of the parents, English is not their strong point. And there is also a pocket of Vietnamese parents who are illiterate in their own language, Vietnamese, so it becomes extremely challenging for them to provide any home support. That's the thing, the teachers are putting a lot of pressure on the parents saying, "You should read to your children at home in order to develop that regular literacy and getting them used to and exposed to literature," but the parents can't read. So it's a bit of a catch-22.

The topic of language and other barriers making it more difficult for school staff to engage parents is described in greater detail in chapter 4.

Cultural differences can result in misunderstandings in classrooms. For example, traditional norms may discourage children from asking questions of adults, which may result in students not getting the academic help they need in the classroom.[18] In more serious cases, the differences can cause the school to feel the need to protect a child's well-being. Based on interviews with refugees and school officials in Edmonton, Alberta, education researcher Darcy Dachyshyn found that:

Canadians often do not understand or appreciate the child guidance strategies used by refugee families. Canadian educators hearing about or witnessing the use of physical punishment, shaming, or ostracism by parents of children in their class may have difficulty knowing how to respond. In Canada, people are legally bound to report to the child welfare authorities if they believe a child is being abused or neglected. Unfortunately, this can set up an adversarial stance between refugee parents and teachers. Teachers feel they must watch for signs of what they consider abuse or neglect, whereas parents feel they must hide, in case their actions are misinterpreted.[19]

In light of this, it is both more challenging and even more important that the staff at high-diversity urban schools engage parents and strive to build trust between parents and the school.

Conclusion

Diversity enhances urban life: the food, the cultural fairs, the art, the music – some of the best things about city life emerge from the dynamic mix of backgrounds and cultures of recent immigrants and their predecessors. Yet diversity, or super-diversity, also introduces multiple challenges to institutions, particularly those that serve youth from low-income families. While diversity adds a wonderful vibrancy to schools like it does to the surrounding communities, training and other support resources are required to help ensure that children thrive in these classrooms.

The elementary schools studied included children of families from all over the world. While some schools had greater concentrations of Chinese immigrants, others had higher proportions of Filipino or Vietnamese students. The schools are now majority-minority schools, like many other urban public schools in Canada, the United States, and Europe. Because of the extreme diversity, high percentages of students in these schools struggle to attain English language fluency. Schools must dedicate substantial resources towards ESL support, even beyond the first few years, in order to overcome this significant barrier.

Having high proportions of students from low-income families adds another dimension to the challenges facing the schools studied (and those like them). Teachers and administrators must address the needs of children who come to school hungry, malnourished, and/or stressed. Gentrification and increasing housing costs, as well as the decreasing availability of affordable housing in East Vancouver, contribute to greater hardships for children from low-income families, even as they benefit in other ways from living near and attending the same schools as children from wealthier families. Some lower-income families are forced to move in order to secure affordable secure housing, increasing transience. And although the neighbourhoods surrounding the schools studied are indeed gentrifying, the residents – poor and wealthy alike – are still affected by urban social problems associated with lower-income areas, requiring administrators to pick up used syringes and condoms from the schoolyard prior to the start of the school day and to take other steps necessary to creating a safe learning environment for students.

Growing diversity in the urban context enlivens communities, even as it introduces new challenges, conferring incalculable benefits for the students, families, and schools within them. Having the educational resources to tackle challenges early is important for fulfilling the promise of diversity, building resilience for children, families and the community.

3 Coping with Challenging Students

What do we do about Frank? He is only 7 years old but is already behind in reading and math. He disrupts class with his poor behaviour, goading the other boys in the class to join in his antics. With a short temper, he frequently gets into fights on the playground and bullies his smaller classmates, and he relentlessly teases the girls. His home life is tough. He lives in social housing with his mother, a single parent who survives on limited social assistance benefits. She only reluctantly comes to the school when the principal calls, and every time she swears her son will not misbehave again.

Students like Frank, whose behavioural issues disrupt classrooms and learning, present a challenge for educators. Other challenges are presented by children who have learning disabilities.[1] Teachers sometimes must also deal with children who come to school hungry, who are frequently absent, or who resort to violence to settle disputes.

Like many East Vancouver elementary schools, New Lake Elementary is surrounded by traffic and congestion. Framing most of the school grounds is a three-foot-high cement wall with a chain-link fence firmly mounted on top. This wall serves to keep out the noisy bustle of the outside world, but when there are acts of aggression on the playground it shatters the calm. During one afternoon recess, a tall non–visible minority boy attempted to wrestle a basketball from two of his visible minority classmates. Meanwhile, in a hidden part of the playground, obscured from view of supervision aids, two black boys sparred with two Asian boys. While all schools experience challenges with occasional fighting, for many reasons violence can be more pervasive and prevalent at urban schools in higher-poverty neighbourhoods.[2]

Every couple of years, the media tends to glorify some "tough guy" principal at an urban public school, someone who decides that enough is enough. Principal Joe Clark was one prominent example in the United States; he was known as the "bat man" because he patrolled the halls of his urban Philadelphia school with a baseball bat and bullhorn in hand to enforce discipline.[3] As student safety issues capture media attention, some inner-city schools in Canada and the United States now have police officers stationed at schools. In the longer run, this approach does not so much change student behaviour as it pushes students with behaviour issues out of the school to other schools or institutions. Despite the popularity of this get-tough approach with some conservatives, it is not an effective way to deal with student behaviour issues in urban public schools, and it may in fact be creating more problems by reinforcing a growing school-to-criminal-justice-system pipeline among visible minority males in high-poverty communities.

While some students are challenging because of their temperament or behaviour, others present challenges to educators due to circumstances completely beyond their control; most are somewhere in between. Recognizing the root cause of behavioural issues is often the first step to addressing the challenge. For example, some low-income children live in shelters or couch surf with relatives or family friends, necessitating that they change to a new school with each move. They might arrive in a classroom in October and relocate by January, when their family secures housing in a different district. Other causes of behavioural challenges can be linked to serious learning disabilities or behaviour problems.[4]

In the case of newcomer students such as refugee families, there can be serious underlying issues such as post-traumatic stress disorder that can have a profound influence on a child's behaviour. Education professors Judit Szente and James Hoot studied the needs of refugee children in Buffalo, New York, through interviews with parents and school staff. They found that "… children show signs of stress in various ways. Some may lose interest or become withdrawn, others may become aggressive or angry. Some may become restless and find it difficult to concentrate on tasks. Some may eat more than usual, some may lose their appetite. Crying spells and nightmares may be common.[5]" Many refugees spend years waiting in camps enduring hardships before being accepted and relocated to North America or European cities.[6] After arriving in Canadian cities, these refugees receive financial assistance from the government for only one to two years, and then they must turn to working in low-wage jobs in the service sector to not only make ends meet, but also to pay back the Canadian government for their travel expenses and often to send remittances to relatives in their country of origin.[7]

In the urban elementary schools studied in East Vancouver, school staff acknowledged the challenges that come with trying to teach literacy and numeracy skills to some students from newcomer immigrant and refugee families. First grade teacher Kerry Reynolds described the frustration felt by teachers at Wellington Elementary:

> You're always sort of trying to improve on things, and I think sometimes you can't really get anywhere in the face of adversity. And no matter how many different ways you try ... you're always looking for different pathways, different ways to reach those children. And sometimes you just try everything you possibly [can] imagine, and it just still doesn't work.
>
> I think there are some of those kids here. And I'm not saying that they're hopeless or helpless or whatever. I'm just saying that sometimes we just haven't found the right way to do it, and often kids end up being placed in programs because they're just not able to cope in our classrooms.

While some special needs students get extra support in class or are taken out of the classroom for more personalized instruction for part of the day, sometimes teachers give up and have these children removed from the classroom altogether. The point at which this happens varies by school, depending both on the teacher's capacity to cope with the various kinds of student needs and on the amount of extra resources that are available to teachers.

The overall trend, though, has been towards integration and keeping children in mainstream classrooms as much as and for as long as possible. In Reynolds' case, she said:

> Wellington Elementary has a fantastic reputation for being an outstanding advocate for children with special needs. It has a really good reputation, and sometimes kids stay here longer than they should just because [the school] can handle it. [However], there are still those kids that you just never can quite reach. I think there always will be, but it's just so frustrating. Why can't we get those kids reading at their grade level? What is getting in our way? There [are] not many of them, but there are a few and

they're a conundrum. And we're always trying to figure out what to do differently… It's challenging.

Compared with the other children, special needs students require disproportionate amounts of time and emotional energy from teachers and administrators. New Lake Elementary teacher Frank Wallace said:

> It's hard. You've got kids who are academically needy for whatever reason, [and] you've got kids who are socially needy – they have social issues [that affect] how they integrate into the classroom. We have a few kids who are severely on meds, [who] have attention and behavioural concerns, and [they] can disrupt the whole class. It just takes one. I can think of one kid in one of [my] classes [whose] got very distinct time-release medication, and you can tell when it's running out because he goes right off the deep end. He can't focus, he's throwing things; he's just not focused. And so, a lot of issues come with that. Inappropriate behaviour, inappropriate touching perhaps; inappropriate interaction with [the] other kids. And all it takes is that one kid.

Although integrating these children within the classroom is usually the best approach, special needs students can disrupt their classmates' learning. One-on-one supports can mitigate this, but they require more resources. Balancing what is best for special needs students and what is best for their classmates is a continual challenge for teachers. It doesn't help that special needs students are frequently absent because of illness and appointments, thus contributing to their own learning challenges.

In many cases, it's possible for the school to address the root causes of students' behavioural issues by providing things like free nutritious meals to hungry kids or proper eyeglasses to those who are far-sighted and can't see the words on a page or who are near-sighted and have trouble deciphering the symbols on the chalkboard.[8] But in other cases more costly interventions are required, which can include extensive English language tutoring and counselling or one-on-one services for students who suffer from social-emotional issues or have other special needs. Some students have attention deficit hyperactivity disorder (ADHD) and can benefit from taking prescription medications, which the school cannot provide them with. The hardest cases are often those in which the behavioural issues exist because of abuse and/or neglect that the child is experiencing at home. In cases like this, things like intervention, support, and counselling can help to lessen the psychological barriers that hinder the child's learning.

Chaos in the Classroom

In a second grade class that I observed at Lakeview Elementary one day, students were having a lot of trouble sitting still, in part because the sun was streaming through the windows and they obviously wanted to be running around the playground instead of watching a *National Geographic* video that was being shown as part of an assignment. Sarah Williams, the supply teacher who had this group of students (who she described to me as "tough") as her first grade class in the previous year, was doing her best to keep the children relatively calm and focused on the video they were meant to be watching, until the outdated and malfunctioning VCR began acting up. Some students became hyperactive and giggly, others distracted or distant. One male student was more unruly than the others.

When the telephone in the classroom rang, the teacher went over and answered it. When it rang a second time, Williams chose to ignore it so she could focus on getting the VCR to play. Seeing this, the unruly and hyperactive boy went over and answered the phone, without permission. The teacher was then forced to deal with the student's misbehaviour and the caller simultaneously. Even after being disciplined for answering the phone without permission, the student continued acting out, repeatedly banging on his desk. Williams threatened him with a trip to the principal's office, but it didn't stop him. Finally, he was sent out of the room. Soon after, I heard loud noises in the hallway as he continued his banging on a table that was out there.

After about 15 minutes of the teacher fiddling with the VCR and rewinding the tape, the video finally came back on. But while it played, several students continued to act up. When the classroom telephone rang again and Williams went to answer it, many of the students left their seats and gathered around another student's desk, where they laughed and played around. At this point, the video was being ignored by most students. One even came over to me to show off a watch he had disassembled into its various parts. When the phone call ended, Williams restored order in the room, turned off the video, and dismissed the class for the day.

She then disappeared for a long time, leaving me to admire the classroom displays and catch up on my observation notes. She returned apologizing for her lengthy absence, explaining that one of the boys in the class had tripped another boy on the way out of the school, and the way the boy landed had resulted in a cut to his arm. While it initially appeared to be an accident, the injured boy's mother claimed that his classmate had also pushed her son earlier in the day, and so the mother was now bringing the situation to the attention of the principal. "A real mess," Williams called it. I also learned in our after-class discussion that the student she'd had to send out into the hall takes Ritalin for his ADHD. Therefore, every day he must go to the principal's office – as there are no school nurses' offices anymore – to take his pill at 3 p.m. According to Williams, by 2:45 p.m., the effects of the morning dose shows signs of having worn off, as the boy's behaviour noticeably worsens.

It was made very clear to me that day how the behavioural problems of one student can impede learning for the rest of the students in a classroom. Even when the issues are actively addressed, they can't be completely eliminated from the daily reality of classrooms. Nonetheless, prevention and treatment can be effective in improving a child's behaviour, thereby improving the child's ability to learn as well as the ability of the other children in the class to learn.

Hungry Students, Failing to Learn

Hungry students find it hard to learn. Not only are they distracted by the growling in their stomachs, their brains need fuel in order to think and acquire new information. At Lakeview Elementary, one teacher related how children used to steal other students' lunches, complaining to their teachers about stomach aches. The school addressed this problem by implementing a hot lunch program. By ensuring that students got at least one square meal per school day, it eliminated the lunchbox crimes while reducing hunger. Most students at the school participate in this program. Each month they are sent home with an empty envelope and the request that it be filled with $50. Parents who can't afford the full monthly amount are instructed to give what they can afford. As long as the student brings back an envelope, he or she qualifies for the nutritionally balanced daily meal. (To avoid stigma, the envelopes aren't marked with a name, so no one knows how much is in each student's envelope.) Encouraged by the success of the lunch program – improvements in both student behaviour and academic achievement – Lakeview also began a school-subsidized breakfast program, which is offered free to the students.

In contrast to the comprehensive and well-established meal pro-grams at Lakeview Elementary, Ashfield Elementary has only recently begun to address the nutritional and dietary needs of their low-income students. Teacher Amy Peterson, explains: "We have hot lunch and we have a breakfast program a couple of days a week run by the First Nation group. But everybody's welcome to come, so whoever is hun-gry can go. So it's just starting up this week." The new food programs aim to address child hunger and a lack of nutritionally adequate food in students' diets.

In East Vancouver, food security is a serious issue for some students. William Coleman, the principal of Pearson Elementary, used to work at Cassandra Elementary, which is attended by students who live in Vancouver's (indeed, Canada's) poorest neighbourhood, the Down-town Eastside. Coleman described the critical role that the school meal programs played in helping those students: "Those kids come to school down there because it's the only sane part of their day. We fed them at Cassandra Elementary. Mind you, we do here too; we have a breakfast program. But we had a breakfast program there and a lunch program, and if the kids didn't eat those two [meals], they probably wouldn't eat till they came back to school for breakfast the next day." According to Coleman, the students "... lived in that SRO [single room occupancy hotel] down there, which is bad because they put all the dysfunctional folks together. I was there [at the school] for four years ... Wonderful kids, but their home lives! What they bring to school and the baggage that they have; how they even get to school is an amazing thing. When I look at that, and I look at [the resources at this school], it's like I've died and gone to heaven. I mean, it's really not fair."

Principal Coleman started as a teacher at Cassandra Elementary in the early 1970s, and he says that it didn't take long for him to notice a pattern. "The kids that I taught [there], they go through the cycle [of poverty]. Their parents were on assistance and welfare, [then] their siblings [were] on assistance and welfare." He felt that the neighbour-hood's social isolation and the cycle of poverty made it challenging to inspire students. "It's really hard in school to try and teach those kids down there that there is another world out there, and that if you just go to school and if you do what you do and you get interested in something, you don't have to be in that kind of a place," he reminisced. Even living only a few blocks from the heart of downtown Vancou-ver's business district, many of the students he taught at Cassandra Elementary were extremely socially isolated: "One year I took some kids downtown, and this is when we still had the old Woodward's [department store] – those kids had never been in an elevator. They had never been on an escalator. I took them to Simon Fraser [University]; they didn't know it existed. Some had never been to the beach and seen sand. That's [the world] that [kids from that neighbourhood] live in. And it's just so criminal."

In some parts of the Downtown Eastside, especially prior to the opening of the Insite supervised injection facility, open-air drug use was common. When I related a story to Principal Coleman about stepping through a crowd of people who were shooting up on the ground at the base of the Vancouver Co-op Radio station in the Downtown Eastside, he replied

> And they are so blasé about it, because it's what they see every day. They don't know that there is this other part [to life]. When I was there in my four years ... there would be horrendous things going on by the railroad tracks; there would be somebody shooting up or somebody murdered in the back alley across the street, and the kids just walked by. 'Cause that's just what [kids in that area] know, and I feel bad 'cause it's robbing their childhood. That's the scary part: the cycle just keeps repeating itself and [the kids] don't ever get out of it ... unless they have a teacher at school who can kind of mentor them along and gear them in the right way, regardless of what happens at home.

Coleman said that, while principal at Cassandra Elementary, "I needed every single penny that I could get [my hands on] to get these kids into after-school programs, to get them into piano lessons, or whatever. I [could] never get enough."

At Coleman's current school, Pearson Elementary, the students historically have come from a mix of economic backgrounds, but the gentrification that's been happening has meant that the school no longer teaches as many children from low-income families as it had in previous decades. This shift, however, has not diminished the necessity for resources and programs to meet the needs of the at-risk students. Principal Coleman explained, "Here, there are a few who are [poor] to that extent [as in the Downtown Eastside], but these kids go to piano, these kids are involved in soccer, these kids go to swimming lessons, these kids go to community centres, and so it's like night and day [compared to Cassandra Elementary]." He feels that the key to schools succeeding with low-income students is to fill "that need for having stuff for those kids, because if we don't give it to them they're not going to get it at home."

Principal Coleman also believes in the value of student mentoring by a teacher or community member. He said, "We had a Youth and Family Worker at Cassandra Elementary and he would go out of his way. If there was a group of girls into basketball or volleyball, he would go on Saturdays and take this group of girls to some tournament here or there. And he actually got three or four of these kids who were in horrendous home situations involved in the BC provincial girls volleyball team. Just for them to know that they can get out, and come be with other people." He went on to say that he really feels that even just having one caring person can make a world of difference in these kid's lives, a belief he gained during a conference he once attended with colleagues. One of the speakers was renowned American educator Deborah Meier, who Coleman says inspired him. "She said, 'One person – all it takes is one person to make a difference in the life of one of those kids.' And that resonated with the staff. And you never know if you're going to be the person."

Research confirms what Meier was saying that day. Long-term mentoring, with consistent tutors and resource-rich programs, has been shown to improve outcomes.[9] Coleman felt that he had made a difference for two students in particular as a teacher. He told me the story:

When I was there [at Cassandra Elementary] as a teacher, little Stacey was in my class. She was in grade 4 at the time and she was always immaculately dressed, but her clothes had holes in them. One day, she didn't come to school and I said to her little friend, "Where's Stacey today?" And she said, "Oh, her mom died last night."

So I found out the long story that there were seven kids in the family and Mom worked at the fish cannery down on the docks there. Mom was like 42 years old, and she [had come] home from work and sat down … They had no furniture, Stacey had a mattress on the floor … [The mom] was feeding the baby [that day], literally a baby, [when] she'd had a heart attack. And so there was Dad, [who] didn't speak any English. He was out of work with seven kids, [including] a baby.

I went to the house and knocked on the door and Stacey answered. I told her, "If there's anything you need, here's my phone number." A couple of days later I checked in to make sure that they [had] stuff, and the day [Stacey] came back to school it was recess and she said to me, "Can I talk to you?" [We were in the] little back room [and] she jumped up on the chair. She put her arms around me and she started to cry and said, "Thank you for caring." Oh god, I was bawling and she was bawling … Long story short now … she had an older brother named Brian and … when I came back to work in September, Brian was in my class and I knew Christmas was going to be tough for [him and his sister], so I had asked [Stacey] to ask her dad if they could come with me for Christmas. Anyhow he said yes, so [when the day came] I went [and] picked them up and – these were the kids I talked about who had never been to Simon Fraser, never been to Woodward's, never been in an elevator – so we did a tour of the city [before] they came back to my house [and] I cooked dinner. My house was like Buckingham Palace [to] them, so when [it was time to take] them back home that night they didn't want to go because they knew.

And [today], 33 years later, Brian is now a lawyer and Stacey is a nurse. We are in contact every year at Christmas, [either] on the phone or [via] a card, [checking in, asking] "How are you doing?" They are just like family. And it's from 30 years ago, so it's amazing. Those are the kind of kids that just stick with you, and you do what you do [to help them]. I just [told] Brian and Stacey there is a better life, you know you can do it, but you have to work hard. They had a couple of older brothers who [had gotten] into trouble, but [these two] knew that that wasn't what they wanted. Brian, when he was old enough, got a job and got scholarships and stuff to go to school. And Stacey did the same thing. And they both have families now, so it just warms your heart because those were two kids who made it, and that's what Cassandra Elementary is all about. So my heart goes back there, [and] I've [gone back] there twice now. Anyhow, time marches on.

Principal Coleman's insights are supported by research that shows that dedicated and sustained mentoring can have a positive impact on the academic achievement and long-term success of students from low-income families in high-poverty neighbourhoods.[10]

Transiency and Student Turnover

North Americans move a lot, especially low-income families. As economic fortunes change, people relocate to obtain work, services, or housing. Sometimes they are forced to leave a rented space and relocated because they haven't paid their rent or their landlord has decided to sell the building. Because low-income families in East Vancouver are particularly susceptible to the factors that necessitate moving, over the course of a school year, several children in a classroom will depart and several new students will arrive, all of whom typically have a very diverse range of backgrounds, experiences, and skill sets.

Katherine Drucker is the principal at Ashfield Elementary, where she claims "We have lots of kids coming in and going out throughout the year. I could get you the exact number, but it's a [continual] revolving door of people coming and going. In fact, right now we are full. Our school is full, and we have 25 people on the wait list to come here who are currently at other schools." She attributed this high turnover among the students to the real estate market, explaining, "In this community a lot of people are renters, so I don't know if there are issues with them not paying the rent or issues with the landlord selling the houses. The housing market's gone crazy. Some of our families move out to the suburbs where they can get a larger place to live that's more affordable for them; some of our families in the [higher] poverty end, they run out of [money to pay rent]. We have several families on the street right now. We also have a whole handful of foster kids who can get moved around."

Foster kids, recently arrived refugees, children from homeless families. Integrating these students into classrooms and getting them quickly on track curriculum-wise poses a challenge.[11] In order to ensure students' smooth transition, high demands are put on school resources. For each new student, the school must track down paperwork, identify gaps in previous education and training, as well as provide extra support to the student to fill in any learning gaps and ease their entry into the classroom. Doing all of this is a real challenge for urban schools in high-poverty neighbourhoods.

Abuse and Neglect

Sadly, students who are exposed to abuse or neglect at home can be found walking the halls of any elementary school, not just those located in urban settings; however, students who attend urban elementary schools have a higher risk of neglect and abuse due to factors such as addiction and poverty. Therefore, staff at these schools must be equipped to identify students who are suffering from being mistreated at home and get them the appropriate help. Besides the emotional trauma caused, if left untreated, the psychological effects of neglect and abuse can hinder healthy child development and learning.

According to the teachers and administrators I talked to, abuse and/or neglect is seldom straightforward. Sometimes it originates in households where children are exposed to crime and violence; other times it can reflect customs and cultural differences around discipline. In some cases it is a combination of both. Katherine Drucker, principal of Ashfield Elementary, explained:

> I don't know if I'm making a generalization, but there are a lot of people who come in to the school and pay [for things] in $100 bills, and so we do know that some of our community is involved in illegal activities. And we know that some of our children are in those kinds of environments. We also know that this whole area used to be "Inner City." When they did all the stats, they said, 'No, it doesn't qualify for Inner City [designation]'. But in reality, I'm told that there are so many families living in illegal basement suites that it doesn't show [in the statistics]. And we do have many families living [crowded] in[to] small areas.
>
> We also have [a] population [of] Asians [who] treat their children differently in terms of discipline. So we have had children with [marks from] hot coins on their back, or children who have marks on their legs from [being hit with] sticks; [these are] common forms of punishing children. So we get the social workers in and we explain and talk to the families about how they need to be treating their children. That kind of violence does show up. I would say it's occasionally brought to my attention. Whether there's more of it or not I don't know, but occasionally it comes to our attention; not frequently.

Regardless of the form of the abuse or the reasons for it, schools play a critical role in identifying and helping address cases of child mistreatment.

How can teachers detect which students are suffering from abuse and/or neglect at home, beyond looking for the obvious physical scars or injuries? According to Susan Fletcher, a social worker who works with students in East Vancouver elementary schools, it is "the children who are more withdrawn and are showing some more internal kind of symptoms of distress or are having some issues. Sometimes [they] get missed, and that's worrying."

Then there is the challenge of getting the students the required help. While Fletcher feels that the teachers are doing a good job identifying students suffering from abuse or neglect, she is frustrated that intervention often stops there. She explained: "I think that the roadblocks are encountered when it's identified that services are needed [but the] services aren't readily available. There are long wait lists for an assessment, [and] there are limitations where they can [be referred to] in the community, or [school staff] are concerned that the family won't be receptive. If the family's not on board, sometimes it's identified but [things] just get stuck there [at that stage]." According to Fletcher, getting the families on board is the key to successful intervention. She explained that, "It's the area counsellor who would reach out to the family and say, 'We would like to make a referral to family services, are you okay with that?' That is typically what happens." In Fletcher's experience, problems emerge "if a family isn't ready to be involved in a program." In particular, she said, "What doesn't work is the pressure that they sometimes experience or feel; sometimes [it's] the sense of a threat [like] 'If you don't do this, this is what's going to happen to your child.' That really pushes families away and, in fact, creates greater problems because they're less likely to reach out when they really are ready and they need something, or [when] there's a crisis."

Fletcher said that, in general, when dealing with students who are experiencing abuse or neglect at home, it is important to be careful not to assume anything: "The other thing that doesn't really bode well is making assumptions around why families are struggling, and I get a sense that this happens. Sometimes there's an assumption that the family doesn't care, you know, [because] they don't come to meetings [and] they never show up to parent-teacher [conferences]. [It's tempting in these situations to think] 'We've tried calling them; they just don't care about the child'." Based on her experience, Fletcher believes that, "there are a lot of other issues that are probably going on for that family, more pressing issues. Sometimes it's just about getting through each day, so sometimes coming to meet with a teacher after school is just less of a priority. Maybe getting work that day or being able to go to the food bank that day is the greater priority."

At the behest of the teachers and in an effort to create an opportunity for intervention where necessary, Fletcher started a parenting skills program at Lakeview Elementary. She explained, "At Lakeview Elementary that was the big thing. [The teachers kept saying] 'These parents need parenting skills. Let's have parenting groups, and that'll solve all the problems.' Well, I would organize parenting programs, and two or three parents would come. Then, again, it was 'Well, they just don't care; they're just not into it.' When really it was about feeling quite threatened, [causing parents to think] 'Why were we selected for a parenting group? Why did I get this letter not my neighbour?' So the approach I don't think was very inclusive. It was quite labeling and threatening."

Although this intervention program failed, Fletcher found success with a different program; one that took place off the school grounds. As she described it,

> One thing that did work was [a program implemented at] the housing project that's right by Lakeview Elementary – the Frank Nichols housing project ... What I did was, I connected with an elder who had lived [there] for years and years. There were a lot of multigenerational families that lived in that housing project, and I asked [the elder], "What do you think [will] help get some families involved in the school? We'd love to have them, they have a lot to offer." She said, "Well, you first have to come here, and they have to get to know you and trust you and build a relationship. And then they're more likely to come to you and pop in and say hello."
>
> So I started a program. They had a hall there, like a little meeting room, [and] once a week we would come together. And I didn't call it a parenting program. I [really just asked them], "What would you like to do?" And many of them just wanted to do art. So I would bring art supplies and I would give some direction but [mainly] let them do their own free art expression. We'd do some movement and just chatting ... building relationships. And from there I would have [casual] visits in my office ... And then they would be more about, "I need your help. I'm really struggling this week." So [the program's success was largely due to] listening to what the elder lady had to say; going there with no agenda but bringing resources that they seemed open to.

In Fletcher's case, a program that was built from the ground up and shaped by the participation of the people targeted really made a difference. In some ways the approach she used for this program, as compared to that used for the failed parenting program, is similar to a community-organizing approach versus a service-model approach. Whereas community organizing focuses on identifying the needs of a community and building the community's capacity to meet its own needs, the service-model approach is simply about providing services such as food or temporary shelter.[12]

English as a Second Language Issues and Instruction

As discussed in chapter 2, the fact that students have very different levels of English language fluency is an ongoing challenge in East Vancouver elementary schools. Principal Katherine Drucker explained how this is an issue Ashfield Elementary:

Obviously language is a huge challenge. Many of our children and their parents speak their native tongue at home. And mothers and grandmothers don't speak English, so that's a real barrier to get the kids speaking and learning English. One of our big challenges is, as you probably know, we have a five-year cap on ESL [support]. So once a child has been in school for five years – that's kindergarten to grade 4 – we don't get money from the government to support them learning English. And so resources are a huge challenge for us because many of those kids don't have a full understanding of English after five years.

Once the five years of ESL resources run out, children must get English language support in other ways.

Principal Drucker feels that English language fluency does not emerge from classroom instruction alone, believing it must be reinforced by engaging in activities outside of class. She explained, "In the area of the whole social milieu, what we find is that a lot of Asian families don't send their children out to play soccer, and they don't send them to Brownies [or] Guides … [The kids] go home after school, and they stay at home. And so they don't have a lot of those interactions with kids to learn more English, to experience our social life, and to do outside activities." This lack of engagement in socializing and extracurricular activities outside of school can limit English language skills acquisition and mastery for some children, in Principal Drucker's opinion. She went so far as to directly link the below average performance of Ashfield Elementary students on the provincial standardized literacy exams to the high percentage of ESL students in her school:

We [are still] working towards meeting expectations because [of] reading comprehension. A lot of these kids can read [words out loud], but they don't understand what they're reading. There isn't a lot of [comprehension]. And when you have a [student] population that is 85% ESL, you have a lot of struggling readers. Our goal at this school, through the early literacy and now the early intervention [program], is to have all children reading [by] grade 2. So we are hoping that in three years all of the grade 2 students will be reading and writing and comprehending [as a result of the] intensive work being put on that age group.

A widespread lack of English language fluency throughout a school's student body means that it can be challenging for teachers to communicate with and engage parents about supporting and improving their child's reading skills.

Teresa McDonald is the principal of Soaring Eagle Elementary. She argues that in the current system there is a lack of resources to help teachers work around the challenges that arise from the fact that a multitude of languages are better understood than English by many of their students and, to an even greater extent, by their students' parents. In her experience, "There are the challenges for recent immigrant families in terms of getting the services that [their children] need, even just trying to have a meeting with them. We share one multicultural worker with about 20 different schools – just try to get some translation services! At report card time, when we have a disciplinary incident, all of those things, it's very challenging. I've had to use senior students sometimes for report card interviews, [and] I use a grade seven student who's reliable to come in and help because I can't get the help that we need for translation." Language barriers can also make it more difficult to address other kinds of issues with parents, such as their child's behavioural problems. Principal McDonald explained,

> Fitting in with, and for us to communicate to them, the integrating process, you can see how slowly it's going. There's where you see poverty issues. You see [families] not being able to access services. So you might have a child that we perceive after a couple of years has a major learning issues. But where do you go from there? That leads to the medical profession, but then it's hard for them to access [those services]. We write consult letters to help the families. All these things are huge time issues [that don't contribute] to those darned FSAs [standardized exams], but they're all the things we need to put in place to help kids in the future.
>
> Life in school is no longer, in my view, academic – not even close. We spend a lot of time with social service agencies. That's the way I see it increasing. Certainly in East Van. I know we have to do it; we all do it. The teachers do it too. Because otherwise we won't get to the academic gains and those other more basic aspects of learning [won't be] in place.

The time spent on the social work and social services side of teaching, especially by teachers in higher-poverty public schools, often goes unrecognized and unrewarded, but it is crucial to improving the lives and experiences of the children who are involved, as well as that of their families. Addressing a child's non-academic problems helps to create a solid foundation for a child's future learning and success. The idea is that if you identify an issue early and address it, it won't knock a child off track. Cracks in the foundation can allow children to slip through, setting the stage for future failure in academic achievement and social development.

Like much of their intervention work, the social work that teachers do to help certain students is carried out in a context of constrained resources and unique challenges, leaving even less of their time and energy for the other students in the class. This consequence of classrooms having high number of special needs and ESL students was something that was acknowledged by several parents who were interviewed. One such parent was Jane Haswell, whose son is in kindergarten at Ashfield Elementary. She said that limited resources and resource cutbacks have her considering switching her son's school. "I went [through] the public school system, so there's [a] part of me that doesn't want to think ill of it because I know the obstacles that teachers face. But at the same time I realize that, due to things like cutbacks, all that kind of stuff, it makes it difficult for them to accommodate special needs [and] they really do the best that they possibly can. I don't fault anyone for it, I just ... I don't think in some ways [my son] fits in as well and I think a different work environment might be better for him."

At the same time, many parents with children who have special needs or who are learning English as a second language reported feeling disappointed at the lack of resources available to help their child. Rochelle Grant, a parent of a student at Wellington Elementary, said she felt her children are not thriving at school because of their lack of English language fluency: "I think [the support for] English as a second language is a big problem. Especially my son, he's in grade 5. How much they want to make him an ideal student, he is not ... Sometimes he is careless or sometimes [there is] the language problem, that's why he is not very good but not very bad ... not speaking. But how can I explain, he's not very good. I think the big problem is language." Formerly a teacher in her country of origin, this parent continues to study and learn to master English herself. "I was a degree holder. I was a teacher, but there is a language problem. I can't understand very well ... So now more than three years, I am living with my kids, so I can't improve my English," she shared. She feels that the school no longer provides enough ESL support for her children, claiming that "In the beginning I feel they are giving extra support, but now I think [because the kids] are older they need more. Now I feel they don't get enough."

The ESL challenge is a critically important one in East Vancouver elementary schools. At East Harcourt Elementary, immersion is the primary method of dealing with students for whom English is a second language. In the early grades these students are quickly integrated into the mainstream classroom but given extra support. Principal Jennifer Newcastle explained, "For the most part the kindergarten, grade 1, and [grade] [students] are simply immersed right in to their classroom. And just the complete immersion is what they get with some support from specialists, but for the most part [the strategy is to] just immerse [them] into the classroom. And through song, and games and stories, and so on, the daily activity of the classroom, they acquire the language."

Generally, most of the specialized instruction these students receive is for basic English, but often it is not enough support and their teachers must then spend time during class giving them extra help, sometimes to the detriment of the other children. That said, children in classrooms with a large number of ESL students also stand to benefit in some ways. One way this can happen is by being exposed to different teaching styles. The approach used by teacher Amy Peterson provides a good example of this. Peterson modified her teaching style to meet the ESL needs of her students at Ashfield Elementary, and in doing so, she more effectively meets the needs of all of the children in terms of their various learning styles. As she explained, "[The kids in my class] really need a routine. [They like me to go] step by step: we're going to do this first, this next, then just sort of work our way through it ... I think that these kids really respond to a routine ... they really respond to small steps, and a lot of repetition. I do a lesson and it has to be repeated; whereas if you teach on the west side, you can do a lesson once and they've got it. Here, you've got to do it over again, [and] you always have to check for understanding." When asked why the repetition was so important, she said, "Sometimes I've spoken too fast [or] given too many directions at one time [for some of the kids to follow]. So I'll say, 'Okay, who thinks they know what to do? If you think you know, you can go. If you have some questions, just stay with me [and] I'll go over it again.' [After I go over it again] I'll say, 'Anybody else who's ready to go, go.' And then sometimes I'll have a small group that I'll just keep with me and [to them] I'll say, 'I'll start you off; let's do the first three questions together.' And then, once they're feeling secure about what they have to do, they go off and do it." Peterson explained how this technique ensures that everyone is keeping up with her lesson: "So it's just sort of breaking it down, giving them opportunities to stay a little bit longer without sticking out like a sore thumb [because] they don't know what to do."

Feeling that it's important for the students to understand that different people excel in different areas, Peterson says, "I always tell my class that they are the 'smart' class and my job is to make them smarter, and that we're not all smart in all areas. So [when I ask them], who's really good at math in the room, or who's a really good reader, or who's a really good drawer, they always know. And we talk about it. I'll say, 'Now, if I'm really busy with a group, who can you ask for help?' So they know who they can go to when I'm really busy." In this way, she encourages the students in the class to help each other:

> They know that if I'm not available and they're stuck, they're really good at helping each other. Because of this, they know that somebody will come to them when they need [help]. [This] encourages them to be willing to ask somebody else for help, and also being willing as a person to help [others]. I say, "You can't tell [your classmates] the answer, but you can tell them the steps that they have to do." So there's just a general feeling in the room that we can help anybody. As a result, I think it [spills] over to the playground. You'll see them out there helping each other when somebody gets into trouble, but that's [just] the way I run my room. Other teachers do other things.

This collaborative learning approach has been demonstrated to be highly effective in promoting extremely high levels of early literacy.[13]

When asked about what she finds most challenging about teaching in an East Vancouver elementary school, Peterson replied: "Well, for me, it's to slow down because I'm always in a hurry. I've been here long enough that I know that I have to re-teach. There are certain kids who I put around me … I'll sit at a table for a while, and I have those kids around me, and just encourage them to finish. Some of them just need to know that they can do it. They don't have that confidence."

This kind of approach, going slow, heavy on repetition, doesn't come naturally to all teachers. While it may prove effective in the long run, it requires teaching in a style that might differ from the way teachers themselves were taught. They must attune their teaching strategy and to meet the unique needs of the diverse students in the classroom.

Teaching in Mixed Groups

Several of the teachers interviewed said that one strategy that worked really well when teaching the foundations of reading and math was breaking up students into small groups, each containing mixed strengths and competencies. Different schools used different approaches as it concerned grouping. Ashfield Elementary, for example, does what's called "family grouping" to more effectively meet the needs of its diverse student population. This entails multi-grade classes, wherein the students have the same teachers three years in a row.

As a teacher at the school, Peterson likes the continuity that this approach affords. "I've always liked family grouping, which is [grades] 1, 2, and 3 [combined]. And I keep the kids for three years. Each year, I get a new group of seven-to-eight grade 1 [students] and I love that. But you can only do that when numbers sort of work," she said. She feels that the year-to-year continuity in terms of teacher particularly helps ESL students. As she explained, "They [don't] have much English, so [that makes it harder for them if they] change to a different teacher every year; they [have] to get used to that teacher and a new teaching style, and same with [getting to know new classmates]. So when you keep them for two years, they get much more confident and [after that] they're ready to work with another teacher."

Peterson noted that there are safeguards in place to avoid some of the potentially negative consequences of the family grouping approach. "We don't work in isolation. Quite often teachers team together, so it's not that [the students] are just having me for three years or me for two years. [There are] lots of other teachers that they're having to deal with at the same time. So it's not that they're stuck with one adult, and maybe a lousy adult they don't like. When I had my [grades] 1, 2, 3, if the parents didn't want them to stay with me for three years, they didn't have to. And if the student didn't want to stay with me, it was fine. I never chose to have anybody leave. I never said, 'I don't want that kid for three years.' I always kept them."

Peterson felt that this multi-year classroom approach worked well for her students: "I always found that by the end of grade 3 those kids, even if they started with academic problems or started with social problems [or] behaviour problems, by the end of grade 3 they were a different kid. Just because of that continuity – they knew my rules, they knew my expectations. So in September I could start right in with that group right away. I didn't have to spend September [and] October getting to know them. So it's a huge advantage."

While the non-traditional multi-grade grouping helps to address some of the challenges of teaching students at Ashfield Elementary, Peterson experiences frustration when children are not able to access the services they need.[14] She said, "The challenge is when you get a [misbehaving] child who really, really needs help, and you [can't get them] the help ... the services that you want for those kids. Somebody with a really bad speech problem [for example], and the speech therapist can't see them. It's those kinds of things that are frustrating to [deal with], not the other stuff because you can move the kids along. You can teach them."

When needed services for children are not available, teachers have to do the best they can with the tools they have at hand, including their experience. In her case, Peterson says,

> The resource teachers have lots of extra training that I don't have as a regular classroom teacher. So they're the people who you really want to be working with those children, but they're spread very thin. So the challenge is getting those kids that need that outside help, [to] get the outside help. Okay, the other kids who [don't need outside help] need resource help [from a resource teacher at the school], because some kids really need that one-to-one for at least half an hour each day. It just gives them a shot in the arm and their confidence goes up.

Observing how much the student's learn over the school year inspires teachers like Peterson. She said, "I mean, I love teaching here, otherwise I wouldn't have stayed. The kids do progress. I can see the difference because we always do testing in September and we do testing in June, and [you really see] the leap from one to the other. You can see it even with the kids who are [Ministry] designated children [with special needs]." This satisfaction is one of the benefits that teachers like Peterson receive by working with students in East Vancouver schools – getting to watch them learn, progress, and develop, often overcoming major challenges.[15]

Students with Special Needs

Similar to the approach used with their ESL students, East Vancouver elementary schools attempt to integrate students with special needs into classrooms (rather than segregating them as was often done in the past) and then provide them with resources and support both in and outside the classroom. But in the schools studied, there aren't always enough resources for effectively managing integration. According to Principal Tim Richards at Great Forest Elementary, "The model was that you needed to integrate the students and then support them with a resource teacher and with staff assistance – with SSAs is what they're called, 'Special Education Assistants'." But, as he went on to explain, resource teachers were no longer being assigned to support these students in the regular classroom: "The support for the integration of the children into regular classes diminished over time, until now it's gone. That's one of the issues that the union is bringing back. They're trying to say those kids do not have the support that they need, and therefore the teachers don't have the support that they need."

Great Forest Elementary has 14 students officially classified as having special needs. According to Principal Richards, "For the 14 low-incident students that we have – that's dependent handicapped, autistic, those with mental [or] physical disabilities … I'm just trying to think of the categories   fetal alcohol [syndrome]. Those kids whose learning and behavioural needs are quite great, they're eligible for a portion of [time with] a [Special Education] Assistant. So we've got 14 "low-incident students" and we've got six SSAs."

While he was grateful for the support they did have, Richards felt that the school required more support staff. But he believes that teachers also have an important role to play in addressing the learning barriers facing special needs students. In fact, he feels that appropriate instruction is key to improving their academic performance, saying, "Essentially it needs to be quality, hands-on individualized instruction to meet each individual student's needs. [This] means that the teacher needs more time to prepare [and] needs to be prepared to spend the time to do that kind of preparation. For the math, [the instruction] has to be hands-on, use of manipulatives; reading and writing and Language Arts programs that we're currently working towards all of our teachers [using], [the literacy programs], they have to meet the needs of individual students."

In this context of declining resources, East Vancouver elementary schools are having to educate more students with special needs than ever before. As Principal Teresa McDonald of Soaring Eagle Elementary explained,

> We are finding hugely, and this is in the last few years, that mental health issues – both [that] of the parents and [that] of the children – are coming to the fore more than any other issue, and this is new. All of us principals are finding this. The amount of time that we are spending on counselling families, plugging families in to services that are hard to access, looking

at learning difficulties – and with learning difficulties often comes social [and] emotional challenges. This is proving to be what we end up doing all day. [And it] doesn't seem to be just the east side of Vancouver.

I speculate that it comes from stress in the home … from the costs of living in Vancouver, so that two parents are very busy trying to provide the basics. Whether or not they look middle-income or not, everybody's still struggling. And children are experiencing that stress and anxiety.

For me, this year I had to hire using my paper budget. I hired an extra Youth and Family Worker because we just couldn't keep up with the volume of that type of referral. Within that referral are children with anxiety, children with severe behaviour that results from [mental illness], and not just acting out and doing stupid things … Everything from video game addiction through to sexualized behaviour – we see a lot more of all of that. I think this comes from media [and from kids] being left alone; [they're getting] exposed [to] the Internet [and] to media more than [they] should be as a young child.

Every day, we have an incident of somebody not being picked up [after school]. A young child not being picked up, and we are worried for their safety. Who's looking after them at home? Are they going home alone at the age of 8? We're looking at those kinds of issues: learning issues that may result may show up looking like ADHD, [but] we don't know if they are or not; helping families access medical services. All those kinds of issues are what we're dealing with as a principal and support staff, hugely.

Many students in East Vancouver schools have special needs despite not being officially designated as such by British Columbia's Ministry of Education.

Principal McDonald emphasized that it is important to remember that not all at-risk children are challenging students to teach, noting that "Some of the happiest [children] in this school are [those who have] foster parents; children with a special need where the parents are together and working on that together with the children and providing [them with] a lovely environment." As she goes on to explain, other children have health-related issues, such as "autistic children, kids with chronic health [problems], kids with feeding issues, diabetic children, and [kids with] mental health issues." These students require extra support, which is essential to their learning in those crucial early elementary years. In McDonald's opinion, "The biggest challenge that we have is the large numbers of children with what we call 'Ministry designation.' So that's children with a learning disability, autistic children, [and] children with chronic health concerns like fetal alcohol [syndrome]. Children with ADHD are not recognized by the Ministry. So, it's like, give [them] a pill … It's seen to be medical, it's not recognized." She lamented that they were lacking the necessary resources to effectively educate these high-needs students at Soaring Elementary:

> There's not [enough] extra support for kids in the classroom. So that's the thing I feel is not working. [We don't have] the expertise that's needed to work with some of these very challenging learning profiles, and on top of that [is] the paperwork that we have to do for it and [the] programming. So in a classroom, to have something that works for visually [impaired] children or children who are mentally in a tough state, or children who are just learning English, they're all together in one room. And [it's such a] feat to try to program for all of those different kids to be successful, I think we're still not there. Everybody is trying; everybody is doing the best they can. But I think that's where we're not successful yet. Meeting the needs of all the learning styles and all the learning issues in each class.

Beyond the 5%–10% of its students who have official Ministry designation, Soaring Eagle Elementary has many children who staff consider to be "grey area" students. As Principal McDonald explained,

> Diversity is a wonderful thing. We love all those kids. But to see them [perform] academically, all of them – this will be interesting for your research. We have a focus at our school for what we call "grey area" children: children that we can't quite figure out why they're not progressing very well. They don't have a special ed assistant – they don't qualify. [We have] 38 kids with an actual [Ministry] designation, so they get extra help. But the grey area children are just not flourishing, for many different reasons. And we went through our class lists, we went through every single student in the school, and in every single classroom we had approximately five to eight children [not progressing well]. Well, out of 23, that's like one third. One third not flourishing! For many different reasons, and we can pretty well tell why. But they're not the children who get extra support. We call them grey area. They're the ones that [the] social/emotional programs target because they've got too much else going on.

Staff at other schools also spoke of challenges posed by students who weren't designated as having special needs but who were having particular trouble learning. For example, Principal Jennifer Newcastle said this about East Harcourt Elementary: "Well, we have a segment of our population that isn't successful. Most of them are boys. We say a quarter of our school population is still struggling with some aspect of their learning, and we're trying to unlock that and figure out why that is. So those are our challenges. We haven't got 90% of our kids reading at grade level and being hugely, completely successful. Our goal is 80%, and we've reached that, but we'd like to keep making that higher and higher. So we still have a group of children that are having some struggles."

What is holding so-called grey area students back? The barriers impeding their learning are usually due to a complex combination of factors that are not easily diagnosed. Without a clear understanding of the causes, it is difficult for staff to identify and address the needs of these students, especially in a classroom where there are students who have other challenges that are more easily recognized and understood. Interestingly, research suggests that achieving early literacy and numeracy competency and skills could serve as a protective factor for these children, building resiliency and a foundation to overcome disadvantages and thrive.[16] What remains an open and vibrant debate is how best to accomplish this goal.

The Failure of Market-Based Approaches to Address the Challenges of Urban Education

One thing is clear: market-based approaches generally fail to improve educational outcomes for students with learning barriers or challenges. As in health care, the least profitable and most-difficult-to-treat cases in education are the ones that require the most resources, and when they are fortunate to get the required attention, they still may have – often – worse outcomes than the cases in which extra resources are not required. So while in education, some profit-seeking entrepreneurs aim to "cream skim" the easiest-to-teach students – those with motivated and engaged parents who will present little challenge in the classroom – the decision to pursue privatized and competitive approaches at a systemic level also leaves the public schools with fewer resources to educate the more challenging students "left behind."[17]

Advocates of charter schools or other privatized educational programs argue that the evidence points to experimental schools rather than other public schools when it comes to being successful at serving disadvantaged student populations; in reality, this evidence is highly contested and overstated. Even in the cases where these programs result in improved outcomes for their students, generally they teach a very different student population than does a typical urban public school in a high-poverty neighbourhood.[18] (One important exception is Geoffrey Canada's Harlem Children's Zone organization, which is discussed in more detail in chapter 6).

Even when a similar percentage of students from certain visible minority groups or from low-income families attend these schools, there are important differences between the student populations (and families) of experimental schools and other public schools. In practice, these differences mean that while some important innovations may be happening in terms of curriculum or technology – such as purchasing a laptop for each student to use – comparing the outcomes of students in these specialized programs or schools with that of more typical urban public schools serving similar student populations is actually like comparing apples and oranges.[19] Experimental or charter schools and programs not only tend to attract students who have more motivated parents – and thus have different home environments than most students in a typical urban poor public elementary school – they also usually exclude most of the challenging-to-teach students, which inevitably are a part of most diverse urban public schools.[20]

Conclusion

As this chapter has shown, special needs arise due to a broad range of factors, and they are factors to which children living in East Vancouver are particularly vulnerable as compared with children who live in the higher-income parts of the city. As students, these children require substantial extra attention and resources, as the failure to meet special needs and provide the necessary resources in the early learning years has long-term negative consequences for academic achievement. Research suggests that drop-out rates of students from some visible minority groups in Canada are shockingly high. For example, geographer Geraldine Pratt found that 40% of Filipino children reunited with mothers who migrated to Canada through the Live-In Caregiver Program fail to complete high school in Vancouver.[21] While social workers and counsellors are increasingly involved with school-based programs in order to help children who need it, teachers in higher-poverty urban public schools must also step up and help students overcome barriers to academic learning.[22]

What kinds of programs for special needs students can help? While some students benefit immensely from counselling services, others benefit from play or art theatre programs designed to help children overcome trauma. Other programs that can help include peer tutoring and peer learning, long-term mentoring, as well as partnerships with parents (described in chapter 5).[23] Some schools bring trained specialists in to work with groups of at-risk youth.

Susan Fletcher is a specialist who organizes intervention programs in East Vancouver elementary schools. As she explained, "We realized that there were many, many children in schools who needed our support or needed counselling services but weren't able to access our program." She said that this difficulty stemmed in part from narrow intake requirements but was also due to a lack of services. "So many children who needed the services weren't getting any support. So we worked very closely with schools and other community programs. We started to look at what could we put together that would really support those kids who we know are at-risk but aren't getting any services."

One of the programs that Fletcher created was for older elementary students who were deemed to be "at-risk." When discussing it, she said, "The outreach component [of the program] is that all the work happens in schools, so we don't have any children come to our office. I have a staff with 10 counsellors, and schools are our referral point. They identify the children through their school-based team meetings [or] through the teacher referral or area counsellor referral. We get a call and a request to come out and work with [the] selected group of children; usually it's between six and 10 children at one time."

This kind of program can help ease the social isolation that many special needs students and their families experience, as Fletcher noted: "Well, what we've noticed that's missing for many of these children and [their] families, that we hope to have them gain by the end of the program, is a sense of connectedness. And quite often that just begins with a sense of connectedness to an adult – an adult who cares; [one who] is available on a consistent basis so there's a stable, safe relationship that's established … I think it really begins with that relationship, and then [they're] able to feel good enough about themselves that they will form relationships with the other children in the group, and there you see a connectedness beginning."[24]

Special needs impedes learning for many students, and so it is essential that elementary schools have the resources to help them if they are to succeed academically. Identifying and then confronting special needs with the appropriate support and programs – ideally preventing them or addressing them before they become more severe – can help establish the preconditions for some children to be able to learn and succeed in the classroom.

4 Engaging Parents and the Community

Increasingly, teachers and administrators are recognizing the importance of engaging parents and the community as partners in children's education. Engaged parents can both directly and indirectly improve their child's learning.[1] Parents support children in all stages of learning and development, and they can often be important allies in identifying and addressing potential barriers to learning. With regard to the broader community, researchers have identified many positive partnerships between schools and community institutions and organizations, including schools that work with neighbourhood-based organizations and institutions to advance early childhood literacy and schools that have partnerships with local community centres to provide after-school care and programs.[2]

Despite the clear benefits to students when schools engage with parents and communities, school staff interviewed at the elementary schools studied in East Vancouver reported some challenges developing these relationships. These challenges include the parents' work commitments, language barriers, and parents' misunderstanding the role they're expected to play in the Canadian education system. Staff are tasked with having to communicate effectively with and engage parents from different linguistic, cultural, and educational backgrounds. Many of the parents must struggle to make ends meet and therefore sometimes lack availability to engage with teachers as a result of working multiple jobs simultaneously. Differing expectations (based on the parents' experiences with education in their country of origin) also creates challenges that go beyond simple language barriers in teachers' efforts to engage parents.[3] Social class differences between staff and parents can add to the challenges, sometimes even creating resistance to engagement on the part of some of the teachers and the parents. Despite these barriers, administrators and staff at the elementary schools continue to make involving parents a priority in students' education, recognizing the important role they can play in improving academic outcomes.

Engaging Parents

Increasing the involvement of parents in the schools and in their children's education is a frequently proposed policy recommendation for improving urban education. According to educational specialist and clinical psychologist Robert Evans: "Of all the ways for parents to contribute at school, by far the most significant is to be engaged in their children's lives and learning."[4] Beyond supporting their children's education at home, some parents volunteer on Parental Advisory Councils (PACs).[5] Some parents volunteer as classroom aides or playground monitors or supervise during fieldtrips. Some do all this, and more.

Parents' Role in Promoting Reading

Parents' role in their child's education can begin at an early age. Regular reading to preschool-aged children, in any language, creates a foundation for early mastery of literacy. Early literacy among elementary school students can also be advanced by parents reading to their children every day, after school and/or in the evenings. This isn't always possible, of course, as some parents themselves lack functional literacy skills, although even just telling stories based on books can help young children become more familiar with books and how stories are constructed. Depending on a family's economic circumstance, it can also be difficult for some parents to read to their children or engage with them over their homework. For instance, low-income families cannot afford to buy as many books as their wealthier counterparts (of course, though, community libraries are a wonderful resource). And some parents, such as those working two or three jobs to make ends meet, sometimes simply do not have time (or energy) at the end of the day to read to their children.

Government-funded literacy programs can help. For example, the province of British Columbia attempts to encourage new parents to read to their children through a public health program that provides new parents with home visits from community health nurses who bring a baby gift bag with a children's book. The national Parent-Child Mother Goose Program and other pre-kindergarten programs offered by community centres and elementary schools also encourage parents to read to their preschool children, in the hopes that they begin kindergarten ready to learn.

School staff in the elementary schools studied all felt that it was extremely important to prioritize reading at home and communicate its value. Principal Katherine Drucker said that Ashfield Elementary is focused on this critical goal: "We also need to get parents reading at home with their kids. Just about every one of our classrooms here has a home reading program with incentives for the parents to [participate]. It doesn't even matter if they read in Mandarin or Vietnamese, we [just] want the children to practice reading and to understand, 'This is a book.' 'Here's how it opens.' '[The words go] left to right.' 'There's a beginning, middle, [and] end.'" The key, Principal Drucker claimed, is to build "that confidence and a joy of reading."

Barriers to Engaging Parents in the School

Engaging parents in their children's education and learning is important, but the dynamics of parental involvement can be somewhat different in urban public schools in low-income neighbourhoods as compared to schools in wealthier neighbourhoods. Why? For one, the parents themselves face greater challenges, and there is greater potential for culture clashes and other tensions.[6]

Wellington Elementary teacher Kerry Reynolds described some of the challenges of getting the parents of her students involved in the classroom: "Parents here, they're busy. They work ... [and] they often do shift work, so some of them never are available." The school organizes conferences and makes it mandatory that parents have to contact teachers in some way. "But they're not here as much as you would probably see parents on a west-side [affluent middle class] school," she said.

Parents working several shifts to make ends meet are not likely to have much time to spare for volunteering at the school. But parents are not the only family members who could potentially be engaged in the schools. At Centennial Elementary, for example, teachers said that grandparents frequently visited the school to check in on children or bring them lunch. In many cases, it is the parents who are not employed who are stepping up to the plate to volunteer. In lower-income communities, school volunteers are generally less advantaged in terms of political, social, and financial capital than those at schools in wealthier areas.

Research in urban schools in the United States suggests that parents whose own academic achievements were limited or marked by failure may be intimidated by the institutional school setting. In her book *Unequal Childhoods*, sociologist Annette Lareau reports that the working class parents she studied felt it was the teacher's role and the school's responsibility to educate their children. These parents believed that their primary responsibility was meeting their child's basic needs of food, shelter, safety, and discipline. In contrast, the wealthier parents Lareau spoke to felt more of a responsibility to play a role in cultivating their children's education. Hence, these parents tended to be more actively engaged in their children's education, both in and outside of the school setting.[7]

Language barriers and cultural beliefs also influence whether parents get involved with their children's elementary school. Principal Teresa McDonald of Soaring Eagle Elementary said,

> That's where language skills come in, if you're not totally comfortable in your English. And also it's cultural. In Asian cultures, the school looks after school things and the family looks after the home things. And they don't really come together usually.
>
> [So these parents] are not used to that, that business of coming to school. They will always come to school if you ask them, they [will come]. The Asian families are there whenever there is a problem or a worry, or they come to parent-teacher conferences. [They're] very interested [then]. But for a PAC meeting, [about] how to fundraise for the school, what should be our school goals, [things like this], they don't feel comfortable. That's the school's job to look after that. You find that in all the schools.

Principal McDonald noted that all Parent Advisory Council volunteers at her school are fluent in English. In the schools studied, actively involved parents tended to have stronger English language fluency and a higher level of education as well as greater financial resources.

According to Principal Jennifer Newcastle, engaging parents of students at East Harcourt Elementary is the biggest challenge facing her school, although she doesn't feel it's due to a lack of caring but to other factors:

> The most difficult thing over the years has been the fact that we don't feel that we have a tremendous amount of parental support. The parents are hard-working, they sometimes work two jobs in order to make all ends meet; and many of them have been displaced. They might have been

teachers [or] doctors – high jobs, high paying jobs – so certainly professionals in their home country. When they come here they aren't qualified for the jobs that they had in their native land, and so they take menial jobs to make ends meet. [Because of this] many [are] in the restaurant business.

[So] it's not that they're not interested [in helping their children], or it's not that they don't care. They care deeply and they want their children to do well. They really do. They have very high standards for their children. They want their children to succeed academically for the most part. But because they're working so hard themselves first of all, and many of them [are] trying to get the language as well and just trying to make money, they don't have a lot of extra time to spend with their kids.

Despite the challenges getting these parents involved in the school during the daytime hours, Principal Newcastle said that, "When we have a concert, they all come in droves. If we have anything at the school where we offer an evening of food, or any kind of entertainment, they'll be here, for sure."

In the case of Pearson Elementary, Principal William Coleman feels "We have to find a better way to hook the Vietnamese folks 'cause I think that's a big thing." His thinking is based on the fact that parents who grew up in Vietnam experienced a very different kind of curriculum and instruction than what their children are experiencing in Canada. He explained,

I think we at the school have to do better to educate particularly the Vietnamese parents ... They think about when they went to school and everything was by rote [memorization] and all that kind of stuff. So here, if we don't send home like 50 million sheets of times tables or whatever, they don't think their kids are learning anything. So it's our job to kind of keep reinforcing the fact that [their kids are] learning, and when they go home if they have a half an hour of homework to do, it should be work that they are finishing up from school, not an add-on thing.

That's a challenge that I always have every time I meet with a Vietnamese parenting group, or a group of them. [I'll hear] "How come they don't have ..." or "My kid can do 37 pages of adding, subtracting, borrowing, and carrying" and all that ... What [these parents] don't understand is, that's all mechanical. [A kid] can add seven and six and make 13 but [not] really understand what "carry the one" means. What we're trying to do is really make the kid understand what [things like that] mean. They can do it on pen and paper, but they don't really understand what they are doing.

But they really *need* to understand, and what we have to do is teach them that they have to understand the concepts. [So] that's a real challenge for us because schools here are different than from where they were – big time, big time.

Another factor that can inhibit parental involvement is that parents often have different expectations of the education system than do school staff, and these conflicting views can create strains in the parent-school relationship. This difference of expectations was reflected in education scholar's Darcy Dachyshyn's research with refugee parents in Edmonton, Alberta. According to Dachyshyn's findings, "Many refugees are thankful for access to quality public education, but struggle with the perceived lack of moral training provided in schools."[8]

In the East Vancouver elementary schools studied, some parents complained that their children were not getting enough homework. Parent Rochelle Grant said this about her children at Wellington Elementary: "Especially in writing, they've got lots of spelling mistakes, no good comprehension. I think if they got lots of homework – not lots of homework, but enough homework daily, some spelling [and] some writing daily, continually – then they can improve these things." Wei Chang, a parent of a third grader at Ashfield Elementary, said that, "I want my kids to bring home more work to do because usually my kids bring no homework home."

School staff at these schools admitted to feeling some frustration when faced with parents who are critical of their pedagogy and practice in the classroom. In the minds of teachers and administrators, active parents aren't always perceived as helpful parents. Whereas Annette Lareau found that teachers sometimes resented the excessive involvement of some middle-class parents in their children's classroom, the issues are somewhat different in higher-poverty urban elementary schools, and somewhat more problematic than some might expect.[9] So while staff at these schools invite parents to become more engaged in their children's education and school life, they also try to channel parental involvement in ways they believe to be the most useful and productive.

Of course, that is if parents are available or wish to be involved. In the experience of Principal Tim Richards at Great Forest Elementary, "We find that one of the biggest challenges we face is that parents do not seem to take enough interest in following through on what children are doing. They don't seem as interested as they should be in making sure their children get their homework done. It seems that it's probably not because they don't care but because they don't understand that it's important." Principal Richards believed this lack of interest in engaging more actively with the school is in part related to parent's financial pressures.

Great Forest Elementary also faces challenges getting parents to attend Parent Advisory Council (PAC) meetings. According to PAC member Helen Welsh,

> You send home a notice, and in the past we have sent it home in up to five languages, but either [the parents] are intimidated to come in and help because they don't know any of us or because they don't speak English. Or, if we sometimes just can't get it translated, you're sending it home in English and hoping that the kids will translate for them, and that doesn't get done properly, or [it] doesn't get done at all and then you've lost your communication right there.
>
> I'd say we have a core of eight [members on our PAC], which is really sad out of a school that has over 500 families. We have a core of eight, although none of those are related to each other, like it's not a husband and wife, so it's actually eight families. It's really hard to get new people on board. Now, we can get volunteers for certain things. Some people are just really keen on certain things, like sports day. I get a million volunteers for that, but I can never get them any other time of the year.

While occasional volunteers are useful to schools and can provide a lot of help around certain events, the benefits aren't nearly as great as having more dedicated parents with sustained involvement.

As was seen to be the case in other instances, some parents simply lack time to get involved in the school's Parent Advisory Council. In order to make ends meet, many parents end up working long hours and even multiple jobs, which puts enough strain on their time without adding more responsibilities.[10] Jane Haswell, a parent of a kindergarten student at Ashfield Elementary, said that she had been to one PAC meeting at the school. As she explained, "I don't think that at any point it [was] never that I wasn't welcome or anything. It's just when I was working full-time I found it difficult to try and get involved too much." Wellington Elementary parent Laura Truella had a similar experience, saying, "I attended [the PAC meeting] at first. [But] because it is a conflict to my schedule, because they usually do it at six to seven [o'clock] at night and [I] work from three to nine, I haven't attended it ever since. But I think they are helpful because they [put] a bulletin board right in the hallway, so I usually look at it, but not all the time." Likewise, Maria Gomez, a parent of a child at Wellington Elementary, said she would like to volunteer more in the school but simply does not have the time. She has never volunteered in her child's classroom or for fieldtrips, although she is interested in helping out. "No, I really want to," she said, "but usually the days when they are going, I have to do something or I have an appointment. But I really want to go with them."

Some of the interviews with teachers and administrators revealed a latent tension between a stated desire and goal to engage parents and what seemed like a simultaneous and occasionally contradictory feeling that the school should be a (middle-class) oasis and safe haven of learning, isolated from the surrounding community. At some of schools, there is a tension between outsiders and insiders. Some teachers seemed to feel that they know best when it comes to education and that it is their job to teach the students, and so they were surprised and dismayed at the perceived disengagement of many parents with their children's education and their school.[11] This can play a role in limiting parental involvement. For example, teacher Amy Peterson encourages parents to be involved at Ashfield elementary school, but she is somewhat more ambivalent about parents in the classroom. She explained,

> I don't have much parent involvement in my classroom, and part of that is because we have so many people coming in. I have the resource teacher; I have an SSW [Student Support Worker] that comes in; I always have a student teacher; and then there's me. So there are [often] four adults in the room, so I don't [want more] ... coming and going; having another one, I don't really need. Sometimes on field trips, we have parents who are happy to [help]. I've had lots of my parents who have worked in the library – they love doing that kind of thing. A lot of my parents have been on the [Parent Advisory Council]. So they volunteer in those sorts of ways, but I don't have them actually in the classroom. Sometimes it's just too much.

For this reason Peterson is selective about parental involvement in her classroom. But while she doesn't encourage them to volunteer in her classroom, she does allow them to visit and observe her class. "They can come in and watch anytime," she said. "In my [grades] 1, 2, 3 [combined class], at the beginning of the year I told the new parents, 'Come in any day, any time, I don't care; stay as long as you want.' And every now and again I'd have a parent come in and do that, but most often they didn't. The parents, once they sort of realized how it worked and what it was like, they didn't [come]. It was never an issue."

Given the fact that many of the parents are struggling to make ends meet, perhaps expecting them to spend many hours at the school is unrealistic. But even so, this doesn't diminish the importance of building relationships and trust between school staff and parents and of encouraging parents to take part in their children's education. This can include asking their kids about their homework or taking them on culturally rich outings that will enrich their in-school learning. This is why, despite the tensions and barriers, the schools studied are actively attempting to engage parents in the school and in their children's education.

Parental Involvement to Reduce Social Isolation

Principal Teresa McDonald feels that a trend towards growing social isolation has made engaging parents at Soaring Eagle Elementary more important than ever. She described the effect that the isolation can have on the parents' approach to parenting: "You're working hard and you don't have anyone to talk to in particular. Lots of isolation. You don't realize that [your kids playing] video games 24 hours a day and then freaking out if the computer is shut off is abnormal. You think everyone is like this. You [lack] a barometer for comparison with anyone." Because of this, she says that at her school,

> We find that we're doing a lot of basic, what we'd consider to be, basic parenting skills for parents. It comes from that sense of isolation ... parents are looking to the school to provide discipline in the home. So the school [will say] 'Shut off the television,' and the parent replies, '[But] my child just turns it back on.' 'Well then, unplug it!' That sort of thing – 'Unplug it, withdraw the cable service. You have to get your children more on to getting their work done, setting up a schedule, routine.' We have huge issues like that here. Basic parenting.
>
> Teachers are finding increasingly that they're spending so much time on giving advice [about] parenting, and helping with the doctor, and recommending doctors, and following through with all those things that, in the old days, used to be quite tangential to your education. [Back then] you came to school [and] the teacher [taught] you ... and the family looked after everything else, and [this is now] blurring. [It] really [is] blurring a lot for us.

Children are also affected by being socially isolated in their own homes. Said Principal Jennifer Newcastle of East Harcourt Elementary: "There is a bit of fear about just being outside and playing outside. They don't feel as comfortable. So you might come to our neighbourhood on the weekend, [and] you might not see a child in the neighbourhood because the parents don't feel safe in letting the kiddies play outside and on the street and so on. So, it's a little different in that way."

Similar to staff at the other schools studied, East Harcourt staff said they encourage parents to take their children to institutions and events in the city as important goals. Principal Jennifer Newcastle explained,

> The parents don't have a lot of energy at night to spend taking their children out to various places in the city. So we find that our students don't have a lot of background knowledge. Many of them have not been to places like Science World and the Aquarium [or] even the parks: Queen Elizabeth Park or Stanley Park. So our teachers, certainly in primary, do *a lot* of that, and try to build background knowledge because [the kids] have nothing to draw on when you're talking about certain things [in class]. We have to do a lot of front-end loading, we call it, making sure that they understand what we're talking about, building the vocabulary, and so on. They're not rich in experiences outside of just their small community. [If you ask them] "What did you do on the weekend?" A common response might be "We went to Superstore," whereas you and I would have taken our kids to do all kinds of things, and so on.

Social isolation and lack of exposure to different kinds of environments and experiences have been associated with literacy challenges in children.[12]

Engaging Parents: Overcoming Barriers

While all administrators said they consider greater parental involvement to be a critically important goal at their schools, they also said that resources were required to overcome the barriers that prevent parents from getting involved. Engaging parents goes beyond sending written messages homes. At Ashfield Elementary, staff reached out to parents by creating a Parent Place where staff can engage with parents at the school. But even so, the school continued to face challenges engaging parents. Principal Katherine Drucker had this to say about the parental involvement: "We do have a very small [Parent Advisory Council].

We're hoping with the [special magnet program] that we'll have more parents on board. And that's another goal, to expand that and to get more parent involvement. We're starting this year to have tea once a month with our Asian interpreters, and [getting] the grandparents and parents that drop the kids off in, just to feel more comfortable in the school because we need them." Many of the East Vancouver elementary schools tended to have relatively small Parent Advisory Councils compared to wealthier west-side schools.

Although they come out in smaller numbers, the parents who do volunteer at these schools were described as being very helpful, often dedicating their time, skills, and heart even when they lacked financial resources. Principal Drucker said, "The ones that are involved all the time in our [Parent Advisory Council], none of them are working. One of them is a father of six kids at home. When he is working, he's not around; [but] when he's not working, he's here and he does a lot for our school – he's fantastic. We have a mom who hasn't worked for years and years but her husband does, and [so] she's here all the time. She does everything, you can always ask her. So there's only a few of them, and they work really closely with our neighbourhood worker Renée, and they're out in Parent Place in the portable, but if ever you need anything they'll be willing to do it for you." Within the context of fiscal austerity, the role that parents and the community play in sustaining and improving programming at many schools will need to continue to increase.

Different elementary schools utilize different models and approaches to encourage parental involvement, sometimes with different goals. At Wellington Elementary, for instance, instead of the Parent Advisory Council being run independently by parents, it is guided by the school administration. Teacher Kerry Reynolds explains, "In terms of an independent PAC, where [parents] organize it and they structure it and they write their own minutes ... They're not very functional. [In our situation the parents] take direction from us more ... I've worked in schools where the PAC runs itself and they don't expect the teachers to be there or anything. Well, this PAC sort of looks to us for guidance." This kind of innovation to make programs and the school more accessible to parents can help enhance engagement.

East Harcourt Elementary reaches out to parents in other ways, such as putting on family evenings. Principal Jennifer Newcastle said, "We have family evenings where we teach the parents how to read with their children. We bring them in and we demonstrate, in K to 7, how to [support their kids] in reading and writing."

Principal Tim Richards of Great Forest Elementary emphasized the need for programs that serve to address the communication barriers to parental engagement:

> Communication is another issue. It's difficult because of the language difficulties. It's both communication and the background, or the socio-economic background, of the families. We have programs like home reading to try to connect with families and show the importance of reading at home, because that's the purpose of it. We've had our staff talk with parents, meet with them about how to find some way to read with their children, even if they read in their first language. That's helped a little bit. We've got our student-led conferences where we invite the parents in and students present their program to their parents in the classroom. We do that, [and] have done that, for years.
>
> We have an open-school policy for parents. We present programs – education programs – for parents. For [the] PAC [members], we invite them in for sex education [and also educate them] on issues related to good home study practices [and] about the importance of education in general. We do things like that. That's one of my own goals for next year, to try to do more of that for our parents because I think that we're finding that we have to engage families more in the children's education.

Richards said that, despite all of the programs the school currently offers, "We have never had a great success rate in getting parents out. So we need to find different strategies. This is not a problem just for our school, it's a problem across the east side, maybe across all schools. But certainly I know it [is] for … the east side schools."

The Benefits of Parent Involvement

Even though the parental involvement is limited at many of the East Vancouver schools studied, some of the parents have made substantial contributions to certain school communities. For example, the eight-member core team of dedicated volunteers on the Parent Advisory Council at Great Forest Elementary has accomplished a great deal for the school. As Principal Tim Richards explained, "They organize all of our fundraising; [they] organize the Book Fair; [they] organize the odd speaker coming in; [and they] connect with anything that's going on in the community. What else do they do? They organize food for Sports Day. They help in just communicating with parents on an ad hoc basis. They're supportive of the school, but they're small [in number], [and] mainly English-speaking."

The parents involved in the Parent Advisory Council also help ensure the safety and security of the students. They created a program called Safe Arrivals. Parent member Welsh explained that at Great Forest Elementary:

> The teachers send out the attendance binders by 9:30 a.m. each morning. The parents go through it, just to see who's away. We have a special [phone] line for safe arrivals. The parents will leave a message if there is a child who is going to be away that day. We go through the messages [to] see if they match any of the kids that have been away, [and] we put little Post-it notes in the attendance binder saying [things like] "Sally is going to be away, her mom called she's got the flu." If [parents] don't phone in, we phone them at home. If they're not home, we phone them at work. We'll phone Mom then Dad – we'll exhaust every phone number we've got until we find out why the child's away. We've only had one child go missing once; she was a runaway. It was a couple of years ago.

After a transition period, students' parents have embraced the Safe Arrivals program, which has helped make the job of parent volunteers easier. "We're making fewer and fewer phone calls every time."

Parents at the school also help out in classrooms and on fieldtrips. As Welsh explained it, "If parents feel uncomfortable coming to a PAC meeting or coming to volunteer, they will volunteer in a classroom, whether [it be to read] with the kids or [do] an art project or [go] on a field trip. I know that [at] our school, we have a harder time getting parents to go "out" on field trips, but I think that we have a lot more parents who come in to the classrooms to help, maybe if we're going to bake that day or if [the kids] are doing a difficult art project, things like that."

While efforts include volunteering and providing on-site help and other kinds of personal resources, the main job of the Parent Advisory Council at Great Forest Elementary, like many other parent organizations at public schools, is fundraising. Welsh said, "[Being a member of PAC], really, is [being a] glorified fundraiser. We do a lot of fundraising. Yeah, any 'a-thon,' we'll do it."

Through their advocacy and fundraising, parents generate programming resources for public schools. These can provide or fund much-needed or desired programs for students, although disparities in political power and resources exist between East Vancouver schools in lower-income communities and the wealthier west-side communities. Yet even in lower-income communities, parents can effectively mobilize for important resources for their children's schools. The PAC members at Soaring Eagle Elementary lobbied the school board for additional funding for extra supervision at recess. Principal Teresa McDonald said, "They go to all the budget meetings at the school district, and they've asked for another supervision aide for us next year. They're really an advocacy group."

The Role of Engaging Parents to Help At-Risk Students

School staff at the East Vancouver schools studied felt that it was particularly important to engage the parents of students at-risk of experiencing academic challenges. Involving parents also provides another resource to help students who are already struggling academically. Staff at Wellington Elementary contact parents when they have reason to be concerned about a student, says Anna Sanchez: "I know they are good to him teaching, and if there is a problem with the kids, they talk to the parents."

As mentioned in chapter 3, Susan Fletcher runs a program that provides counselling and support services to at-risk youth in Vancouver elementary schools. She acknowledged the need to engage the parents of these kids: "How do we connect the family? Now that's one area that we don't feel we've really done very much in. In the last five years, we've been so focused on the kids and the schools that we haven't done a very good job of connecting with their parents, [but] we know that for the impact to be sustained we need to bring families on board. I think the connectedness that the kids feel is lacking for many of these parents and families. They are very isolated, so we need to bring them on board with the school." When asked about the challenges in getting the parents involved, Fletcher said,

Well, I think a lot of the issues are based around trust. Many families who haven't perhaps had very positive experiences in schools or with community agencies [like] social services aren't as likely to reach out for help or attend parenting programs in schools ... For some families, it's because they are new in the country. They are really unaware of what's available to them, or they are fearful. They're fearful that if they talk about some issue that might be happening in the home [then] they are at risk of losing their kids. So they feel that sense of losing control in their families.

Fletcher also felt that language issues and poverty played a role, saying,

Language barriers are huge, [as] many meetings in schools and communities are [conducted in] English. I think there are definitely socio-economic issues in terms of accessing services. We have a lot of moms who want to come in to our children's program in the office, but they don't have any money for childcare. They don't have money for a bus pass. Agencies, like family services, have to look at what do we need to put in to make these services accessible. Now we put in childcare for every group we run in the office. We have bus passes available, but we can only do that when we have funding or grants to support that.

Having a multilingual staff also helps, as does having connections to social agencies and other organizations that work with newcomers.[13]

The Parent Coffee Club

Sometimes building trust can be a particularly difficult challenge. In these cases, strategies that aim to engage parents where they are, rather than where the school wants them to be, can be more effective. For example, New Lake Elementary has reached out to parents by creating a parent coffee club. Program Coordinator Claire Winslow created this club out of her desire to engage parents in order to build relationships as a proactive way of preventing problems, instead of only turning to parents when problems with their children emerge.

The goal of the coffee club and other parent programs at New Lake Elementary go beyond engaging the parents in the school and in their children's education. The programs also aim to make the school a resource for the parents. Winslow said her inspiration to create the coffee club emerged out of a feeling that "there's a sense of mistrust [among parents] out there … Culturally, there's a lot of mistrust [that causes them to think], 'Someone is not going to understand me and my cultural values. And they're not going to understand me because I don't speak the language very well'." She hoped the coffee club would bridge the divides of language, religion, and culture by bringing parents together around their children.

New Lake Elementary is also offering courses and other programs for kids with the purpose of engaging parents. According to Winslow, "Here the kids get opportunities to be exposed to some performing arts and that sort of thing. How many times do parents get a chance to do that for themselves, [or how many] may not have [ever] had [the] opportunity? Even what may seem very simple and basic things [related to] cooking or arts and crafts programs."

These educational opportunities help to build the relationship between the parents and the school. Winslow said, "It's not necessarily about what you're cooking [or] what you're making. It's about the fact that a group of us are sitting there having that small talk [and] developing a relationship; developing a support network. I want to have fun with the parents. We're not there to dictate to them." Winslow felt that the informality of the club was important. "It's informal in order to be comfortable. It's like walking them into your home [and saying], "Have a cup of coffee or tea, have a little treat …". [It's] just about making it a warm and inviting environment," she said.

Despite its informality, the coffee club achieves the important goal of building trust and a sense of community. As she explained, "It is opening that door of communication with those parents [so that they will feel comfortable] saying 'How do I get access to this?' or 'How do I find out about this program?'… or 'I'd like my child to come into this junior kindergarten class; how do I go about it?' or 'How do I get support for this? How do I learn about what booster shots my child needs?' That sort of thing. Some very basic things." In this way, by providing information and resources in an informal environment, the coffee club is able to reach some of the more difficult-to-engage parents.

Without these kinds of programs, Claire Winslow argued, "[Parents] don't come in to the schools. [And] if they don't have a place to go, you find fewer parents attending things. And certainly it is my experience that the more they feel comfortable coming on to the school premises, then the more comfortable they will to [get] involved in advocacy for themselves and for their children."

Based on participation, Winslow's parent coffee club appears to be succeeding, even attracting involvement from parents of children enrolled in surrounding schools.[14] The program helps defuse some of the mistrust and miscommunication between parents and the education system.[15] When it comes to engaging parents in diverse communities, school staff may underestimate the level of distrust, anxiety, and uncertainty that some parents have regarding schools as an institution. Parent coffee clubs and other kinds of parent engagement programs can create safe places for communication and relationship building.

Getting parents involved with their children's school through programs such as coffee clubs can result in countless benefits. Parents can provide useful volunteer human resources, and through their fundraising efforts they can help to provide financial resources for special programming and events. Furthermore, by having a relationship with parents, teachers can gain a better understanding about the kids in their class, which can be very helpful in preventing or addressing problems that that may be hindering learning.[16] While far from a panacea, engaging parents remains a critically important factor for elementary schools to improve early learning and outcomes.[17]

Engaging the Community

The elementary schools studied in East Vancouver reach out to and receive valuable resources from both the immediate community as well as the broader community.[18] In her job at Wellington Elementary, resource teacher Kerry Reynolds focused explicitly on outreach to parents and the community. She said,

> Because we are an Inner City school, we get so many things coming from the community, and one of my roles is to liaise with the community. Another [of my roles] is to build school spirit and self-esteem in the students. I work with the Drake Shopping Centre, which we have a lot of things going on with because it is in our community. I work really closely with the PAC [members]. I go to all the parent meetings and we talk about what we can do make our school better. I organize events like our walkathon, where we raised over three thousand dollars that we'll use for outdoor initiative camps and things like that for next year.

It takes substantial staff time to ensure that these donations and other resources are put to good use, as Reynolds explained:

> Williams Elementary [on the west side], for example, they support us financially. They give every kid in our school a Christmas present. We have an Inner City team I am a part of that includes Mark Brown [the principal];

myself; Wanda Lowell, who is our neighbourhood worker; Melissa, who is our Youth and Family Worker; [and] Gabriel who is our First Nation worker. We all meet once a month to plan events and to organize the Christmas hampers, organize the Christmas presents … It's almost mind-boggling how many things come in and through our school, and without a project teacher a lot of these things would just be gone.

Yesterday, for example, I organized a free field trip for every class in our school for next fall. They'll all walk down to a museum, and the government is actually paying for every child to go. Well, we are fortunate because we can walk there, so it's absolutely a free field trip for our kids. As a project teacher I coordinate that so the teachers don't have to. They've got enough on their plate, so I just sort of make life as easy as possible for the teachers.

At times Wellington Elementary is so overwhelmed with offers of help that they actually have to turn some down.

Some community-sponsored programs are designed with the goal of improving literacy. Reynolds said,

We've got the firm Goldman and MacDonald. It is a law firm that comes to us throughout the year. Each week, there's usually four lawyers that are attached to one class. Over the whole program, they have fifty lawyers that come throughout the year. They rotate, so they only come once a month, and each time they come they bring a book that the firm has purchased for our school. So [when] they come they read this book, and then they spend one-to-one reading time with the K to third grade students. And they make these connections with these kids. It's very rich, and [the kids are] focusing. When they are not reading to the whole class and sharing the book and talking about the book, they are a reading volunteer with the kids who need that extra one-on-one time, [those who] often don't have a parent at home who will take that time.

Programs like this that provide individual mentoring can really help to improve student learning, especially in the case of struggling students.[19]

Of course, mentoring relationships can also exist within schools. For example, older students can act as mentors or reading buddies for their younger peers. When I observed Heather Mansbridge's third grade class at Ashfield Elementary, the kids were eagerly awaiting their grade seven "buddies" who provide one-on-one mentoring.

Wellington Elementary is located near the New River Community Centre, which partners with the school to help address some of the needs of the students and their families by providing them with assistance and special programs. According to staff member Tricia Thompson, the community centre just started offering before- and after-school care offered through the early childhood development program for students from three nearby schools: High Point Elementary, Soaring Eagle Elementary, and Wellington Elementary. As Thompson described, the programs offered are developed by provincially licensed early childhood educators and include "mathematics, music and movement, literacy, science, and there's lots of sensory stuff."

According to Thompson, the community centre aims to meet the basic needs of students in need by addressing hunger and malnutrition through a family dinner program. She said, "Our family dinners are quite inexpensive. They are three dollars for a dinner. The family can come and enjoy a nutritious dinner and be with other families." In addition, the community centre also helps connect parents to subsidized childcare. As Thompson explained,

> When they walk through the door, we have a representative from the Westcoast Child Care Resource Centre, an outreach coordinator. This representative is solely responsible for helping these families go through the whole subsidy process, which kind of relieves a lot of responsibility from us. Just being able to sit down with a family, we just don't have time to have somebody here [to do that]. When families come in to access your programs and they can't afford it, [having that resource on hand] is great. We can actually bring [those families] upstairs and they can speak with someone to get started – somebody who has all the information to help them make the phone call and to help get the information sent to them.

The New River Community Centre offers extensive childcare and youth-oriented programming. They also provide programs for adults, on topics such as legal assistance and refugee processing in Canada. Thompson explained further:

> We provide services for children from birth up, to seniors and adults. We have different programs, so there's [the] ECD [Early Childhood Development] program, which [offers] the preschool, the daycare, the drop-in family support programs, and [the] family dinners. We then we have our youth program, which has children typically from 13 to 15; programs [are

offered] after school for them and on the weekends. And then we also have our adult programs … [including for] adults with disabilities, which is our Go Forward program. And we also have senior programs. A little bit of everything is going on, we offer a lot of services. We have Food Bank donations that are available to participants and for people in the neighbourhood, and we usually have snacks and coffee for them all the time so they can come in and warm up in the winter. [There's] lots of resource referral that goes on as well.

Thompson said that the language mix of their community presents a challenge. She said,

We try to do a little bit of everything, but nobody is perfect. We've offered programs in Cantonese, Mandarin, Spanish, and also in English, but [they're] kind of done in a split. We have some families who speak English and some who speak Spanish, and they all want to come. We're lucky enough to have facilitators who speak a lot of different languages, so we're able to offer [our programs] in a lot of different languages. We have a lot of other agencies as well, like Building Blocks coordinated by MOSAIC [an immigrant services organization], and they do the interpretation. Language has always kind of been a barrier in this area, so you just have to find a way to make it all work. Staff matters.

These kinds of community–school partnerships make a huge difference in the lives of students from low-income families in the East Vancouver area. According to teacher Amy Peterson at Ashfield Elementary, the community centre and the neighbourhood house near the school both provide invaluable services for the students. She explained,

… [the community centre provides] before-school, after-school and all-day care. They have a program here [at the school], but they also take the younger ones back to the [Grant Williams] Neighbourhood House. They do lots of programs for families [there] now, which they hadn't done before. There's language instruction; they have activities for moms that are at home with their younger children who aren't in school. They do a community fair carnival thing and notices go out all over and people come to that. It's just a fun place for the kids. They have lots of summer programs. For the kids, I think it's a good place. Rising Sun Community Centre is the same thing. They offer lots of programs now for kids and families.

Childcare. Language courses. Programs for stay-at-home parents. Low-cost, subsidized physical fitness courses. These are only some of the kinds of programs these centres offer to help children in urban schools.

Getting the families to make use of community resources requires marketing and extensive networking, and schools do their best to inform students and parents about the programming available. When asked if she felt that the families at her school access the available programs and services, Amy Peterson replied:

> Some families are ... The families where the parents are both working and grandparents are raising the children, sometimes they're mostly in the house. [But] some of the grandparents now are getting used to taking the kids, because the kids find out about Rising Sun Community Centre, because [there is] ice skating there. And so once the kids see the ice skating rink and where it is, then they take their parents there. Or they take the grandparents down there. They're getting into realizing what's available in the community. We promote that at the school ... when the notices come out from Rising Sun Community Centre or Grant Williams Neighbourhood House, we always read them out to the kids and make sure that they really understand them.

Peterson also encourages parents to take advantage of the short-term childcare. "I tell them how much money it is per day," she said. "Quite often, when they look at spring break and they see a week at such-and-such a price, I say, 'Well look, that's five days.' And I divide that [amount] up by five days and I say, 'Now that per hour, it's only this much per hour. That's way less than babysitting.' So we do sort of encourage the kids to get out and do other things in the neighbourhood."

The services offered by the community centres and neighbourhood houses for children who attend East Vancouver elementary schools are often the key to families balancing work and family, with supplemental before- and after-school programming, summer camps, and other early childhood education programming, which is often heavily subsidized for lower-income families. Coordinating programs and working with schools helps these schools meet the needs of children and families.[20] By partnering with local elementary schools, these community institutions are helping meet the childcare, recreational, and educational needs of children and families in their communities.[21]

These community institutions often begin to play a role even before children formally enrol at school. The New River Community Centre, for instance, offers programming to help children begin school ready to learn. According to Tricia Thompson, "We participate in the Ready, Set, Learn [program] in the school systems. We do that every year. We also work within the program planning of the preschool and daycare; they do a kindergarten-readiness program, which starts around January. It focuses on the letters and numbers and pronunciation ... [helping the kids to start] being able to recognize combinations of words and sounds, getting them thinking about pre-reading and going off to kindergarten."

The Ready, Set, Learn initiative is a provincial government–funded program that operates in East Vancouver elementary schools in partnership with local community centres.[22] Principal Jennifer Newcastle explained how important it was for East Harcourt Elementary:

> We have the Ready, Set, Learn program, which is [funded by] government money, $2,400. [This year] we gave it to the Richard Owen Neighbourhood House ... two women have come and run a preschool for us twice a week for six weeks, Monday and Friday mornings. It's a parent-participatory preschool [program] and it runs for two-and-a-half hours twice a week for 3- and 4-year-olds here at East Harcourt Elementary. We also have every Wednesday morning the little 4-year-olds come, and have been now for several weeks, with their parents. These are the new kids that are going to start in September.

Principal Newcastle argued that, in combination with other early learning and preschool programs, children who have been a part of Ready, Set, Learn are more comfortable beginning school and better prepared to learn to read:

> We [also] have Books for Breakfast, in which we have beautiful picture books put out on the table. The teachers do a demo [for the parents] each Wednesday morning: 'This is how you can be reading with your child,' [they'll say]. 'This is the kind of thing to do.' We even do a little workshop on writing with [the kids], and get them to pretend that they're writing the grocery list. 'What do you want mummy to get at the store when she goes?' [we'll ask] and the kid will, they can't write, but will pretend that they're writing.
>
> What the teachers have found when we brought in the Ready Set Learn and the Books for Breakfast [programs] is that when the children come to school in kindergarten, they're more ready for school. They're more settled. We have fewer tears, and the parents also know what school is about.

Preschool children who will attend Soaring Eagle Elementary also have access to the Ready, Set, Learn program through a neighbourhood house. According to Principal Teresa McDonald, "The Grant Williams Neighbourhood House runs a before- and after-school care program at the school, right in the school. There's a program we do [in partnership with them] called "Ready, Set, Learn" and it's a preschool program. It's one morning a week, Thursday mornings, in our school. So families can start coming to school before school starts and get familiar with the school procedures and ... [they and their] kids [can become] familiar with the grounds. They get lots of help for where to go in the community for services and all that kind of thing."

Universal access to high-quality preschool with trained early childhood educators is crucial for preparing children, particularly those from disadvantaged backgrounds, to begin school read to learn.[23] High-quality early childhood education programs are increasingly being recognized as key to ensuring high levels of academic achievement in early elementary education, with disproportionate benefits going to children from low-income families. Longitudinal research has followed randomized groups of children enrolled in preschool programs compared to their non-enrolled counterparts, and the findings demonstrate a host of positive outcome benefits, including higher rates of high school completion and lower rates of juvenile arrests.[24] Early childhood education programs are a valuable long-run policy investment, with analyses suggesting between $6 and $10 in cost savings realized for each $1 invested.[25]

Corporate-, Private-, and Institution-Sponsored Programs

In addition to the resources provided by community institutions, some East Vancouver elementary schools reported receiving substantial corporate and private donations. For instance, through a corporate partnership with a major bank, approximately 80 students at Wellington Elementary are fed breakfast each morning. In addition to providing things like mentoring, some partners, such as the Goldman and Mac-Donald law firm, provide the school with fiscal resources. For example, the school librarian makes a list of books she wants to add to their collection, and they are supplied by the firm. In terms of private donations, Principal Mark Brown said: "The more advantaged parents also end up covering the expenses of their less fortunate classmates. For example, a recent camping trip sponsored by the school cost $150 per child. Only a few families were able to pay even a portion of the cost. So one family paid $300 so that another student could attend. No child was denied due to non-payment, and this is true for all school-based activities."

According to Vancouver School Board consultant Angela Myers, private sponsorship ensures that children get fed in some schools. "Well, there are some big picture things like the hot lunch programs," she said. "We're sponsored by an outsider who has continued to support that, even though some of the funding [is] gone. That's an Inner City school thing, because schools themselves can't afford it on their own. There's a corporate sponsorship involved in there."

Principal Jennifer Newcastle spoke about a literacy program at East Harcourt Elementary that is funded by the BC Lions: "You've probably heard about the Read Write & Roar program with the BC Lions [football team]. They send out little books for the children; lovely little clear sketch books basically. Any child from K to third grade can have that. And it's just to encourage them to read a book and draw a picture about what [they've] read. And then they will give a certificate to [the kids] based on how many books [they] read over the summer [or] during spring break. They put the books out this year, and the kiddies wrote and put pictures in [them]."

Despite successful initiatives like this, some school staff reported challenges mobilizing resources and other kinds of support, from the private sector in particular. Principal Tim Richards said Great Forest Elementary had not much success in this area, despite his efforts. "A lot of the poorer neighbourhood schools get that kind of support that we can't, such as King Elementary and Cassandra Elementary. I haven't spent a lot of time trying here, but I [did] at my last school. It's tough to get that money. They tend to put it towards the even more needy communities. The Moose Lodge has given us a little bit of money over the years. That's the only other [source of donations] I can think of."
It may be more difficult for schools in lower-poverty neighbourhoods to fundraise from certain private-sector sources.

Unique Models of Community Partnerships and Engagement

Some of the most innovative and interesting partnerships build on the strengths of the community. Vancouver School Board consultant Angela Myers offered a good example of this:

> One of the things that has been a wonderful bonus for a whole school is the artist-in-residence programs. The school that [came] up with this new model of support for learners a number of years ago had an

artist-in-residence who they very creatively used across the whole school, and the result was that they created a book of their heritage. First of all, they created these incredible pictures – they were collages, and in the middle was a picture of their family and around it were various elements. They had a conversation with an elder of their family. It was an Aboriginal focus in terms of the elder, but basically every culture has elders, right? And so the children had to have a conversation with an elder, and then there was something written on one side of this book that they created from the elder's perspective about how these young kids are or aren't the way they used to be and then something [was] written from the child's perspective, who created the collage with the help of the artist-in-residence and then they had this sort of opposite each other. [The collages] were in [the] Vancouver Art Gallery for a while. Then they got funding somehow to create this book and it's lovely. It's called *We Are All Related*, I believe. It's very nice.

These kinds of community partnerships keep children engaged in school, and help them develop their critical thinking skills and creativity; yet the precise impact on early literacy and numeracy skills acquisition is difficult to measure. There is no doubt that the programs contribute to children's early learning and enthusiasm for school, but the benefits are difficult to capture given limits in terms of data collection and evaluation tools.

Many East Vancouver elementary schools have successfully built partnerships with immigrant services organizations to help children transition into the schools. In Principal Teresa McDonald's case, she developed a set of programs at Soaring Eagle Elementary with two prominent Vancouver-based immigrant settlement organizations. The programs provide support, including a multicultural worker, to help the school engage with immigrant families. These kinds of partnerships are promising and should be expanded. More should be done to build relationships between the organizations that help immigrant families and the elementary schools where the children from those families learn.

Sometimes schools need to go beyond simply providing services to families and reach out to work with the local community organizations, institutions, and residents to solve problems that are affecting the school. In the case of Pearson Elementary, street crime and disorder near the school were negatively affecting the learning environment. As a result, the school staff joined a coalition of community leaders, activists, and concerned residents to "take back the street" near the school. According to Principal William Coleman, the school hosted meetings attended by up to 300 people to demand action. He reported that the mobilization and community action was effective: "A group of neighbourhood people and parents from the school have kind of taken over the neighbourhood. They moved out all the hookers and all that street trade stuff. They do walking patrols at night, they do bike patrol, they do driving patrols, and they do community events to bring people in the school … together."

Engaging in a community campaign to improve neighbourhood conditions can be an effective strategy, as this example shows. Working with local community organizations and businesses can improve the lives of students by providing resources or helping to reduce crime, and build power to mobilize policies and programs that will meet the needs of vulnerable students and even reduce poverty and hardship among the families of their students.

Conclusion

Urban public schools in lower-income communities can and should engage with parents as well as with community organizations and institutions to help improve students' educational outcomes. Yet, even when these kinds of partnerships exist, it doesn't eliminate the fundamental inequalities between lower-income and wealthier school communities. For example, some East Vancouver elementary schools need to fundraise even for basic supplies, which are simply taken for granted at wealthier west-side schools. And schools in these lower-income neighbourhoods face greater challenges in terms of engaging parents, particularly working poor parents who juggle several jobs to make ends meet. Language and cultural barriers also contribute to the challenges. But it's worth the effort to engage parents, as they yield important benefits through their volunteering and the financial resources they garner through fundraising. Community institutions such as community centres and neighbourhood houses also provide important resources for children and families in low-income urban regions, including before- and after- school care, summer programming, and weekend programming.[26] Even the broader community plays an important role in some schools, from providing mentoring to new books for school libraries. But more can be done, particularly for the sake of improving children's literacy achievement. For example, local fire stations and small businesses could celebrate and reward reading milestones.[27] In urban public schools in lower-income communities, engaging parents and the community requires already over-stretched staff time and resources; however, this investment is well worth it, as it generates positive rewards for students and, most importantly, enhances children's learning and skills acquisition.

5 Addressing Needs and Supporting Resiliency: Programs That Matter

Sometimes the dynamic-sounding program introduced by a new principal does have a galvanizing and perceptible effect and one that lasts for more than just a few years. In other cases, it is really just an avalanche of words and short-term measures that temporarily establish a degree of calm within a school and sometimes brings sudden spikes in test scores or graduation rates, although the academic gains more frequently than not turn out to be short-lived and, in some cases, they have proven to be spurious.

— Jonathan Kozol, *The Shame of the Nation* [1]

Although Jonathan Kozol presents a somewhat pessimistic perspective on school reform efforts, his views are based on decades of following trends and outcomes of school reform, particularly for poor children. He reminds us that real positive change in schools is not easy or quick, and it generally requires many resources.

The issue of school reform is divisive and extreme; rhetoric flies freely – largely unhelpfully – from both the ideological right and the left.[2] Many on the right seem convinced that teachers unions are the cause of most of the problems in schools, and they shamelessly seek to put forward measures that sap teacher morale or introduce private sector notions of added value and pay-for-performance competition as mechanisms to magically utilize the invisible hand of the market. Unfortunately, on close scrutiny many of the gains based on these proposals turn out to be illusory.[3] For example, while it is true that some innovative urban charter schools work well for some students, these schools also rarely educate the same diverse mix of children found in typical urban public schools. Those students who are difficult to teach are excluded to a greater extent in schools outside the public school system. But even in public schools, the rate of exclusion increases, unsurprisingly, when competitive models such as rankings based on standardized exams are implemented. That is one reason why, when successful "experimental" models are replicated more broadly or applied more generally, the positive effects often tend to fade out or even disappear.

Arguments on the ideological left can tend towards knee-jerk reactions against any form of standardized assessment or testing of students, or against school reform programs that aim to provide basic foundational reading and math skills through what some view as "rote" or structured curriculum methods. Most educators would argue that the angry, divisive tone of the education debate is largely unnecessary. Clearly, magic bullets and quick-fix programs do not exist. By and large, principals and teachers at urban schools do their best to successfully educate their children, at times against staggering odds. Schools face unique circumstances locally, and one-size-fits-all solutions are not appropriate or likely to succeed. Given this context, what kinds of programs and policies help students learn foundational literacy and numeracy skills? Administrators, teachers and parents in East Vancouver elementary schools described some enthusiastically supported programs.[4]

The Inner City Schools Project

The Inner City Schools Project in British Columbia is built on the premise that schools with high percentages of students from low-income families require additional resources to meet the unique needs of their students. The project provides schools with the necessary support to implement programs to meet students' basic needs,[5] such as resource teachers and hot lunch programs. For example, Inner City program funding and an anonymous donor allow Lakeview Elementary to provide a free breakfast in the school cafeteria for all students.

The Inner City program allows selected schools to hire more staff as well as provides connections and resources to enable the mobilization of additional resources from private, non-profit, and other partners in the community and the city. With Inner City funds, schools can hire resource teachers to work individually with at-risk students.[6] By providing extra one-on-one attention to these students in a wide range of areas, these resource teachers offer the kind of tutoring that can prevent students from falling behind their peers in the early years, especially when it comes to mastering the critical steps for learning to read.

Resource teachers at Inner City schools receive training and work directly with classrooms to teach literacy, in addition to doing their one-on-one work with students. For example, as part of the Literacy Innovation Project (LIP), teacher Kerry Reynolds attends specialized workshops and training sessions, and then she helps coach other teachers at Wellington Elementary as well as leading classes with the other coaches and librarian. "They don't have to plan for a sub to come in," Reynolds explained. "We'll go in, and we'll do some of these great things that we've learned in workshops, and focus on literacy. For example, making all children make connections with books." She says that during that time the coaches have the "opportunity to plan and to work with other teachers [who teach the same] age group. If it's a [grades] 2/3 class and a [grades] 3/4 class, those two teachers can meet and talk about group planning, and they can mark their assessments together because the two coaches, myself and Natalie Courso [the librarian], will go in to their classrooms."

Wellington Elementary has adopted a Reading Powers program. Reynolds says that, as a result of the program "… the language [around reading] across the school is the same. All the teachers are trained in the Reading Powers language, so we all have posters – the same posters – so the kids see them from grade to grade to grade, and all the teachers are talking, 'Okay, let's make connections. Let's make connections.' It's a common language in our school, and I think that's important."

In addition to literacy education, resource teachers also manage other kinds of programs. For instance, Reynolds introduced the Action Schools program, where she has "trained peer leaders to go out at lunchtime and teach games to kids and bring skipping ropes. And I've set up a circuit so that kids go out there and just be active out[side] at recess and lunch." Reynolds helps organize assemblies, talent shows, a student choir, cartoon clubs, and pottery classes, also matching students with after-school care at the school and at nearby community centres.[7]

Community of Schools Programs

Other programs provided extra resources for schools with high proportions of at-risk students. For example, the Community of Schools program funded by British Columbia's Ministry of Children and Families provides extra resources in terms of staff as well as connecting the schools to the community. Principal Tim Richards reported that, at Great Forest Elementary, "It's connecting kids. It's connecting schools. It's supporting vulnerable children." Part of the program funding provides a half-time Youth and Family Worker, who "supports kids' emotional needs [and] social needs." The Community School Team provides many different kinds of resources at Great Forest Elementary, including creating and funding cultural and physical activity programs. Principal Richards explained,

> We have lots of after-school programs that are organized through that Community School Team ... Last year, for the first time in a long time at this school, we had [a] summer camp run for the kids. They were able to come up and sign up for a week or two weeks or three weeks and participate. That'll be going on again this year, and it's very cheap. If the kids can't pay for it, there's always a way to find the money for them. We've got basketball happening after school. We've got various programs, [including] arts and crafts programs [and] dance programs, that happen intermittently throughout the year.

In addition to programs available to all students at the school, the Community School Team has created a new program targeted at students who are facing learning difficulties. As Principal Richards went on to explain,

> We have also got a project here that we started this year, called the Greenhouse Project. And it is to support kids who are learning-disabled. There is a designation called LD [Learning Disabled] for kids who are just having difficulty with one aspect of their learning. From the money from the Community School Team, we hired our Speech and Language person to work more in our school; only half a day more, but to support a more intensive mediation of children's learning. It's called Greenhouse [in] the sense that you nurture; you provide support for a more condensed amount of time in 10-week sessions to try and teach kids how they are learning and how to pay attention to their own learning, through "mediated learning."

The Community of Schools team also connects the elementary school to the secondary school where many of the children will continue their education after grade 6. One program mobilizes secondary school students to act as mentors for elementary school students. Through mobilizing networks, relationships, and the community to create and fund universal and targeted programs, the Community of Schools teams represent another innovative and positive reform improving early learning in East Vancouver elementary schools.

Full-Day Kindergarten

Reforms such as enrolling kindergarten students at an earlier age and extending the school day for young students as well as high-quality early childhood development programs represent important steps in the right direction. The research literature on the benefits of early childhood education shows positive gains in student achievement, which sometimes fade out, although subsequently reappear when students get older.[8] The data suggest that investments in early childhood education should be followed up with extra resources and support through the early years of elementary school to prevent these students from falling behind. According to education sociologist Karl Alexander and his colleagues, "High quality pre-school experiences need to be followed up by high-quality, full-day [k]indergarten,"[9] which especially benefits students from low-income families but also helps working parents from across the socio-economic spectrum.

In terms of preschool education, the province of Ontario is expanding universal early childhood education by moving towards full-day kindergarten and by lowering the starting age for kindergarten down to 4 years old. In British Columbia, initial reforms to extend all full-day kindergarten to 5-year-olds was initially delayed due to funding constraints for several years, but then finally implemented in September 2011. Yet recommendations to extend kindergarten to 4-year-olds and even 3-year-olds appear to have been shelved.[10]

The full-day kindergarten option is popular in the East Vancouver elementary schools that already offer it. Anna Sanchez, a parent of a kindergarten student at Wellington Elementary, gave the school an "A" grade in part because of full-day kindergarten: "Well, I heard from the other school that the kindergarten is only from 8:30 a.m. to 12:00 p.m., but here [it's] 8:30 a.m. to 3:00 p.m." She said she likes the program because, "my son will learn a lot and how to communicate with the other kids." As she works during the day, full-day kindergarten also means she will not have to pay for childcare or other arrangements for the full afternoons.

Although this policy reform requires substantial resources, allowing all children to begin kindergarten at age 3 would help more students achieve foundational literacy and math skills early in their education.[11] This program would benefit all students and many working parents too, while disproportionately benefitting vulnerable students.

Multi-Year Classrooms

Some teachers argued that multi-year classes – where the students stay with the same teacher for several years – created a continuity that results in strong relationships between children and teachers. One example is Heather Mansbridge's classroom at Ashfield Elementary. When I observed the class, the students were completing a literacy exercise called "Mmm, Cookie." Based on a Robert Munsch story, the children were asked to chronologically order eight pictures and then write one sentence to describe the activity in the picture. There was little need to stop and ask the children for cooperation. Only a few words of instruction kept the children on task and focused on their activities. Mansbridge valued the year-to-year continuity created by multi-year classrooms. The advantages included students starting the school year having already familiarized themselves with her routines and teaching style.

Teaching a multi-year classroom involves some innovation to address the diverse needs of students at different educational and developmental stages. Another lesson I observed in Mansbridge's class was called "Big Five Math" (the title refers to a review of the previously completed unit of math, and includes five main questions). The children retrieve miniature green chalkboards, circa 1960s, and take a seat on the carpet. They are then asked to write down math questions and work independently to solve them. Once a student's math exercise is complete, they discuss the answers and then return to their seats to complete more questions around similar math concepts.

While they concentrate on solving the problems, Mansbridge moves from student to student to see how they are doing, and provides assistance to those who need help solving the problems. One student employed a strategy using a ruler to solve an equation involving the nine times table. She is adept at this strategy and it clearly works well for her. Another girl who was struggling with the same equation was offered an alternate strategy using her hands to solve the nine times table. It was clear that Mansbridge had provided the children with several different strategies for solving math equations, and they could be called upon by the children easily and with confidence. One student,

Sofie, used a multi-method approach in the math-based lesson. She reviewed the problem, worked on her chalkboard, solved the problems independently, and then moved on to math-based games.

Principal Coleman explained that at Pearson Elementary: "The whole school here is multi-aged. Three grades in every classroom: K/1/2, 2/3/4, 5/6/7. We choose to do that because we believe in older kids helping younger ones. They stay with the same teacher for three years. So the teacher really gets to know the kids and the families." Interestingly, he argues that the effectiveness of multi-age classrooms is contingent on the motivation: "In other schools where they put two grades together, it's only because they don't have enough kids to fill the class, so they'll have one class with grade 4's and then they'll have to throw in a few grade 5's; that's because it's a numbers thing. Where[as] we do it because it's a philosophical thing. So that's different," he claimed. These multi-age classrooms focus heavily on advancing literacy.

Curricular Innovation

East Vancouver elementary schools offer a diverse mix of programs with the goal of meeting the special needs of students and advancing basic skills learning.[12] School staff highlighted certain programs they felt were important for advancing the goals of early literacy and numeracy skill acquisition. While one program or approach to early learning is not the magic bullet, opportunities for teachers to train, learn, and experiment with innovative approaches and programs can improve classroom learning. Some programs may work better for some teachers, and others may work better with a different mix of students and learning styles. Professional development and other kinds of resources should be generously available for teachers to learn and experiment with different kinds of innovative programs. Empowering teachers to select their own professional development programs in terms of curriculum innovation will help them match their ongoing training to their own teaching style and the unique needs of their students. There is no one-size-fits-all solution in terms of a program that meets the needs of all teachers and students, but this only underscores the importance of providing resources, flexibility, and ongoing professional development training opportunities to improve teachers' effectiveness in educating students.

Some administrators and teachers spoke about specific curriculum programs as being useful and important. For example, Alison Dunn, a first grade teacher at Centennial Elementary, championed one particular math program based on blocks, describing it as a "a cutting-edge program." She felt it worked especially well for children in the first grade. Today children in early grades are expected to beyond simply learning times tables. The new emphasis on solving word problems and developing critical thinking skills led Dunn to conclude that these kinds of math programs are important to improve learning. When asked if she thinks other programs in numeracy have similar positive results, she said: "At the moment, I would say this is it. I've seen a lot of programs."

Other teachers did not favour following strict or highly structured curriculum programs, instead preferring more flexibility. Teacher Jane Sorrento contrasted literacy education at Centennial Elementary with the way literacy is taught at another East Vancouver elementary school: "Grandview [Elementary] moved to a very structured reading program. What I was so happy about when I came here is that Centennial Elementary has not. It has resisted that sort of thing and instead has offered a very wonderful literacy program through the sorts of things that I value. Literature-based programs. Lots of good material."

Although some teachers strongly support particular programs, others resist what they find to be restrictive models. While teachers do not support rigid curriculum programs, it remains important that teachers have access to curriculum training resources and professional development opportunities, as well as resources for classroom materials.

Literacy Programs

While many programs are school-based, some of the most important programs for promoting early literacy originate at the Vancouver School District level. Centennial Elementary teacher Jane Sorrento explained, "The district has a literacy initiative. If schools want to be part of [it], they [have] to make a commitment to upgrading and working on literacy within the school environment. It means going to conferences. It also means some assessment of writing ability and reading ability pre-assessment and then post-assessment, and also meeting and discussing the results and taking a look at where we need to go and goals and that sort of thing."

The Vancouver School District provides resources for literacy programs and training, particularly for teachers in the primary grades.

Sorrento explained how the program inspired her to create special records to assess her students' reading abilities. She said,

> The first thing [I do] is assess the student. At the beginning of every year, I actually do "running records" with all my students. I do them myself. Sometimes you listen to a student read, and you record word-for-word how they do. Then you identify which strategies they're using. So, for example, they might be sounding out. Are they using context clues? Are they using word substitutions? Are they substituting words? Are they good substitutions, or are they senseless substitutions? Are they just looking at the first letter and then guessing? Identifying the reading strategies, that's what that's supposed to be doing. Then trying to target where they might be reading for the literacy assessments for literacy program.

These assessments of a child's reading patterns are then used to match them with appropriate books. "We use Developmental Reading Assessment (DRA) testing, and we also have a book room. The primary children have a book room filled with wonderful children's literature, which we've worked hard to sort of upgrade in the last couple of years, and then also with some books that are targeted at DRA levels. So people can use those if they want, and after a while you get a sense of what level 30 is and what level 18 is. I assess at the beginning of the year and then decide who would be best going and working with the resource people."

In addition to intensive one-on-one reading programs for first grade children who are not yet reading, matching books from the book room to the students' reading levels can advance literacy skills development. Using regular assessments by teachers to match students to books appropriate for their level helps build skills and confidence in reading. Sorrento adapted the guided reading program into what she calls a "book club" in order to develop more in-depth understanding of the materials. She explained, "Once I've done all my reading assessments, I group [the kids] into book club groups and we work there on meaning and discussions. It's not necessarily just working on decoding but just getting a little bit more in-depth, although with certain children, certain groups, I take a careful look at what reading strategies they are using if they need that help."

Sorrento said her program differs from "guided reading" as it is more of a broad-based literacy program: "It looks at other things. So, for example, you might have somebody who's reading quite fluently but needs to do a little bit more in-depth discussion. So you might put that [child] with a different book club, or you might look at their personalities. You can shift these around all the time. I suspect many teachers that use them [guided reading programs] just put children in groups based on reading ability, and they're left there all year and that's it. But that's not really how they were initially meant to be used."

Placing students in diverse ability groups can also advance literacy. Sorrento said she does "lots of other sorts of reading, shared reading, [and] buddy reading. We have poetry books where I give them poems that are semantic such as slow poems or winter poems. We read them together. We do drama with them, so just part of what's a full-literacy program." Teachers at Centennial Elementary also insert literacy education into a wide range of curriculum activities. Incorporating literacy programs into other areas of the curriculum beyond reading has been a successful strategy to improve early literacy acquisition.

Many schools used the district-wide resources for literacy but adapted them in ways to build on their own school communities' strengths and meet their specific needs. Principal Teresa McDonald of Soaring Eagle Elementary also emphasizes the importance of school district level leadership, particularly in literacy. She said, "The district has an Early Literacy program where we share, not physically share, but we share good practice, teaching practice. We share our data between schools and for the district. We have a consistent assessment tool that we use so we're able to take a look at children all across the district and see where they are in their growth and reading skills. I think all those are very important."

Opportunities to discuss successful experiences and literacy lessons across schools are critically important. The school district also provides a useful assessment tool that helps teachers understand where students are in terms of reading. "You need a broad and comprehensive program," said Principal McDonald. "And the fact that we work with other schools is huge. The Early Literacy program in Vancouver is huge. With consistent tools and consistent techniques, I think it is a big one."

At the same time, Soaring Eagle Elementary implemented its own literacy program for struggling readers. She said, "We have an Early Literacy program in addition to our regular learning system to target the kids who still aren't getting the basics of reading. So sounding out, recognizing letters, and it's very targeted. It's just small groups of children. And that goes right through to grade 3 with our kids that are struggling, K to third grade. They get extra time in an Early Literacy [program]. Very strictly phonological, [asking them] "What is the letter? What is the sound?" Hearing sounds, using sounds. It's basic writing. We target those kids so that our school-based team can make recommendations early."

Principal McDonald also emphasized the importance of balance and a mixed-methods approach to teaching literacy: "The other thing is to have good balance in the classroom [when it comes to] ways of teaching reading. You need the phonetic approach, but you also need the whole language approach of being exposed to a number of different fiction and non-fiction sources. You need a variety of techniques for children, [including] lots of writing. You need good oral language development programs, lots of talking. Lots of linking language to literature and linking language to writing." The same mixed-method approach is also useful for math, as she goes on to explain: "For math, the same thing goes. You can't be using textbooks for everything that children need to know in terms of [numeracy]. So, again, you need a balanced program, lots of hands-on activities, practical uses of math". Mixed-method approaches help build skills for students who have diverse learning styles and strengths.

While many school staff oppose the standardized FSA exams (as described in chapter 7), this does not mean they do not embrace the importance of assessment as a tool for improving learning. According to Principal McDonald, "Riding above all of those [important factors] is a close evaluation of kids to see who is understanding and who is not. And enough services [are needed] to help those who are lagging for whatever reason, struggling for whatever reason. So that comes from the classroom teacher and [from] the support services." The key is to identify students who are falling behind and immediately provide the kind of support that will allow them to keep up in the classroom.

A Common Language around Literacy?

The Vancouver School District has been promoting continuity and a "common language" to build year-to-year consistency as children master the fundamentals of reading. Principal Jennifer Newcastle of East Harcourt Elementary explained, "We have now a common set of strategies that we use and common language that we use throughout K to seventh grade in order to teach reading. So when the teachers talk about visualizing in your head, or predicting, or building on background knowledge, all the kids know what we're talking about." East Harcourt Elementary has built on the common language, tools, and resources provided by the school district in order to develop their own programs to advance teaching of literacy skills.

The teachers adopted a visually oriented approach to teaching reading, which Principal Newcastle feels works particularly well with ESL students at East Harcourt Elementary:

> What it has done has really improved not only [students'] interest in reading but it's also improved their writing so incredibly. We think this is what the ticket to success is: to just have a common way of speaking about literacy and a common understanding.
>
> Now, having said that, some schools have gone to a type of … guided reading. We haven't done that. We've really gone to [using] fabulous picture books. So rather than the kids just sitting and plunking their heads into a novel and you don't know whether they're understanding anything they're reading, we've gone to large and really wonderful picture books, and … the pictures are there that help with our non-English speaking kids. It's really been a hugely successful for us.

The success of this approach in literacy has inspired staff to shift to using more visually oriented math instructional materials as well. Principal Newcastle explained, "The common set of strategies for literacy has worked for us. In grade 3, for math, we have new textbooks here and we're trying to do more hands-on [activities] to increase understanding of what they're doing. We're finding that the textbooks put out nowadays are so language-based that it's difficult for a student to understand them, to be able to read them. So we are trying to make it so that it is more hands-on so they really understand."[13]

In some cases, early literacy programs did not turn out as successful as hoped. Principal Tim Richards of Great Forest Elementary voiced his frustration that district literacy initiatives appeared to make a difference in learning but not in standardized testing scores. "The teachers work together to try to improve instruction, and we're finding that we're making some difference. But it's not as big a change [as] we were hoping to make in the academic levels of our children. [They are] not materializing at this point," he lamented.

Putting Literacy First: A Top-Down Commitment to Promote Learning to Read

East Vancouver elementary schools implemented focused campaigns to elevate literacy as a school-wide priority. Principal Katherine Drucker said that at Ashfield Elementary: "We are very focused on two goals that we have for our school. I would like to think if you asked people in the school, including children, they would be able to say to you: "Our school goals are social responsibility and literacy." And we know if you get everybody focused on those kind of things you can make a difference in a school. So this is our third year going in [with] those two goals." Principal Drucker described the Early Intervention Program as an important program for improving early literacy skills at the school: "We're so excited. We are one of six schools. It's just started this year ... We were chosen because our school has been part of the early literacy program; we're in our fifth year. You'll be able to see it in action [in] the guided readings, the one-on-ones, all the group stuff, all the strategies, pre-reading strategies; all of our primary teachers have committed to that. But now they've taken it a step further and, of course, we realize that if we catch these kids when they're in kindergarten and grade 1, we're going to be able to help them." Teachers at the primary levels across the school have adopted similar methodologies to teach reading.

While Principal Drucker feels that the Early Intervention Program is "very powerful" for improving literacy, Ashfield Elementary has not adopted a similar program for math, given their current focus on literacy. The school is guided by district initiatives that brought in greater consistency in terms of math instruction: "What the Vancouver district finally did is they got everybody on board for the same math textbook. The majority of the schools in Vancouver are using the same program, which is really helpful so that when teachers move [from] school to school, they're not learning a new program, and more so for the kids when they're moving from school to school, they're not learning a new program. Down the road will we focus on numeracy? You bet. But what we find with a lot of our immigrant kids is they're good at math. They can do math except for the problem solving because it's language-based."

Other administrators credit a combination of school-based and district programs for improving literacy education. According to Principal William Coleman, it is the mix of programs and reforms that is effective for improving literacy at Pearson Elementary. "We've got lots of programs. We're hooked up with the Grant Williams Neighbourhood House. They provide after-school programs and they provide something akin to a Mother Goose program for the 3- [and] 5-year-olds on Fridays. They come and they do a drop-in kind of thing ..." Principal William Coleman went on to say:

> The teachers are part of the Early Literacy Program. They've had to undergo some training. They've had to bring in new resources in the classroom. They've had to look at their own teaching strategies. And we've created something here at the school called a professional learning community, where we have grade groups that meet together and they talk about curriculum – what they need to do better, what they do well, how they can share ideas. We meet once a month and then they meet on their own time. Then we have the literacy mentors from the district who come in and do demo lessons. I'll select teachers to go and watch, and then they get a chance to sit down and talk. So they're constantly looking for classes and trying to make sure that we're improving what we're doing for the kids to make sure that they're improving. So it's kind of an ongoing [process] ... It's a lot of work.

These innovative strategies are organized around a broader focus on literacy at the school. Principal Coleman explained: "They have a lot of games for kids. We have a strong literacy program. We're part of the urban literacy project with the Vancouver school board ... It's a real community; it's a home for kids here. They are given lots of opportunities for leadership. We have a student council staff volunteer to take kids through various things. We have a peer helping group, and a peer leader group. We have a playground leader group that help the supervision of the kids outside."

Principal William Coleman described creative strategies to meet the challenge of teaching ESL students to read: "Each classroom teacher here teaches ESL. We have an ESL teacher, but she is specifically for kids off-the-boat, so to speak. But the classroom teachers, they have to devote part of their teaching day to the ESL kids in their class, and they have to responsible for what it is they are teaching them so we do a little bit of organization around our staffing to allow everybody to do that." He points to other assets for supporting early literacy: "We have a full-time librarian, which other schools don't have, and a full-time LAC [Learning Assistance Centre] teacher ... [who provides] learning assistance for kids who have difficulty ... She works with small groups, one-on-one, and then she will also work in classrooms with teachers to make sure that you get kids with what we call Ministry-designated, they have learning disabilities. We have some autistic kids in the school that we have Special Ed assistance, for we have some other kids that have some health problems so they get some extra assistance through Special Ed support." According to Principal Coleman, the secret to Pearson Elementary's success is constant evaluation, re-evaluation and improvement.

Multiple programs at East Vancouver elementary schools target the needs of the students. Wellington Elementary, for example, partners with nearby New River Community Centre as described in chapter 4. They also have the Ready, Set, Learn program as well as enrolment for full-day kindergarten. The Read Well programs are also highly effective. Overall, Wellington Elementary currently offers 57 different programs over the year. These included the Artist-in Residence program, visits by authors, pottery artisans, cartoonists, and a commitment to the 3Cs (Care, Consideration and Courtesy), and LOVE, a student-led United Way program for grade 6s and 7s, which stands for Leave Out Violence.[14] While many of these programs generally help all students in a school, other programs are more targeted at meeting the special needs of specific students.

School-Specific Programs to Help Students with Special Needs

Certain elementary schools have special programs that serve students with particular kinds of special needs. These programs are critically important. Parent Helen Welsh described one such program at Great Forest Elementary, called Rays of Hope:

> It is a program for kids who might have a learning disability of some sort, whether it be ADHD or dyslexia or whatever. I think we only have 10 kids in that class. They have a main teacher and two support workers in the class. Other than that, these students] participate in everything in the school – every fundraiser, every assembly, every function. But until they've reached a certain stage in their program, they won't intermingle with their grade. It's a multi-grade level [group]. It's kind of a reverse of a multi-age cluster class in the gifted program. It's the reverse of that, where they are struggling and need help. They come from all over the [the Vancouver region]. It is my understanding quite a few of them are bussed in.

Effective programs for special needs students can attract families and students from across the city as they provide the specialized programming to effectively educate these youth.

Many programs that provide support and counselling for at-risk students at elementary schools in East Vancouver positively impact student learning. The Helping Children Thrive program, managed by Susan Fletcher, a social worker who works with East Vancouver schools, is an, "outreach program for at-risk children in Inner City east-side schools." The program targets fifth to seventh graders. Even though this program targets older elementary school children, it provides a model for earlier intervention. Does the program work? According to Susan Fletcher, the evidence suggests that the program reduces absenteeism, disruptions in classrooms and improves learning: "It's not one of the stated goals or objectives, but certainly we understand from research that children that are happier, that aren't worrying, that are less anxious, that are feeling grounded and supported, are going to be open to learning and they're going to retain information, and they're going to be confident, and do better in school. We understand that, so one of the unintended outcomes that we set out to try to achieve is that kids would have academic success. Many of these kids were kids that are just not making it."

High rates of absenteeism are one barrier to learning and achievement for at-risk children. Fletcher explained, "One of the things we heard very early on that was interesting is that for some children, particularly boys who weren't coming to school, the day of group was the only day they were coming to school consistently for the 10-week period. If group was Tuesday, Tuesdays they were at school, when every other day [teachers] hardly saw them. That was something we first heard at Cassandra Elementary, but now it's been a bit of a theme that we're hearing in other schools." Fletcher said teachers report students being less disruptive in the classroom when enrolled in the Helping Children Thrive program. "We hear teachers say that kids are getting along better, so there's less disruption in class. So they're staying on task and they're doing their work. They generally have a more positive sense or feel to themselves," she said.

Yet Susan Fletcher admits it is challenging to generate quantitative data to back her claims that the program is having these effects. When surveyed by the program, many teachers said they simply did not know or could not say if the program was making a difference. She said, "That was one of the questions that our evaluators asked, and teachers said they didn't know. If you tried to get some hard data – this is all sort of narrative and qualitative stuff that we hear – the hard data didn't show that because the answer predominantly was, 'can't say.' 'Can't say' that the academic was impacted and sustained. So that's something that, for year two as we increase the rigour of the study, the assignment, we have to look [at]." According to Susan Fletcher, it is challenging to evaluate the impact of such a program.[15] At the same time, this program appears to help at-risk children by providing some of the stability that is missing from these children's lives. That stability helps improves behaviour and facilitates learning.

Social/Emotional Development Programs: Creating a Learning Environment

Many East Vancouver elementary schools had explicit goals and targeted programs to promote social responsibility and social-emotional competencies of their students. While at first glance, these programs might appear disconnected from teaching early literacy and numeracy skills, they were described as a crucial part of creating the conditions for learning.

Principal Katherine Drucker emphasized the link between these programs and academic achievement at Ashfield Elementary: "We know that academic achievement is directly connected to self-confidence and good self-esteem, those are the two biggies. And liking your teacher is up there too," she said with a laugh. "So we put a huge emphasis on social responsibility. When I think social/emotional, I think about the child, right? The child's behaviour, the child's attitude, the child's effort. When we think social responsibility, it's always the child interacting with others. It's about other people too."

Principal Drucker described some of the many ways that teachers and staff attempt to promote social responsibility among the students at Ashfield Elementary:

> We have regular assemblies at our school that focus on virtues. In September, we started out with compassion because the Dalai Lama was here, and so we have students that go on the PA every day at one o'clock with announcements, and they always have a message. Right now it's compassion: What does compassion look like? What does it sound like? What does it feel like? One of our goals this year is to connect our literacy to the social responsibility goals through writing. In the past, we asked each

teacher after the finished [were] announcements to talk a little bit about compassion and this year what we're going to implement is writing. It's called a school-wide write. Each day after you've heard the announcement, they will do some writing about one of the virtues.

Despite their importance, maintaining momentum around these kinds of school-wide initiatives can be challenging. According to Principal Drucker, "I've learned from my past experiences [that] if you don't have a team of people keeping those goals alive, that social responsibility goal alive, it's such a big [challenge]. [Saying] "Okay, everybody be socially responsible," it doesn't keep alive. We have a leadership team of staff, not just teachers, [who] meet on a regular basis and plan events and get resources for all the teachers and put them in their boxes around the virtue that we are working on." In light of the high turnover of principals, administrators must engage teachers and other staff as leaders in these programs, especially those who have been working at the school for many years. Drucker explained, "What we're trying to do is start all these leadership teams here. A third of our staff have been here over 30 years. In some of the bigger schools, there's usually a group that's been there a long time. And another third of our staff have been here over 15 years. What happens is they become sceptical, right, because some of these people have seen 15 administrators. They become sceptical. Now we're trying to get in and say 'You're the leaders of this school. You've been here. You know this community, you know these children.'" Both staff buy-in and resources are important for sustaining these programs.

The Vancouver School Board provides training and support for social and emotional development programming for school staff.[16] The goals of these programs are to foster self-esteem and self-confidence and to help children learn critical problem-solving skills.[17] Heather Mansbridge's third grade classroom at Ashfield Elementary has one wall dedicated to a virtue; the school focuses on six virtues throughout the year and presently, it is compassion. Each of the children has prepared an illustration and completed the sentence which begins with, "Compassion is …" Other classroom walls have posters on various issues related to social responsibility and literacy including: "Don't be a bulldog!" and "Fill your brain with reading power!"

At Great Forest Elementary, students learn about bullying and appropriate behaviour and how to respond. The school also has a program to encourage students to watch out for each other to prevent bullying.

Parent Helen Welsh said: "We also have a buddy program. An intermediate class buddy [is matched to] a primary class. So, of course, if you see someone picking on your buddy, then you say "Hey, hey, hey, that's my buddy, don't pick on him." So I think that's worked really well and, like I said, I think we have kids who are way off the charts ... I think we have very little bullying at Great Forest Elementary, very little." As bullying enters the cyber-age, it is increasingly important that curriculum and programs address issues around bullying and violence. Frightened and traumatized children who are bullied or harassed are distracted in class, and face serious barriers to learning.

Principal Teresa McDonald listed the social-emotional programs as some of the most important at Soaring Eagle Elementary:

> We have a Life Skills program for kids who are not successful academically, and we give them success in looking after themselves – safety, building things, organizing things. [It's] something that [doesn't require] a high[-level] academic focus but a hands-on type focus. One of our teachers has developed that, and it's brought our behaviour problems with some of our kids down. There's huge success there. They feel really valued in that program. They can do everything. I'm very happy with it. It's more common in high school, but we needed it here. We have a lunchtime program that the same teacher has set up for kids who have behaviour problems outside, where they can come in and just be in a smaller environment. Play board games. [It's] a mixed group of kids and they're invited to come in for that program.

Sometimes these targeted programs can help, especially if children do not feel labelled or tracked as a result of their selection.

Programs that prevent and address behaviour issues help set the stage for learning. At East Harcourt Elementary, Principal Jennifer Newcastle also described the importance of social-emotional programs: "In our school, we have a Youth and Family Worker, and we have a counsellor, and so with those two people, we also have a Roots of Empathy program here. We have social responsibility as one of our goals. We never stop working in this area of social/emotional, and we bring students who we are particularly concerned about, we bring them before school-based teams on a regular basis to talk about what more we can be doing about [for them]. I do a lot of work in this area with the students, as well." Both universal and targeted social emotional development programs were described as important because they providing students with useful skills they can draw on over the long term, both inside and outside the classroom.

Providing students with leadership and service opportunities was also described as an important part of building social emotional competencies. Principal Newcastle argues that the outcomes of these kinds of programs cannot be measured by a standardized testing: "All the wonderful other programs that happen in schools, all of the time in the school that aren't measured by writing a test, just students' participation. One of the things that we do here is we have a lot of opportunities for students to serve their school. At the end of the year we give out recognition awards and service awards. I'll show you one, what it would look like, for a grade 7 student." Principal Newcastle pointed to certificates covered in stars that reflect the service students had provided to the school, such as, "when they were [a] reading buddy, if they were at the science fair, or a telephone monitor, or in the choir, or the library, or monitor, or peer helper ... We're very proud of all the many things. We give our students a lot of opportunity."

Some parents extolled the virtues of these kinds of social-emotional development programs even more than the more focused literacy programs. For example, Rochelle Grant, the mother of a child at Wellington Elementary, said she would recommend the school to a friend because: "They are working hard with our students so they try to make them good students and good citizens. They try to make them responsible. They feel responsibility. Many times when they make a mistake they have a sheet that reminds them next time we will be careful we have to be careful about the other person so their feelings are not hurt."

Beyond academics, schools play an important role in socializing and shaping the values and outlook of their students. Tolerance. Compassion. Civic Engagement. Empathy. These are the kinds of values that undergird a vibrant democratic community life. One of the programs that focuses on these critical social values and deserves special mention is the Roots of Empathy program.

Roots of Empathy

Observing Roots of Empathy programs in action is simply amazing; the program engages a classroom around infant development, which holds the students' attention and imparts valuable lessons. Principal Teresa McDonald of Soaring Eagle Elementary said that of all the important programs, "I guess the biggest one of all is Roots of Empathy."

Roots of Empathy is a social/emotional development program, which involves each classroom "adopting" a baby belonging to a family in the community, and using the experience of that baby to learn about development, safety, and other issues over the school year.[18] I had the good fortune to observe the program in action at Lakeview Elementary. The classroom was friendly and welcoming. The walls were covered with posters displaying numbers, a calendar, numbered hands, and shapes. The ubbies were filled with blocks, bricks, puzzles, and games, and there was the kids' favourite: play houses. Books like *Cat in the Hat*, and *I'm Still Here in the Bathtub* sat on the shelf wall. One sign read, "Today is Friday. Yesterday was Thursday. Tomorrow will be Saturday."

On the morning I observed the classroom, there were approximately 27 students from kindergarten and the first grade sitting on the floor in the front of the room, facing a storyboard. They were listening to Dr. Amita Singh, a medical doctor in her early 30s, who was reading from a story book. The majority of the students were visible minorities. The children sat transfixed by Dr. Singh's story. I observed the back of their heads, a sea of shifting colours and textures, from jet black to blond hair. A baby doll lay on a large pink blanket on a low table off to one side. Today's lesson was about the milestones of a baby's development.

The story Dr. Singh was reading was about a baby. It is difficult to capture in words how engaged the children were in the subject. They loved the story. During the reading, one girl exclaimed, "She's growing up." With each illustration, Dr. Singh asked questions, and the students raised their hands to answer. Sometimes they got so excited they blurted out their answers without waiting to be called upon. They were full of curiosity and asked questions like, "What's happening to her face?" Other enthused exclamations included, "She can walk now!" and "My cousin's baby, she can stand."

As they went through the baby's stages or milestones of development, one girl concluded, "That's a beautiful book." Resource teacher Sarah Williams took over leading the class and went through the book page by page, while Dr. Singh glued a cut-out drawing next to each word. Their classroom teacher, David Simmons, encouraged the children to pronounce each vowel clearly. They repeated each word: 'Safety,' 'Smiles,' 'Rolls over,' 'Sits,' 'Crawls,' 'Stands,' and 'Walks.' He then asked, "What does 'walking' start with?" He was met with a chorus of "Ws" from the students. Simmons also connected these stages of a baby's development to Lily, the classroom's adopted 'baby.' "Can she walk yet?" he asked. They reply in unison, "No, not yet!"

Using the baby doll as a model, Dr. Singh also demonstrated some of the phenomena described in the story. She asked, "What can happen if a baby rolls over, and no one is watching her?" As the life-size baby doll plummeted off the table with a crash, one kid shouted, "She can really hurt herself!" Another girl sitting nearby spontaneously jumped up and grabbed the doll's fallen hat from the floor and placed it back on her head. In the discussion that followed, one student proposed putting the baby on the ground so it wouldn't fall. Another child became concerned, "What if the baby was in the backyard and rolled out onto a street and was hit by a car?" Williams nodded empathetically and said, "Yes, that's why we always have to watch the baby." Another concerned child exclaimed, "What if a bad dog took the baby?"

The kids discussed a myriad of ideas centred largely on the fear of children being hit by cars and attacked or taken by dogs. When talking about crawling, another child said, "It would not be safe if the baby was crawling and the gate opened, and the baby crawled out and there was a car." Another said, "What if I left the baby alone, and a bad dog or a nice dog bit the baby?" These learning opportunities were used to explain to the children that they have to be careful around cars and dogs.

Over the course of the session, the students espoused many creative ideas. At one point or another, almost all had their hands up and actively participated in the ongoing discussion. A first grader, Van, asked, "What if the baby crawls around and falls down the steps?" Dr. Singh moved a chair over, and the baby doll was used for a demonstration. She fell down again, off the table, onto the short plastic chair, and then onto the floor, as the children in class looked on in intensely. "Then she would get hurt!" they exclaimed. Dr. Singh then asked how the problem of crawling off the stairs could be prevented. The children weren't sure at first, so Dr. Singh gave them a clue. When told it rhymes with plate, they shouted out the correct answer: "a gate!" Using their collective concern over Lily, their "adopted" baby, they built a bond with experts like Dr. Singh. Through the lesson, they engaged in discussions about safety: the first milestone.

Around noon, it was time for the kindergarten kids to go home. On their way out, Simmons had them sing a song from the "Buddy Sing-a-long" book. The boys stood in one row with the girls in another and they put their arms around each other, their shoulders forming two long lines. They began to sing. As they left for the day, their voices rose up with glee. Even as the kindergarten students collected their things to leave, they continued to sing along with the remaining first grade students. At the end of the song, everyone clapped vigorously, and the kindergarten students departed beaming from ear to ear.

Many school staff were extremely positive about the Roots of Empathy program.[19] According to consultant Angela Myers, Roots of Empathy helps connect with difficult-to-engage children:

> And it's absolutely amazing, this goes back to the whole idea of relationships. I'm working with a grade 6 class at Victoria Elementary. Grade 6 teacher, really nice bunch of kids. There's one kid in there who has got a gang [sign] branded on his forehead already. He's got slick hair and the cool look and all that stuff. I'm thinking, "This is going to be interesting." But they are extremely well-behaved. The teacher has them very well trained. The mom [of the adopted baby] came [to the class]; she was kind of hesitant. Her English wasn't very good. We went through it, everything was fine. This little [baby] girl took a shine to this particular boy, to the punk kid, and for one of the first times, he'd made efforts to interact, even though he was still too cool for this. She turned and she gave him this brilliant smile. Well, you should have just seen that kid melt. He just melted, and over the school year, no matter what, every month when that baby came for a visit she singled him out, and by the end of the school year that kid had totally changed, it was just phenomenal. So that's one of the values of Root of Empathy.

The program engages students emotionally and uses the relationships between children and the "adopted" baby to develop analytical skills and to teach important life skills about community.[20] Unsurprisingly, the Roots of Empathy program created by Mary Gordon is widely popular, and school districts across Canada and globally are incorporating it into their curriculum.

While some schools follow standardized programs, staff at other schools develop their own versions or programs. Principal Teresa McDonald of Soaring Eagle Elementary said, "Roots of Empathy, all of those kinds of programs, have a standard curriculum. You have to be trained to teach them, and you have a standard curriculum for them. For our own social responsibility programs, we develop them as a staff. For the Life Skills [and] Early Literacy [programs], they've been developed by staff. It's not standardized in the sense that [a program] exists out there and anyone else could have it." School staff argued that it is important to have both the flexibility and resources to adapt or even create new programs to meet the needs of their schools and kids.

School Magnet and Other Special Programs

Some East Vancouver elementary schools have "magnet" or other specialized curriculum programs that can provide opportunities for motivated students whose parents elect to enrol them. In the United States, sociologist James Coleman and others argued that the introduction of selective schools and special school programs are important for attracting middle class families back into the urban educational systems, which have suffered from neglect, underfunding, segregation, suburban sprawl, and white flight.[21] These programs often tend to attract students from more educated and motivated families. They can track students from an early age, which can reinforce future inequalities.

While these programs may keep students in the schools, students in specialized magnet-type programs are often isolated from the mainstream student body. These programs can also act to "cream skim" some of the highest achieving students and highly motivated and experienced teachers from the system, leaving those left behind worse off. In many Canadian schools, French immersion programs are one example of a program that attracts motivated parents to enrol their children.

Teacher Amy Peterson at Ashfield Elementary expressed some reservations about the appropriateness of French immersion programming for ESL students. She argued, "I think it's a mistake to take our ESL students and put them into French, because they don't speak English well enough, and [in the case of] a lot of them, their parents don't speak their own language well ... Then add another language on top. That's just my opinion. I just think these ESL kids need to learn to speak English. They're going to be living in a city that's English-speaking, [so] they need to speak it well, read it well, write it well." While there may be lower interest in French immersion among parents of ESL students, they are increasingly enrolling their children in French immersion. Specialized magnet programs tend to attract students whose parents are motivated enough to sign up for the lottery to get a coveted spot.

The nature of these programs as both exclusive and selective – with fewer spaces than interested students – means that they tend to attract a group of students who are different from the rest of the student population. Many programs, such as French immersion and dramatic arts magnet programs, are open to students from a much broader catchment area than the regular school program. In some cases, motivated parents must not only register in advance but also arrange transportation so that their children can attend these school programs.[22] As a result, these programs can result in allowing an advantaged group of students to opt out of the mainstream school classrooms within the public system and attend classes with fewer challenging or special needs students.

Despite these serious equity issues, the presence of these programs also attract and keep motivated teachers and students in the urban public school system. If these programs did not exist, some motivated parents might be more likely to enrol their children in private school. All in all, these special programs clearly appear to have an important place in public education. Yet the deleterious consequences of cream-skimming resources or of creating segregated schools within schools should be actively addressed or even partially redressed at every stage, from selection processes to resources. For example, schools should provide preferred or expedited selection to students with certain characteristics to ensure diversity and to make sure that the benefits of these programs help more than just privileged students.

Critical Resources: Program Cuts Hurt

Funding cuts were frequently described as having negative consequences for the quality of education in East Vancouver elementary schools. For example, a dramatic cut in per-school funding – from $80,000 to $25,000 per year – devastated the Inner City project team at Wellington Elementary, which previously funded a Youth and Family Worker, a neighbourhood worker, a primary staff assistant, a part-time area counsellor, and a part-time speech pathologist at the school.[23] To make matters worse, the reduced level of funding had to be supported by evidence of "student improvements," which Wellington Principal Mark Brown suggests is challenging given a transience rate of 26% to 27% per year. In other words, many children supported by these programs soon leave the school and therefore are not available for assessment and follow up.

Principal William Coleman of Pearson Elementary describes the devastating effects of recent cuts: "With $100 million dollar budget cuts, we're reeling. This year, it's the worst it's ever been. You call downtown to the [Vancouver] School Board, and there is nobody to answer the phone anymore. All the consultants and all the help that we used to have, we don't have anymore. So we're kind of flying on our own now. So I think that's a real issue, just the resources and the help to get us there."

When I asked about more examples of the consequences of the cuts, Principal Coleman said:

> I don't even know where to begin. Like everything we've lost, I don't even know where to start. Stuff that we used to have in terms of special needs that isn't there anymore. Stuff we used to have in terms of music and the arts, there's no one there anymore to do that. Someone around literacy. We used to have like a billion people, and now we have one person trying to do the whole system, and a couple of mentors who work a couple of hours a week. Yet the need is greater than ever, in terms of support for us as administrators and in terms of professional development. We have some support, but it certainly [isn't] to the extent that it used to be before.

Cutbacks create a desperate atmosphere that causes teaching and administrative staff to feel deflated and frustrated. Cuts mean there are fewer resources to address the needs of at-risk children and help them to be ready to learn.

Outside of the school system itself, funding cuts also hurt the programs that support the children and families who need the most help. Susan Fletcher, a social worker who works with East Vancouver elementary schools, commented that there simply were not enough resources to provide the kind of critically important individual services and counselling to address the needs of at-risk youth in the lower-income areas in Vancouver. She argued,

> My sense is that if we had enough resources, if there were more programs, more staff, we would be doing much more outreach. By that I mean starting with letting schools know this program is available. We just don't have the resources … The programs that I work with, everyone is stretched to the max. I think there are some great innovative programs, but if people don't know about them – families don't know, schools don't know – there are tons of families that go with their needs unmet. Then when we do get somebody who calls us and we're full, we've tried creating a wait list. But then, we can't find many of them at the time when we do have a space.

Fletcher described the example of a specific under-funded program for women and children who've escaped from abusive situations: "For example, in another program I manage, we work with women and children who've been in abusive home environments, and it gets full very quickly. We only have 1.1 counsellors for all of Vancouver, right?

That's what we get from our funding from the government to run that program. So by the time we call them they've either left the transition house, we have no way of finding them, or they're back in an abusive environment. That's the problem: it's lack of awareness and lack of resources. When people are ready the service is not always available to them." The consequences of under-staffing of support programs are that too many children are falling through the cracks and not getting the services they need.

Despite the widespread understanding of the central role of early literacy acquisition for the future success of elementary school students, resource cuts means that almost all of the elementary schools have restricted access to their school libraries. At Lakeview Elementary, they can only afford to keep the library open three school days per week. At Ashfield Elementary, Principal Katherine Drucker said, "Our library is open, yes; it's open through the lunch hour." But that's it. Despite these limited hours, she remarked, "We have one of the highest turnover of books going in and out of the library in Vancouver. That may be because we're one of the biggest schools, but the kids are really encouraged to take out [books] … I think they can take out five books at a time, and they do." Despite funding cuts, at Ashfield Elementary they continue to buy new material and keep the library open. Principal Drucker said, "Our parents have supported that. Some of our [BC government] casino money[24] each year goes towards the library. [The librarian] always requests a certain type [of books]. Last year it was non-fiction, Canada, and the year before it was non-fiction, animals. So he focuses in on one area, and the parents have been great about supporting it."

At Centennial Elementary, the library is also only open for limited hours during the school day because they can only afford a part-time librarian. Teacher Jane Sorrento explained, "Our librarian is here on a part-time basis. The library is open Mondays, Tuesdays, [and] Wednesdays for signing out books and returning books. So I built in a library time for my kids. They go 10 [students] at a time to exchange books." When I asked about the library limitations at her school, Sorrento told me,

> Do you know what's been happening with libraries the past year or so in Vancouver? There have been terrible cuts, and times when staff has had to prioritize. Do we keep our music program or do we keep our librarians? So a lot of adaptation a lot of compromise has had to be made now.

The other thing is too, a number of us have worked very hard and quite loudly [fundraising] the last couple of years to build up the resources in our library. When I first came to Centennial Elementary, I was horrified at how outdated the books in the library were, and how few resources there were compared to other libraries that I'd been in, I've used and been in, and also the libraries that my children had access to in their own schools.

Cuts that keep school libraries closed much of the week affect students' early literacy skills acquisition. Sorrento said the budget cuts result in:

Terrible resources and schools without music programs. Schools without art specialists. Schools without libraries and librarians. The libraries just sort of sitting there. So that's had a definite negative impact. And that's sort of one of the fundamentals of expecting and wanting children to be literate and fully educated and literate human beings is that they have access to books, really good quality books. And we as the primary staff have really beefed up our own primary book room, so we've got tons of wonderful children's picture books that ... teachers can sign out and use. So that's just for the primaries, in addition to what's even in the library.

Funding for these staff and programs – from libraries to arts and music instruction – may be viewed by some as "extras," yet they are critical for developing a love of school and learning that promote long-run literacy and numeracy skills acquisition.

Principal Tim Richards of Great Forest Elementary feels that cuts have hurt the quality of instruction at his school. He explained,

We have less flexibility because our staffing levels are stretched so thin that we cannot use a piece of a teacher to teach band, for example. We cannot use a teacher to do hands-on instruction for a small group of students ... We don't have enough resource teachers to support the needs of our most needy kids. That's been cut. Our librarian is still only at 80%. We don't have enough money. We don't have enough staffing to staff our library at 100%. Up until this year, resource money to support classrooms with resources was pretty thin ... Support for teacher assistants isn't high enough. The schedules of our SSAs [Support Service Assistants] who cover kids is just ludicrous, what they have to go through. They will go from classroom to classroom to try and support as many kids as possible. And the nightmare of timetabling of teachers, getting them when they need them, is difficult.

Several parents spoke about the impact of cuts and the need for their children's schools to have greater resources to effectively educate the students. Parent Helen Welsh highlighted budget issues as a top concern at Great Forest Elementary:

> I mean, ESL is definitely our number one. Number two is budget. I mean, we're trying fundraisers … My dad was on the PAC when I went to Great Forest Elementary, and they were fundraising for the extras. Now, we're fundraising for *necessities,* so that's a huge difference. I mean we're fundraising for things that the government should be providing … art supplies and field trips. Now, granted, in Vancouver they do have a policy [that] no child will miss a field trip; technically they say the [school] board will cover it, but really what they mean is that the principal now has to take money from another source, another pot, and put it into the field trip pot.

Adequate funding levels, when they exist, allow for the human resources required to provide extra help to special needs students. Welsh explained: "In my son's class last year, we had one special-needs girl who had full-time care. So it was kind of lucky for our teacher, she was able to help with other people as well. But we also had three other kids in there who were supposed to have extra help, but we couldn't afford it, so they didn't have it. I only know of three of them because I know their parents. There could have been more." Without dedicated in-class support, teachers and parent volunteers must attempt to fill the gap, which can detract attention and resources from the other students in the classroom.

In urban schools in low-income neighbourhoods, administrators have to be financially savvy to make limited budgets stretch as far as they can to meet the student's needs. School staff also must creatively stretch limited funding to make it go further towards meeting needs. Welsh related how, at Great Forest Elementary, the vice-principal stretches limited resources: "I think it's been great [that] our vice-principal can make a penny into a nickel. He's fabulous! He works our budget unbelievably. We're shocked sometimes at the deals he gets and how [the teachers] work it. We have a very generous staff. We have a staff who, I won't say all of them, but we have a staff who will stay late, who will come in early, who will come in on their day off because they know that this kid needs more help. We have an unbelievable staff at Great Forest Elementary."

Welsh has also observed the negative consequences of cuts first-hand: "One of the main reasons is that a teacher who wants to do something, even remotely elaborate, a project or anything, they don't have the funding. They don't have the resources to give the kids anything. And because we are somewhat of a low-income school, a lot of the kids can't get their parents to buy it for them. The teachers know this. So if they can't supply it for everybody, it's something that we may not be able to do. It affects them in the way that the teachers have to completely alter their programs to fit in with what they can afford to do."

Funding shortfalls also translate into a lack of high-quality teaching and learning materials in the classrooms. Even basic supplies have run short in some East Vancouver elementary schools. Welsh explained, "We have a lot of kids who can't take their book home because we only have 24 for the class, and if one goes missing, we're short. So, it's 'you do your math now or you don't do it at all.' And as a PAC with casino money [from the provincial government], we're not allowed to use that gaming money for textbooks. The things that we really need, we're not allowed to use it for. It's a dumb rule, but it's a rule."

In order to save money in light of funding cuts, resource teacher positions have been shifted towards entry-level teachers, who often remain in their position for only one year. According to Vancouver School Board consultant Angela Myers, "The biggest thing that isn't working is the fact that resource teacher has become an entry-level position. Every year I spent the majority of my energy training a new cohort of entry-level positions because if you have a 0.47 position and somebody offers you full-time, of course you're going to take it. And then I've got a new cohort that needs to be trained all over again, and they're like the deer in the headlights."

Funding cuts to ESL programs also harmed the quality of education in East Vancouver elementary schools. Many of these programs were eliminated as a result of provincial funding cuts in the early 1990s.[25] Cuts were so severe that the school district no longer provided any ESL support to teachers and students in schools. Subsequently, some of these ESL instructors were rehired as additional school district–level consultants and shared by several schools, yet even these positions face the constant threat of elimination.[26] Cutbacks have also hurt teacher training and the ability to provide literacy support for ESL students.[27]

Some of the biggest challenges facing East Vancouver elementary school teachers with ESL students result from a lack of training or support. "The teachers haven't had the opportunity to have the training.

They've hit the deck running, and they're doing the best they can. So the kids are getting the very best that the teachers can give them, but they're not getting what's optimal because the infrastructure is not in place to give the teachers the appropriate training," Angela Myers argued. Professional development opportunities have also been reduced as a result of cutbacks.[28]

One of the most direct and pernicious ways that funding cuts harms student education is by reducing the number of staff available to work with special needs students. Principal Teresa McDonald of Soaring Eagle Elementary explained that the biggest challenge facing her school is "… giving enough individual attention to all the children in the school. As I mentioned, [there are] the high mental health needs of many families at the school; the large number of special integrated, special needs, children at the school. So making sure that we're providing for all those individual needs [is a big challenge]."

Principal McDonald argued that having an adequate number of on-site trained staff is important for success:

> The key thing that works the best, even though it's hard to get because it's costly, is personal contact – staffing. Having the people who are specially trained on-site, not the drop-in people who you can call in an emergency to come in, but people who get to know the children and the families; [who] are here on-site and are able to go into classes to talk, to give kids some extra counselling time, to help families access services, to be that extra help, to take on a mentoring role outside of the classroom teacher and administration. So I find that's the most effective out of everything. All of the things I mentioned are effective, but if I had to choose the one that makes the biggest difference I've seen over time, it's the staffing, particularly the Youth and Family Worker role.

Yet these positions are often the first to face the chopping block in the face of funding cuts, reducing the human resources available to meet the needs of students.

Conclusion

While unfortunately there are no easy answers for ensuring universal early acquisition of literacy and numeracy skills among elementary school students, adequate resources to fund programs that meet the needs of the student population and foster the conditions for learning are centrally important. There are currently many important programs running in East Vancouver schools to help address these needs. Clearly, programs that provide extra resources to schools to meet the needs of their students, like the Inner City Schools Project, are especially important. As described earlier, these resources allow for the kinds of programming and support required by special needs students. Other essential programs include before- and after-school care as well as free breakfast and hot lunch programs. Community-oriented literacy fairs and extra resources for struggling individual students, such as newly arrived ESL students, are also important. When these programs are cut or underfunded, vulnerable children are at risk of falling further behind. Sociologist Karl Alexander and colleagues argue that, "Preschool and [k]indergarten can help children arrive at first grade ready to learn, but to help them keep up, extra resources and enrichment experiences will be needed along the way."[29]

Ensuring that students are ready to learn by the time they begin the first grade requires high-quality universal access to early childhood development programs, and full-day kindergarten is arguably one of the best ways to achieve this goal.[30] Currently, many elementary schools also reach out to preschool-aged children and families. For example, Pearson Elementary and Centennial Elementary, among others, include a Parent-Child Mother Goose Program as part of the Ready, Set, Learn programs that engages parents and toddlers in the neighbourhood to help provide parents with child development insights including nutrition, creative play, and early learning.

It is impossible for school staff to meet all of their students' needs by themselves. They need extra help, including school board resources and collaborative community programs. East Vancouver elementary schools partner with nearby community centres to provide after-school care and other programming for students. Other important programs include those that provide instructional resources for teachers, and those aimed at teaching social-emotional competence. These programs foster tolerance and pro-social behaviour in diverse environments. Another great program is the Community of Schools program, which creates links between the different elementary schools that feed into a secondary school. For example, at Centennial Elementary, the Community of Schools program promotes mentoring and teaching of elementary students by secondary students, who lead cooking and other kinds of lessons. The program also creates floating teachers and support staff that work with the elementary schools, helping children who are falling behind and preparing kids for secondary school. Principals, teachers, and parents who were interviewed extolled the virtues of these programs. While the sheer number of programs – from preschool to curriculum-based programs – can seem overwhelming, they provide important resources to address the needs of at-risk students in East Vancouver elementary schools, helping children master early literacy and numeracy skills.

While there are serious challenges facing education researchers and school staff to evaluate these programs, a multidimensional approach that includes quantitative and qualitative data provides more illuminating evidence than do limited approaches. The resources to support local and district-wide initiatives are fundamentally important and are essential to achieving the goal of universal early literacy and numeracy skills mastery at an early age. These programs play a central role in helping children overcome barriers that limit their ability to learn and achieve academically.

6 Standardized Testing: Here to Stay?

The tests, however, like it or not, are hanging there like sharpened swords above the heads of principals and teachers, and since the scores, when they are finally released, are widely publicized in press accounts and on TV (the lowest-scoring schools are often named in horror stories in the tabloid papers – 'Halls of Shame ... the worst of the worst ... the dirty dozen,' for example says *The New York Post* above a story on twelve of the city's lowest-scoring schools), educators live in terror of the days scores come out.

– Jonathan Kozol, The Shame of the Nation[1]

As a social scientist, I love data. Generally speaking, the more data that is publically available, the better, right? Yet when it comes to high-stakes testing data, I hold conflicting views. While testing can and likely should play a role in education, the current use of standardized testing regimes, especially when the data is used to evaluate school performance and rank schools, remains highly problematic, not to mention ineffectual. After exploring the problems with the current high-stakes accountability testing regime, I will propose some new reforms and models that require working with educators to improve student learning and outcomes.

The role of testing and data can certainly be an important one in improving education and identifying challenges. Under the much-critiqued No Child Left Behind legislation in the United States, each state is required to submit "accountability plans" that mandate the publishing of standardized test data, including performance figures broken down by ethnic and racial categories. While very controversial, this legislation has advanced our understanding of disparities in school performance. As urban sociologist and education scholar Pedro Noguera argued: "Even the fiercest critics of the Bush Administration must acknowledge, that despite its many flaws, No Child Left Behind has, in an odd way, moved the national conversation about race and education forward, because for the first time in our nation's history, schools are required to produce evidence that they can serve all students."[2] The production of this data could theoretically help identify problem areas and help measure advancements after the implementation of effective reforms.

Yet the current standardized testing regime and the publication of printed rankings of schools based on the data remains highly problematic in many ways, and may be poised to get even worse with new trends (such as pay-for-performance schemes and social investment bonds). These fundamental problems with the current testing regime in British Columbia schools parallel those of other jurisdictions globally.

In the United States, the No Child Left Behind reforms were based on the notion that testing, ranking, competition, and market forces will somehow – through the magic of the invisible hand – improve school performance and students' educational outcomes. The fundamental problem with this approach is that public education, similar to health care, is not the same as the markets for most goods. Thus the invisible hand creates perverse incentives and generally fails to enhance outcomes for struggling students. Fundamentally, also as in health care, the recipients in most need of expensive services are generally the least able to afford to pay the costs themselves, and also the most likely to perform poorly in terms of objective outcome measures. Students with learning disabilities or special needs and those from troubled home environments, for example, require more resources to thrive educationally, and the higher the need, the less likely the result will be "above average" in terms of outcome testing.[3]

Other problems with standardized testing have been extensively discussed in the research literature, and some findings merit repeating.[4] The negative effects of standardized testing regimes are both deep and broad ranging, as education scholar Stuart Green commented: "Indeed, a considerable amount of research has demonstrated that No Child Left Behind (NCLB) has actually undercut the goals of democracy, equity, and social justice. For example, the curriculum in schools seems to have narrowed to accommodate increased testing and accountability, so that children do not have opportunities to engage in a wide range of literacy practices. Moreover, the ways assessments are used have perpetuated the stratification of our schools by race and class, enforcing both the exclusion and containment of minority students."[5] Standardized testing–based accountability regimes fail to live up to the promises put forward by advocates when they are put into practice.

One important finding by sociologists Douglas B. Downey, Paul T. von Hippel, and Melanie Hughes in their article, "Are 'Failing Schools' Really Failing: Removing the Influence of Nonschool Factors from Measures of School Quality" published in the journal *Sociology of Education*, is that the effectiveness of schools educating disadvantaged populations is likely underestimated by standardized testing.[6] In a novel approach, they create an "impact factor" that attempts to measures the difference between the rate of learning during the school year compared to the rate during the summer, when children are not in school. Using data from the Early Childhood Longitudinal Study, they find that a majority of the schools scoring in the bottom 25th percentile on standardized test score averages are not actually poor performers in terms of their impact factors. In other words, they found that children are learning a great deal when in school, even in many schools that appear to be "performing poorly" based on the ranking of schools by overall standardized test score averages.

In Canada, economist David Johnson has attempted to address this fundamental problem with the current standardized testing and school ranking regime by recalculating rankings of schools in the Canadian provinces of British Columbia and Ontario based on their standardized test scores, taking into account the socio-economic characteristics of the catchment area.[7] Theoretically, the idea is that the recalculated scores would better reflect school "performance" given the socio-economic demographic of their student populations. These recalculated rankings, while available online from the C.D. Howe Institute think tank, are not the rankings distributed by the Fraser Institute, a right-wing think tank, published annually in the *Vancouver Sun* and studied by parents and the school administrators in Vancouver. While these alternate revised measures and rankings are certainly an improvement, they only begin to address the fundamental problems with standardized testing for school performance assessment.

Standardized testing has been shown to problematically change the way teachers teach, encouraging them to "teach to the test."[8] Research on the impact of testing in the classroom has uncovered some serious causes for concern. Based on 300 hours of observation of a reading specialist in Texas to examine her response to the implementation of the Texas Assessment of Knowledge and Skills (TAKS) standardized exam regime, Lori Assaf reported that standardized testing changed the way reading is being taught, with the emphasis being on teaching students to pass the test. What is lost when teachers teach to the test? Based on her observations, Assaf found that discussions of books gave way to "systematic, low-level, drill-and-skill-building instruction."[9] Students who failed the exam were pulled out of classrooms and enrolled in summer school for test-preparation instruction. Others were retrained, but with a focus on passing the test. She concluded that, "imposing a high stakes test, even in the case of subsequently increasing test scores, does not equate to increased learning."[10]

Teaching to tests may improve scores, but it does not improve literacy, numeracy, or the outcomes that testing is supposed to measure (and improve). It also does little for students' love of learning. Once tests become published (or worse, schools are ranked based on test results), several predictable things occur. Depressingly, schools begin manipulating and inflating results through a variety of practices, from categorizing more students as unfit to take the tests and encouraging students to stay home who have a high potential to fail, to literally, in some cases, cheating: biased marking, giving out answers, and having teachers fill in answers.[11] While none of these strategies improves actual student learning, they increase test score outcomes.

Publishing the scores and ranking schools based on the results does not appear to be creating the kind of positive changes in literacy and numeracy skills acquisition that policy makers and some think tanks had hoped would occur. For example, we are not seeing advances in the performance of Canadian schools in Organisation of Economic Co-operation and Development (OECD) educational performance outcomes or rankings after the implementation of these testing regimes in many provinces.[12] The research evidence suggests that, despite high hopes, the current trend towards increasingly employing standardized testing as a tool to create competitive pressure and improve school performance remains highly problematic. Part of the problem is that many of the fundamental assumptions about school performance behind standardized testing accountability regimes simply do not reflect reality.

Why Standardized Testing and Ranking Schools Fails to Improving Learning

Standardized testing of students has long been touted as a way to boost student learning and skills acquisition. When reviewing examples of the uses of standardized testing regimes, it quickly becomes clear that – in contrast to the ideology of those who believe that market forces and competition will improve the quality of education – the absolute worst use of standardized testing is to try to "shame" poor performers.[13] One example was the labelling of New York City schools with poor test score profiles as "failing schools" in the early 1990s, and the subsequent threat to shut them down if they did not miraculously improve, even in the absence of extra resources. Often the performance worsens as negative labelling causes students with resourceful, motivated parents as well as good teachers to actively pursue alternative options, thus leaving the worst off behind.[14] Despite threats, these schools are rarely actually closed down. When they are, we don't generally see miraculous improvements in student performance.

Problematically, when schools are ranked by standardized test score outcomes, these results get conflated with school performance, without any of the contextual information that would be needed to even begin to accurately assess what the scores mean about the quality of instruction provided by the schools. These lists do not, for example, account for the percentage of students from very low-income families in the school. They also do not report on special programs that might be attracting disproportionate numbers of students with special needs or talents.[15] Regrettably, when the data are also "bad" data and incomplete, the usefulness of the testing is further limited in terms of improving school performance, which is technically the purported goal of the program.

In Vancouver, the newspaper stories accompanying the school rankings every year follow a pretty typical pattern. Some articles describe handwringing over the low percentages of students "meeting expectations" or passing at urban schools that serve extremely high-poverty neighbourhoods. Other accompanying articles include a (often smug) celebration of the success of resource-rich schools serving privileged children in wealthier communities. Another short article might focus briefly on a school whose test scores have dropped, usually pointing the finger of blame at administrators. There is also usually an article profiling a school whose scores soared compared to the previous year. These articles generally highlight factors like leadership, corporate sponsorship, or, as in the case of Grandview Elementary, a "back to basics" phonics curriculum. Of course, rarely are there follow-ups to these stories when the test scores at these same schools subsequently reverse and decline. What is lacking from these accompanying newspaper articles is an accurate portrayal of how schools are actually changing, including the new challenges they experience, and how they are attempting to address these new needs and challenges.

In British Columbia, the results on the Foundation Skills Assessment (FSA) standardized test exams at a school level vary from year to year, although schools with higher proportions of students from more privileged socio-economic backgrounds consistently perform better overall than schools with high percentages of students from low socio-economic backgrounds.

Over the course of the research, many of the 10 East Vancouver elementary schools studied experienced quite dramatic swings in scores since standardized testing of fourth and seventh graders began. Some schools also experienced fairly dramatic annual changes in the "excusal" rates – the percentage of students at the school not sitting for the standardized exams. These year-to-year changes in excusal rates reduce the comparability of scores from year to year and also reduce the overall utility of the test scores for assessing how well a school is performing.

For example, Lakeview Elementary experienced dramatic increases in its FSA standardized test score results over the study period. In only a few short years, the school went from below 50% of its students passing to almost 90% of fourth graders tested meeting or exceeding expectations in reading. At the same time, the participation rate of students at Lakeview fell from 100% to 80%, which likely means that a higher percentage of students were excused from taking the test. This change alone, which has nothing to do with school quality, likely partially explains the upward trend in outcome scores between the two years, especially if we imagine that those students excused were more likely to fail to meet expectations on the exams because they were ESL or designated special needs students.

Instead of testing a small sample of randomly selected students, all enrolled students at the fourth and seventh grades are expected to take the standardized exams. In practice, this also means that schools are being evaluated and ranked on the basis of relatively small sample sizes, where a few students' performance make a big difference. In Vancouver, a typical cohort of fourth grade students is usually less than 150 students, even at most large elementary schools. At some elementary schools, fourth grade cohorts can be less than 40 students. Hence, the difference between 12 students and 17 students failing to meet expectations in literacy or numeracy skills on the exam dramatically changes the school's overall average, and therefore its published ranking. If there were a way to guarantee full participation or at least random non-participation, we would still expect some cohort variance in passing rates between years, which would have little to do with school quality. Yet there are varying rates of non-random non-participation in the exam. In other words, a larger number of students are excused or absent for the test than in other schools, and in some schools, those who are excused or absent are the students most likely to fail to meet expectations on the exam. Together, these two factors mean that relatively small differences in terms of actual numbers of children not passing the test – at least differences that could theoretically be explained by cohort effects, selective non-participation, and a host of other reasons – are instead extrapolated as reflecting school quality or trends in school quality.

At Lakeview Elementary the average number of students in the fourth grade taking the test is approximately 30 students. In this case, the relatively small number of fourth graders available to be tested meant that the performance of only a handful of students had a substantial impact on school-level results. For example, Wellington Elementary went from 56% to 72% of fourth graders tested meeting or exceeding reading expectations from one year to the next; but exam participation rates in the second year plummeted. Similar to Lakeview Elementary, if the students not taking the exam were more likely to fail to meet expectations on the test than those who sat the exam, then the increase in scores between the two years does not actually reveal improvements in student learning at Wellington Elementary. The percentage of students meeting or exceeding expectations at several East Vancouver elementary schools, including Wellington Elementary and Soaring Eagle Elementary, were highest when participation rates were at their lowest.

Overall at the schools studied, the percentage of students meeting or exceeding expectation rates in reading scores among fourth graders who sat the exams ranged from the low 60% to a high 80% range with no consistent pattern, demonstrating the low year-to-year reliability of the FSA standardized exams as a measure of school "performance."

With a fourth grade cohort of approximately 60 students taking the exam each year, Great Forest Elementary highlights this variability. In one year, nearly 20% of students were excused from participation. Subsequently, nearly 60% of fourth graders at the school did not take the exams. This does not reflect changing policies at Great Forest Elementary but instead reflects the decision of many parents to keep their children at home on testing day in the protest against the standard-ized testing accountability regime.[16] Interestingly enough, these wide swings in participation rates in this case did not result in much change in the percentage of students meeting or exceeding expectations in lit-eracy among fourth graders at Great Forest Elementary over the study period.

In contrast, Ashfield Elementary had consistently high participation rates. Yet one year, the percentage of students meeting or exceeding expectations in literacy among fourth graders fell by 25 percentage points; that year, only 50% met or exceeded expectations in literacy. Ashfield was not the only school to experience dramatic variations; the percentage of students meeting or exceeding expectations on the reading standardized plummeted in some cases and spiked in others nearly 20 percentage points compared to the previous year in many of the schools studied, with no reasonable pattern or explanation linked to quality of education or instruction. Even the most consistent "top performer" among the East Vancouver elementary schools in terms of fourth grade reading test scores had one year where the propor-tion of students meeting or exceeding expectations in literacy fell over 10 percentage points *below* the provincial average. Overall, the schools that tended to post the most consistent higher passing rates since the 2000–2001 school year, when the standardized testing began, are also, unsurprisingly, the ones where the student body and community are the most middle class.

Another way to understand the dramatic variability of the results is to consider the rankings of these 10 East Vancouver elementary schools based on the percentage of their students meeting grade-level expecta-tions on their exams. Among the elementary schools studied, only a few had stable test scores from the base year (2000–2001) to the pres-ent (2012–2013); others dramatically fluctuated up, down, and in both directions. The elementary school that had the worst passing rate in fourth grade reading in the 2000 to 2001 school year – with a below 50% passing rate – had the highest of the group in the 2004 to 2005 school year, with 86% passing. The strongest performer of the group of schools studied in the 2001 to 2002 school year – with a passing rate of 81% – was among the worst performer in the group (third from the bottom) in the 2004 to 2005 school year. In other words, some of the "best" per-forming schools in the sample according to FSA exam results for fourth grade literacy at the introduction of this testing regime became some of the "worst," and vice versa, only a few years later. This variability alone suggests the fundamental unreliability of standardized test results in terms of assessing the performance of these schools.

While some schools performed more consistently in the 2000 to 2001 school year as compared with the 2012 to 2013 school year, others had substantially different outcomes between these two points in time. Yet the school testing data at these two points in time are *not* reflective of the overall trends the schools experienced during the intervening period. More basically, changes in rankings of these schools also do not take into account the changes in percentages of students who were excused or who simply did not come to school on testing day.

The longer the standardized testing continues, the more it becomes clear that the current FSA standardized testing regime in British Columbia does not provide much useful information about how a school is performing in terms of the quality of education provided to students or in terms of student learning, particularly in comparison to other schools serving similar student populations. The regime of standardized testing and ranking, overall, does not appear to be improving the quality of basic skills education. Stepping back from the 10 East Vancouver elementary schools that I focused on, the most interesting information generated over time by the testing is that pretty much consistently, over the years, schools with fewer students from low-income families tend to also have higher percentages of students who meet or exceed expectations on the standardized exams.[17] A well-known sociological fact, but one that does not immediately advance student learning in classrooms.

Given the lack of accuracy and reliability of the FSA standardized test scores in the current testing regime, one of the most negative uses of passing rates is their annual publication in ranked lists by the Fraser Institute and *Vancouver Sun*. This ranking of schools does not take into account other predictors of test score outcomes, such as the percentage of students from extremely low-income families or recently arrived ESL students, or even which schools teach substantial numbers of children with special needs. When socio-economic factors are taken into account, a very different profile emerges as to which schools are "successful" and which are "struggling" to improve literacy and numeracy.[18] Even when socio-economic status is taken into account, how do we understand variance in outcomes on these standardized tests? Do different schools take different approaches? If so, in what ways and why? And if not, are there other differences beyond socio-economic status that explain the variation between schools? The test results do not provide any answers.

Many of the school administrators and teachers interviewed felt that the FSA standardized tests failed to provide an accurate picture of student progress and achievement. Teacher Jane Sorrento at Centennial Elementary explained why she does not like the FSA exams: "I think that it is very limited, and I think that it only gives you a very limited picture of where students are and how they are doing … The best way to prepare for any of the standardized tests is just to keep doing all the really important experiential activities that we keep doing. I don't really believe in preparing children for those sorts of tests." Teachers complained of feeling pressure to teach to the test. Others said they felt the test was useless.

Principal Tim Richards of Great Forest Elementary described the FSA exams as "not valued by the teachers. They're not valued by the principal because they're used for mainly for political reasons." He also explained that many teachers "send home notices to the parents indicating that if they wish their children to not write, they just have to fill in a form and send it back." As a result of these notices, Principal Richards said only 40% of the eligible seventh graders actually take the standardized exam at his school. He said, "It's a question of, politically, the parents being told that the FSAs are being used to evaluate schools, and the parents are listening to that and asking that their children be excluded." When the key stakeholders in the system actively resist the tool, it further reduces its usefulness for improving education.

Parent Helen Welsh, whose children attend Great Forest Elementary, argued that there is a bias in the standardized tests against students from low-income or ESL backgrounds. "We're not a school that teaches to the FSA. We're not a school that studies for it. We don't stop all the rest of the curriculum [during] FSA week and study for FSAs. That's not what we do. I think that any scores that we get on the FSAs are because the kids have had good learning in the classroom – any of the high scores. Some of the low scores are low because the questions are not for kids who come from low-income families or kids who are ESL." Welsh went on to say that she felt the test questions reveal a middle-class white bias: "Some of the questions and some of the pictures [display this bias]; like, what is a normal meal that you would have for breakfast? And there's oatmeal, bacon and eggs, and French toast. Well, half of our ESL kids don't know what any of those are because they're [used to] having an Asian meal [where they have] rice with something. Part of it is that the whole thing is in English. You're not allowed to help them, so an ESL kid has no hope if he doesn't understand a word. One word is going to throw him right off." Welsh said that minor details such as the time of day the students take the test can also impact the results. "It depends on when you take the test," she said. "Some kids take it fresh, first thing in the morning. Some kids take it in the afternoon after PE [Physical Education] or what have you." Overall, Welsh felt of the tests: "I hate them, hate them, hate them, hate them."

Many staff voiced strong opposition to the way standardized testing was employed in British Columbia schools. Vancouver School Board literacy consultant Angela Myers said, "The FSA is such an arbitrary snapshot of where a kid is at on a particular day, in a particular mood, in a particular climate. It's ridiculous. What's the metaphor ... it's like taking the tire pressure, while the car is in motion. What do you really learn from that? Not much." She argues that the FSA exams fail to measure important factors related to learning:

> What should we be measuring? There's the big thing about relationships, and you can measure how successful you are in building relationships and a sense of community by how the kids act. The social responsibility piece.
>
> The other thing that we need to measure, we need to measure kids' capacity to access the learning they need, when they need it. The learning how to learn piece. What we should be teaching kids is not a bunch of data, but how to access the knowledge they need when they need it. So they need the skills and understanding and attitude of how to go about finding what they need to know, when they need it.
>
> It's like trying to tell high school kids that they have to decide what their future career is going to be, and, well, they're going to have about five or six most likely. You know, let's get real here. Are you doing what you did at 18? I'm sure not.

Critical thinking skills, social responsibility, research skills, the ability to communicate effectively. These are all alternative metrics that could perhaps be measured quantitatively and qualitatively. Myers goes further to question the concept of success. "Whose version of success? When you add culture into that component you get a real rat's nest," she said.

In the end, the conflation of FSA exam results and "school performance" in British Columbia is even more problematic than the use of standardized tests themselves. How did the province end up with such a flawed system? School reform efforts generally have a better chance of success when they include buy-in from the major stakeholders, who include administrators, teachers, and parents. Without this support, unpopular regimes are vulnerable to political activism. For example, the BC Teachers' Federation is so opposed to the current testing regime in the province that they have asked parents to keep their children home in protest on testing days. This further erodes the already questionable value of the current testing regime. Rather than imposing unpopular accountability approaches, those that are developed in partnership with key stakeholders are much more likely to achieve the goal of improving educational quality.

Scholars who are critical of standardized testing in education focus on several important issues, including how class and cultural biases favour the privileged, and the deleterious consequences of teachers shifting to teach to the test.[19] In the worst cases, researchers have found outright manipulation of results by excluding certain students from sitting for exams to literally filling in answers for students, as happened when high-stakes testing was implemented in the United States (and described in Steven Levitt and Stephen Dubner's popular book, *Freakonomics*). Jonathan Kozol described the depressing evidence of cheating in Houston, Texas, where principals instructed teachers how to cheat – in a school system where testing-based reform was heralded as a success story. According to Kozol, "nearly 300 Texas schools are now suspected of having cheated too."[20]

Beyond cheating, another incentivized response by school staff has particularly negative consequences for vulnerable and special needs students. In many systems, the implementation of high-stakes standardized testing has been associated with increasing expulsion rates. Getting students who will perform poorly on the test out of the school, or even the school system, becomes a strategy of "dealing" with problem students, rather than addressing issues and focusing on how to help these students learn. Clearly, pushing poorly performing, at-risk, and disadvantaged students out of the school system does little to advance their education. More broadly, the problematic incentives created by high-stakes testing go beyond a few bad apples or cheaters and actually comprise a predictable and systematic consequence of adopting a standardized testing regime, and other neoliberal marketizing reforms to improve education.

Judged by the measures I have discussed here, such as validity, reliability, fairness, usefulness, and accuracy, the FSA standardized testing regime as implemented in British Columbia has not been successful. With little evidence of benefit, the costs of the current regime are simply too high. While theoretically FSA standardized test score results could help identify some schools with extremely high rates of students failing to meet expectations and result in additional resources and improvement, in reality, the challenges facing these high-challenge schools – often with extremely high percentages of inner-city poor and First Nation youths – are already well-known to educators and school boards.

While the publishing of ranked lists of schools based on standardized test scores in the media provides information to parents, it does little to improve the education in poorly performing schools. While school administrators did not describe parents storming into their offices demanding that more be done to improve the passing rates of their students, the publication of these rankings has likely quietly increased cream-skimming, whereby motivated parents place their children in alternative schools, private schools, or magnet programs. These processes tend to enhance inequality between schools in terms of outcomes. The market model fails to realize hoped-for improvements in outcomes at the school level or at the aggregate level.

Recently, the success of the schools in Geoffrey Canada's Harlem's Children Zone (HCZ) in closing the minority-white achievement gap demonstrates that improvements in educational achievement among visible minority youth in high-poverty urban neighbourhoods are possible. The success of Harlem's Children Zone has made it the model of school reform across American cities. While it incorporates a mix of reforms – from charter academies, extended school days/years, and partnerships with other community institutions – the fundamental basis of its success is resources. The improved academic achievement of HCZ students supports the claims of teachers, administrators, and parents in Vancouver: educating students from high-poverty urban neighbourhoods requires a substantially higher level of resources to address and overcome challenges hindering academic achievement. In this case, standardized test score results confirm the importance of heavy investment in urban schools for improving academic achievement. The challenge, then, is developing the political will for government and other sectors to dedicate the resources required to create the foundation of learning for disadvantaged and vulnerable at-risk urban youth.

Making Testing Work to Improve Student Learning

Despite these serious theoretical and practical challenges, system-wide standardized testing will continue to be a major part of school reform efforts in British Columbia, as it will in other parts of Canada and globally. The fundamental opposition of teachers to the current FSA standardized testing is largely due to the implementation of the testing regime and widespread publication and promotion in the media of the results in terms of annual school rankings. This current publication outlet does not allow for reflexive and mediated analysis of the data.

The BC Teachers' Federation has proposed randomized testing as an alternative, which would provide a sense of how the public schools in the province are doing *overall* in terms of teaching reading, numeracy, and writing skills. The data would not be broken down and reported at the school level. While the proposed reform would helpfully move away from the current ranking of schools by test score data, it would still involve employing a problematic tool to measure progress. As the data would be collected at the provincial aggregate level, it would also not provide the kind of useful assessment data assessing the differences between school populations or schools.[21] It would not provide any indication of educational inequality and it would also be somewhat limited in providing greater resources for struggling schools. At the same time, working collaboratively with educators and other stakeholders to address concerns and create buy-in has the potential to greatly enhance the effectiveness of testing for improving outcomes.

One fundamental problem with the current standardized testing regime in British Columbia and many other parts of Canada and other countries, is how the standardized test results are being (mis)used as proxies for school performance. A new approach to evaluation and testing is critical for making testing effective for improving early mastery of literacy and numeracy skills.

What kinds of features would increase the likelihood of an effective testing regime that would actually improve student learning and achievement? First, it is critically important to have stakeholder buy-in, particularly from teachers. Working with teachers, teachers unions, and other stakeholders should be the first step to reimagining a testing regime that could work.

Certain suggestive patterns have emerged in the testing and assessment literature. One is that teachers are more supportive of "portfolio" type assessments than rigid multiple-choice, fill-in-the-blank standardized-type exams. According to John S. Lofty, who completed a qualitative study of teachers in the United States and England for his book *Quiet Wisdom*, one frequent complaint about standardized tests is that the questions aim way too low in terms of the level of material that they are testing for children at a particular stage. Summarizing George Hillocks Jr.'s research on writing assessments, Lofty comments: "One notable exception is the Kentucky Portfolio assessments which feature a broad spectrum of writing, and emphasizes writing for different audiences and purposes. More Kentucky teachers spoke positively about their state assessment than the teachers of other states."[22]

While it is important to change the kind of tests used and the evaluation procedures, it is also important to consider a more multidimensional assessment of school quality, as argued by urban sociologist and education scholar Pedro A. Noguera in his book *The Trouble with Black Boys*: "But individual outcome measures (such as grades, test scores, or graduation rates) are used to grade progress, while more nebulous indicators – school climate and perceptions of safety, the morale and collegiality of teachers, the quality of relations between a school and the parents it services – are ignored."[23]

Collecting a wider variety of data through the use of multiple methodological approaches would clearly provide a more multidimensional picture of a school's strengths as well as the challenges it is facing. This could include observation, parent surveys, and so on. While some of these assessments already do exist, the results should be prioritized and ranked equal to other evaluation tools. This broader mixed-method multidimensional approach would be more likely to earn stakeholder buy-in and thus be more useful for actually improving academic achievement in schools.

One potential model for a better way forward is the current approach employed by Professor Clyde Hertzman and his research team at the Human Early Learning Partnership (HELP) at the University of British Columbia. The collection of data on all children using the Early Development Instrument (EDI), conducted by kindergarten teachers who assess the social-emotional well-being of all of their students, is now also being carried out in other provinces across Canada, Australia, and other jurisdictions worldwide. The model of evaluation is fundamentally different than traditional standardized testing approaches. While it encourages teachers to think about some of the basics of how their students are doing in terms of social-emotional factors and readiness to learn, data are collected at a macro-level, not in a child-specific way. Rather than standardized exams, teachers provide assessments of their students on the basis of rigorous and tested scales.

The aggregated data are also not published as extensive league tables, with rankings from best to worst in terms of child development. Instead the data are published in colourful map form. Rather than sitting in a report or league table, the data are then brought to those stakeholders in the community through a series of meetings with stakeholders from a variety of sectors including education, early childhood development, health care, and non-profit, as well as to academics and policy makers. These stakeholders discuss the outcomes in their community, and work on strategies to address these needs. Rather than data being used to shame and rank, the data illuminate issues and challenges, and help mobilize support to improve outcomes in a cooperative, non-stigmatizing way. Longitudinally, it remains possible to track trends and progress.

Thus far, HELP's Early Development Instrument assessments have not generated the kind of vitriol and backlash among teachers, administrators, and other stakeholders that the current FSA standardized testing regime has. Instead, advocates for children and child well-being have, in general, been excited to have easy-to-understand evidence to use in order to argue for more resources and to help guide and measure reform success in a longitudinal way. In this case, rather than data being used to rank and criticize, they actually become a tool for mobilizing diverse sectors to focus on a critical issue in the community: the challenges facing vulnerable children. On a local level, hundreds of programs and initiatives have emerged to address specific needs identified by the assessments, including programs to ensure that kids are not coming to school hungry. Beyond these programs, the engaged advocates for early childhood development found allies from all sectors of society and successfully lobbied local and provincial government for more early childhood education resources.[24] Unsurprisingly, this model has gained national and international interest, and has been adopted by other provinces and countries for assessing and improving early childhood development. The EDI model is one potential model for assessing learning and school children in elementary school and beyond.

While the success of the EDI model employed by HELP can be measured in programs created to meet student needs, it is also reflected by a growing number of multi-sector coalitions advocating to improve access to high-quality early childhood education. By building power, they created political will to begin to address some of the more fundamental challenges facing vulnerable children. For example, these coalitions have been instrumental in pushing for policies to extend universal schooling through making kindergarten programs available to children at an earlier age in Ontario and to bring full-day kindergarten to both Ontario and British Columbia.

While a growing awareness of the importance of early childhood education culminated in a proposed national early childhood education program with agreement from all of the provinces, unfortunately this program was scuttled with the election of the Conservative minority government, which replaced this universal access program with a tax credit that provides all families $100 per month (taxable) for each child 5 and under.[25] Yet there remains intense interest in improving child development outcomes at the local and provincial level in Canada, with coalitions emerging around reducing childhood vulnerability and helping children begin school ready to learn, and several provinces extending full-day kindergarten down to age 3.

Although the EDI assessment employed by HELP could prove to be a model for a new system-wide version of standardized testing of literacy and other basic skills acquisition in the early years, it admittedly also works better in many ways because the underlying foundation and assumption of causal mechanisms about measured outcomes are different than in standardized testing. Urie Bronfenbrenner's ecological model, as described in chapter 1, is at the heart of the Early Development Instrument assessment, where a child's development is influenced by interacting factors from the family to the community and society level. As the data are based on teachers' evaluations of their kindergarten students, the EDI assessment does not carry with it underlying notions that what is being measured reflects upon the performance of the school itself as an institution. I would argue that this underlying, and often incorrect, assumption about the predominant influence of school quality on academic achievement is the one major problem with standardized testing as implemented across so many school systems today. Standardized tests presume to measure school performance, when what is actually measured is the socio-economic status and cultural capital of the children at the school.

How would a reformed system of standardized evaluation work? Teachers could evaluate their students' reading and provide data about those who are struggling to meet certain foundations on the way to attaining literacy or numeracy skills. These data could be collected and mapped, similar to the way child development data are mapped by HELP at UBC, and presented to local stakeholders in the education, public health, and non-profit sector so that they may work together to address problem areas, including mobilizing resources and adopting strategies to reduce the percentage of students who lack the necessary skills. Bringing in teachers as centrally involved stakeholders in the assessment process, rather than as individuals who will be judged by the passing rate of their classroom, is one important lesson for making testing useful for actually improving literacy and numeracy acquisition.

The current political climate shows promising signs of support for rethinking the role of testing. The Conservative government in the province of Alberta has now led the way in implementing a suite of reforms to standardized testing that reflects many of the principles described earlier. New computer-based standardized tests (reflecting the growing importance of technology in education and work) will be given at the beginning of the school year, so as to identify opportunities and challenges, but also to avoid the conflation of test scores with individual "school performance."[26] In the United States, the Bill and Melinda Gates Foundation has been helping to bring together teachers' unions with school boards and policy makers to rethink high-stakes testing and work towards a new system that has buy-in from key stakeholders and will be effective for measuring and improving learning.

Standardized Testing: Where to Go?

My research set out to go beyond statistics to understand and explain differences in academic achievement outcomes between elementary schools with similar student populations in East Vancouver. I found more than simplistic differences between schools; rather, I observed a set of schools in the midst of dynamic and exciting transformations. While there were clearly differences between the schools, the differences could not easily be classified as factors that explain variations in school "performance" or effectiveness. These schools could not simply be ranked on a reified list of factors and compared for clearly defined differences, nor did the school-specific programs or implementation of these programs reveal clear explanatory pathways for understanding variation in standardized test score results. Rather, over time, the weakness of the underlying assumptions about the standardized testing regime became apparent. As scores soared in one school, or stagnated in another only to mysteriously reverse course again, the unreliability of the current FSA standardized testing regime in British Columbia to accurately measure school "performance" or improve outcomes became abundantly clear. Similar problems plague high-stakes standardized testing in many other provinces and countries.

The differences between East Vancouver elementary schools in terms of programs or features generally did not point to causal pathways or clearly reveal what factors are important for early literacy and numeracy achievement. Instead it was frequently the similarities that were the most interesting and relevant. These elementary schools teach extremely diverse student populations, typical of many urban public schools in lower-income neighbourhoods in Canada, the United States, and internationally. The diversity in these schools brought a richness, a vibrancy, and unique resources, but also real challenges, from high proportions of ESL students in classrooms, special needs students, and the challenges of poverty. Meeting these challenges requires effectively used resources, which are all too often in too short supply.

East Vancouver elementary schools educate high proportions of visible minority students, including newcomer immigrants, refugees, and second- and third-generation children.[27] These schools often teach disproportionate amounts of ESL children and those with specific learning challenges, such as ADHD and other learning disabilities and behaviour problems. The student populations at these schools have been in flux through their histories as new waves of migration intersect with early or advanced stages of gentrification. At the same time, these elementary schools teach many students from near-poor and low-income families. Some at-risk students at each school begin school with significant unmet needs, from hunger to social isolation. These needs bring similar challenges for each school, although often in a unique mix.

According to school staff and parents, what mattered most for early literacy and numeracy was having the resources to identify and address these problems, ideally preventatively or as early as possible. Many spoke of programs and reforms that are making a difference on the ground to improve learning, especially that of children from low-income households. As institutions, urban schools need to have the flexibility and resources to educate students with diverse needs.

Imagine a classroom where 80% of the students who begin the school year will no longer be in that class by the end of the year – dropping out or changing schools because of economic circumstances – and they are replaced by a cohort of new students who arrive throughout the year. Imagine a classroom where every week or two a new student arrives – sometimes having recently come to Canada from a war-torn country or a persecuted family – with limited or no English fluency. Other students have unmet medical needs, including dental and vision issues. Some have undiagnosed and untreated behavioural or attention deficit disorders or learning disabilities. Others are traumatized by unstable and insecure home lives. Others are coping with much more serious issues, such as abuse and neglect or violence.

Standardized testing of students is only one – highly problematic – tool for assessing and improving "school success." Sure, some general trends are clear from test results. In Vancouver, year after year, schools in the wealthy west side and in suburban West Vancouver have the highest rates of students in the fourth and seventh grade meeting or exceeding expectations in literacy, numeracy, and writing, while schools in the highest-poverty schools on the east side generally score the lowest. Standardized tests can also help identify schools that have serious problems. For example, if only 20% of students are passing a basic literacy or math test, the results can serve as a flag that something is going on that needs to be addressed.

Yet the strategies to improve test scores often fail to increase the literacy and numeracy skills of the students in question. Sometimes, addressing the students' basic needs or implementing social/emotional competence programs – programs that may not initially appear to be directly relevant to reading and math – is what is needed to create the classroom and school conditions where children can thrive. These programs can be more effective than curricular reform at helping children develop critically important skills.

Most problematically, standardized test score results are used to evaluate the "success" or performance of specific schools. On the one hand, a massive improvement in test scores – such as the 45% increase in passing rates that occurred in the much celebrated case of Grandview Elementary between 2001 and 2005 – can indicate improvements in curriculum, leadership, and programming. But as already indicated, on the other hand, given the small size of fourth grade cohorts in many Vancouver schools, relatively dramatic changes in test scores can actually reflect shifting school policies such as who is excluded from taking the test, or they can be the result of a non-random sample of students being encouraged to stay home, or literally be due to a small group of students failing in a given year. Substantial improvements or declines in pass rates on standardized tests can also reflect non–school related factors, such as particular politics or gentrification. Rapid gains can also erode just as quickly, as we've seen subsequently at Grandview Elementary and other once-celebrated exemplars.

With increasing importance being placed on standardized exam results, the focus becomes the test; hence, it's not surprising that the trend in overall test performance would be expected to improve, even without any real improvement in the quality of student skills or learning. Educators adopt a variety of strategies to improve performance on standardized tests, such as teaching to tests, encouraging certain students to stay home, and even cheating. Indeed, some argue that these strategies can lead to an actual decline in the quality of education.

Conclusion

Taking school reform seriously is essential to improving opportunities for students. All too often, aspects of the school system – from institutional inequalities and failure to meet students' needs to administrator and teacher bias and diminished expectations of children from certain backgrounds – combine to create a tragic self-fulfilling prophesy. As described by Lisa Delpit in *Other People's Children*, "It is a deadly fog formed when the cold mist of bias and ignorance meets the warm vital reality of children of colour in many of our schools."[28]

There are many problems with relying on ranking schools according to standardized testing in order to gauge and improve performance. Issues with validity, reliability, and dramatic over-time variability rendered the FSA standardized test scores virtually useless for assessing the school performance of 10 elementary schools in East Vancouver. The standardized testing regime has also failed to generate useful data that could be constructively used to improve actual student literacy and numeracy learning or achievement. The "name and shame" annual publishing of ranked lists of test score results in local media has shamed and stressed many principals and other school staff, but the invisible hand of school competition has not magically led to dramatic improvements in student mastery of basic skills.

Yet these failures do not mean that data from standardized testing could not be a tool to improve academic achievement; the system would have to be implemented differently and the data used in less problematic ways. For example, testing in classrooms at the beginning of the school year can help ensure all children master the basic fundamentals of literacy and numeracy on their way to mastery of these skills. On a broader level, teacher assessments of their students' skills could be aggregated to provide valuable data to help target additional resources. A much more comprehensive picture of a school and its successes and challenges emerges from a multi-method approach to evaluating a school, especially an approach that is supported by the most important stakeholders.

A new testing evaluation regime in British Columbia makes sense and could even contribute to mobilizing the coalitions required to generate the will to meet the needs of children. Ideally it would be developed collaboratively with administrators, teachers (and teachers' unions), and parents as well as other stakeholders. Unfortunately the often proposed teacher pay-for-performance "merit" system that is the new educational reform idea of the moment does not address the weaknesses of standardized testing as it's currently applied, including vulnerability to manipulation and teaching to the test. One possibility is an evaluation regime that would involve teachers assessing their students' skills acquisition in literacy and numeracy, and subsequent mapping of the data, which would then be brought back to community stakeholders with the goal of generating programs to address weaknesses and improve future outcomes.

Created with the collaboration of system stakeholders – from administrators to teachers and parents – a new standardized testing regime could provide valuable data that could improve learning, especially for the most vulnerable. This kind of approach would have to be collaborative, not combative, and based on a respect and mutual cooperation, not antagonism and largely unhelpful notions of accountability and merit. Testing that works could potentially mobilize resources that would address real barriers to early literacy and numeracy achievement.

7 Conclusion: Improving Early Literacy and Numeracy Skills Acquisition in Urban Schools in Low-Income Neighbourhoods

> Urban schools can become a powerful resource for community development and facilitate other forms of political and economic empowerment that can ultimately transform the character and quality of life of urban areas through bottom-up / grassroots initiatives.
>
> – Pedro Noguera, *The Trouble with Black Boys*

Urban schools are a centrally important public institution in many communities. They can create opportunity or cement inequality. Similar to many urban public schools in advanced industrialized countries, elementary schools in East Vancouver, Canada, educate diverse student populations, including high proportions of visible minorities and students from immigrant and low-income families. While many celebrate the diversity of their students, and rightly so, these elementary schools also grapple with some associated challenges. These challenges do not, in general, emerge from cultural issues, value differences or ethnic enclaves, but rather from broader social issues and barriers such as poverty, the effects of which do not stop at the schoolhouse door. In practice, this means that teachers at these schools teach higher proportions of ESL students with different levels of fluency, students with recognized or unrecognized special needs, and students from struggling families as compared to other schools in wealthier urban neighbourhoods or suburbs.

Newcomer immigrants and the second- and third-generation students are not intrinsic "problems" for these schools. Research suggests newcomer immigrants are less likely to engage in crime than native-born Canadians.[1] Another study of UBC science students found that public school students from East Vancouver outperformed their peers in first-year physics and math classes than those who had attended Vancouver-area private schools.[2] Yet this good news can obscure some more difficult issues. Not all members of these groups are sharing in the success, and even within broadly successful groups, some subpopulations are experiencing challenges and disappointing outcomes. For example, ESL students in grade 12 in Metro Vancouver are much less likely to graduate than non-ESL students.[3]

Most of the real barriers to classroom learning in East Vancouver elementary schools involve the challenges of teaching children who have needs for which there is a lack of resources to address. Soaring real estate prices and gentrification contribute to housing instability and changes in the student populations. In an era of budget cuts, many East Vancouver elementary schools struggle to meet the needs of their students in order to build a foundation for early mastery of literacy, numeracy, critical thinking, and social/emotional development in the first few years of elementary school. East Vancouver elementary schools help their students by developing resiliency, in part by providing them with the foundational skills that serve as the basis for their future education.

While the research for this book did not uncover a magic bullet to address all barriers to learning in East Vancouver elementary schools, the findings contribute to our understanding of common challenges facing urban schools, and provide the foundation for recommendations, including policies and reforms to help these schools achieve the ambitious and important goal of universal mastery of early literacy and numeracy skills at an early age.[4] In our digital tech-driven and service sector based economy, these skills are a requisite basis for full participation in social and economic life, and the effectiveness of education thus fundamentally shapes the health of the city and country's future economy and democracy.

Helping Students Achieve Early Literacy Mastery in Diverse Classrooms

The field of urban school reform is both dynamic and all-too-often ideologically polarized. On the right, advocates of "school choice" and high-stakes testing and accountability argue that introducing market mechanisms into education is the ideal solution for school systems.[5] Others see it simply as a way to give motivated parents a chance to send their kid to a "better" school. A more pragmatic approach would be to support innovative experiments, including charter schools and magnet programs, but with ongoing evaluation and a goal of learning lessons to be adopted by other urban public schools.[6] Steps should be taken to minimize "cream skimming" and compensate for some of the negative consequences for students unable to take advantage of these programs. Other reforms should include smaller class sizes in urban schools to allow for teachers to give students greater attention.[7] Some argue for smaller schools, where teachers and administrators have a better chance to get to know colleagues, students, and their families.[8]

In *Tinkering toward Utopia*, David Tyack and Larry Cuban lament the long history of education reform in the United States based on "decree by remote control," singling out solutions like "competition" and "choice." After reviewing decades of school reform trends, where reformers vacillate from hopelessness to overconfidence about education, they conclude that the key to successful reform is helping teachers improve instruction from the inside.[9] Teachers need additional resources and training to help children master critical literacy and numeracy skills in diverse urban environments.

One important factor for improving early mastery of literacy is preventing students from falling behind or through the cracks during those critical stages when children are learning to read. In diverse classrooms, this can be challenging, for many reasons. For example, in a given classroom, some students might be advanced as compared to others in terms of mastering skills. A tension can exist between allowing advanced students to move ahead, with the goal of ensuring that no student falls behind. At the most extreme case, allowing advanced students to move ahead can become an early form of informal and even formal tracking that can exacerbate inequalities in student achievement. While there remains debate about the merits of tracking for older students, it is even more problematic for younger students. Especially in the early grades, research evidence suggests that it is better to go at a slower pace in terms of teaching foundational skills for reading and math in order to ensure that no student falls behind.[10]

There are some practical options available to address the pacing dilemma in diverse classrooms. One is to have trained resource teachers available to provide mentoring to students, without removing the children from mainstream classrooms, until they master a foundational step and are ready to move to the next step. Some literacy programs in inner-city communities in the United States and internationally, including the well-known Success for All program, include resource teachers as a critical component to provide supplemental one-on-one or small-group instruction to students.[11] Students in multi-grade or multi-age classrooms can be divided into smaller groups based on reading or math achievement levels for those lessons, although this incurs some danger of tracking.

The use of frequent and detailed student assessment coupled with individual mentoring and support is one potential strategy for improving literacy mastery in early elementary education. Testing students, in this case, allows for the identification of specific concrete problem areas or stumbling blocks that can be addressed early. It provides extra resources at the point when they matter the most. And when students master a skill, they and their parents as well as the teachers can celebrate the tangible evidence of success from the exam results, which often is more meaningful to build grounded self-esteem and confidence than verbal compliments or empty rhetorical flourishes. This is very different than most current standardized testing regimes.

Training/Professional Development for Teachers: The Example of ESL

Improving classroom instruction in diverse classrooms can involve improving teacher's training and professional development opportunities. Vancouver School Board consultant, Angela Myers, argued that training should occur at two stages. The first is during the teacher training process, at education schools, before teachers enter the classroom. She said this kind of ESL training currently gets short shrift in education schools: "It chagrins me to say that my alma mater calls me every spring, 'Would you come and talk to our kids before they go out on their practicum about ESL?' 'How long do I have?' 'Two hours,' and I'm kind of going, 'Pardon?' Yes. In teacher training at UBC, you can choose to do an ESL concentration. Which was the only way you could do that a few years ago. The only way you could do that is if you did it in the evenings while you were on your long practicum." Training for working with urban poor and diverse classrooms should be an integral part of the teacher training curriculum. And, ideally, this kind of training should be combined with some practical hands-on experience outside of the classroom, such as being a volunteer mentor for an ESL first grader.[12]

While the results of better training would make a difference in the longer term, another important policy in the short term is to provide greater training opportunities around teaching ESL students for current teachers.[13] This training should not be something that teachers are expected to do on their own, outside of school hours, but an integral part of professional development. These kinds of training and skill development opportunities are an important part of improving overall levels of literacy and numeracy skills acquisition by students, particularly in diverse schools.

Funding Issues

Money matters in education. Surprisingly, this is a controversial and much debated point in the sociology of education literature. I am not going to delve into this debate here, which is discussed in more detail in chapter two. For those who study or work at urban schools, the reasons why money matters for the quality of education are abundantly clear.

In chapter 5, I outline some of the ways that critically important programs were cutback or eliminated as a result of provincial budget cuts to education in British Columbia. These cuts disproportionately affected support programs that were operating in East Vancouver elementary schools. As these schools teach high percentages of children from low-income families, ESL students, and students with other needs not being met elsewhere, the cuts negatively affected the quality of education. They resulted in shuttered school libraries and cuts to arts and music classes. They even led to shortages of basic supplies and texts in the classrooms. Thankfully some of these cuts have subsequently been reversed. Yet the recent commitment to expand kindergarten to full-day for 5-year-olds and eventually extended to 4-year-olds and 3-year-olds has been scaled back or stalled in light of the climate of fiscal austerity.

Public school funding in Canada is not tied to local property taxes. Rather schools are funded on a standard per-pupil rate, set at a provincial level in Canada.[14] These rates include extra funding for high need students. This funding system is much more equitable than the US system because schools in inner-city areas actually get additional resources to meet their greater needs as compared to more privileged communities.[15] Unfortunately, these extra resources are not generally enough to meet the high level of need in these schools.

Programs that target schools with high percentages of poor students, like the Inner City Schools Project described in chapter 5, provide critically important resources for schools with many at-risk children. In the case of British Columbia, it would make sense to also extend extra resources to schools teaching a high percentage of ESL students, regardless of catchment area income average or poverty rate. While the extra financial level support is crucial for ESL students during their first several years of school, the challenge of an extremely diverse classroom in terms of degrees of language fluency should also be recognized. Perhaps some of these extra resources could come from federal programs, including settlement and integration funding that currently focuses mostly on programs for adults, given the important role these schools play for "integrating" students into society.

What are some of the most important uses of additional resources and funding? One is the hiring of support staff and resource teachers to work with at-risk and struggling students. While programs at a district level are worthy and make sense for certain forms of support, programs and staff targeted to specific schools or groups of schools appear to be the most promising for addressing the needs of the students. When funding shortfalls means there are not enough school staff, libraries sit unopened during the school day, music programs falter, students can't get the help they need, and overwhelmed teachers can't meet the needs of their students, and address barriers to learning.

Funding constraints also prevent the comprehensive implementation of potentially successful reforms and programs. Educational researchers have put forward policies and practices that could improve student performance.[16] The Success for All program, for example, restructures pre-kindergarten, kindergarten, and early years' elementary school programs to teach and reinforce basic reading and math skills. Through a combination of one-on-one tutoring, reading re-grouping by skill level and not age, frequent assessment and family support teams, the program has empirically demonstrated that it can significantly improve the performance of urban minorities in urban public schools across the United States and internationally.[17] Some critique the rigidity of the program, and it is clearly not appropriate for all schools.

Another promising Canadian program is *Pathways to Education*, which provides extra resources, mentorship and incentives for visible minority students who live in social housing, such as Regent Park. This program appears to be very successful in high poverty Toronto communities, and is being piloted in other Canadian cities such as Winnipeg, where a high proportion of students are First Nation. This program targets older students, who are entering secondary school, but early results point to dramatic increases in post-secondary graduation rates and other positive outcomes.[18] Resources are required to pilot, evaluate, and build on successful intervention and reform programs.

Look beyond the School: The Broader Context

Increasing economic inequality and urban poverty create new challenges for East Vancouver elementary schools, even as some neighbourhoods are simultaneously being transformed by immigration and gentrification. Schools are an important institution in these dynamic communities, and a site where some of the challenges of poverty can be partially addressed, for example, through lunch programs that feed hungry children.[19] Yet ultimately, poverty and social exclusion, especially concentrated disadvantage, create challenges for schools. Sociologist Karl Alexander and his colleagues argued that in the United States, "Despite many exceptions, as a group, poor children and disadvantaged minority children already are behind when they begin school ... And barring a mid-course correction, the prognosis is that over time they will fall further and further back mainly because of hardship outside school."[20] Improving education outcomes for children from low-income families would be less challenging if policies – from indexing and increasing the minimum wage and refundable tax credits to lower-income families as well as expanding access to high quality affordable childcare, housing assistance, and union representation for low-skilled service sector workers – were enacted to reduce socioeconomic inequality and improve the quality of life for the economically disadvantaged.[21]

Research has linked improved school performance by children directly to poverty reduction.[22] The Canadian federal government commitment to social programs has stagnated as a percentage of total spending and per capita GDP, and this financial commitment needs to be ramped up in order to provide the resources for provinces to take the bold steps needed to reduce poverty and inequality. Based on her research on education reform in Newark, New Jersey, schools, Jean Anyon argued that more than just reforming schools is required to address the challenges of urban education; reforms must also address the concentration of poverty and other urban issues, especially segregation.[23]

This echoes the call of education scholar Charles Ungerleider in Canada in *Failing Our Kids*. He argues that as schools can only play a limited role in reducing socio-economic inequalities, what is needed are social policies such as fair minimum wages, universal daycare and early childhood education, and fair employment standards.[24] Working families with young children need more support. (The Canadian province of Quebec provides an excellent model, with extended paid maternal and parental leave and universal access to affordable early childhood education programs). Providing universal access to extended paid parental leaves and early childhood education promote greater equality of opportunity, and is an excellent investment that has shown promising dividends in terms of future outcomes.

In the new post-industrial economy, urban public schools are more than just places of learning and education. They are also critically important public institutions that provide help and support, particularly to vulnerable children and their families. Urban public schools in low-income neighbourhoods often have disproportionate numbers of students with special needs, and they require extra resources to meet the needs of these students.

Providing support to families includes offering parental skills to parents to help them cope with challenges in the home. The issues facing students at home and in the community do not stop at the schoolhouse gate. Education sociologist Jean Anyon argued, "Failing public schools in cities are, rather, a logical consequence of the U.S. macroeconomy – and the federal and regional policies that support it ... an unjust economy and policies through which it is maintained create barriers to educational success that no teacher or principal practice, no standardized test, and no 'zero tolerance' policy can surmount."[25] Schools do not only provide academic instruction; the line between school and families and communities has continued to erode.

Given the central importance of basic skills as a foundation to mastering the higher order analytical and critical thinking skills that will be key for students' success in the globalizing economy as well as enable them to be actively engaged participants in their communities and democratic society, it is imperative that schools work to identify and effectively meet the needs of students. Addressing these needs head on, from the beginning, sets the stage for a student's future academic achievement.

Leadership

In the popular media and in school folklore, leadership is frequently held up as a key factor driving school success. In the movies, run-down urban schools are turned around by tough principals who enforce norms of discipline and academic achievement, and help teachers and children focus on learning. Clearly these stories hold widespread appeal and resonance, but they should be viewed with cautious scepticism. According to long-time school administrator, Theodore R. Sizer, "Books are written celebrating the inspirational teacher of the axe-handle-wielding Principal or the stern but loving school head or the management-bedazzled follower of some organizational guru. Like most testimonials, these portraits are partly persuasive, partly myopic, and to a veteran like me largely unconvincing."[26] At the same time, when many East Vancouver elementary schools experience a dramatic improvement in test scores outcomes and ranking, credit is granted to the principal.[27]

How do we evaluate claims that leadership matters? Many teachers, staff and parents described the key role of leadership.[28] Yet effective leadership was described in very different terms than celebrated in the aforementioned Hollywood films. Instead of a bat, effective leaders were described in terms of passion, commitment, interpersonal skills, and organizational and problem-solving skills.

Leadership itself is incredibly difficult to measure. How many models are there for success? Are good, even great, leaders born, trained, or do they learn from experience? In the educational context, can professional development improve leadership? Do leadership differences explain why similar programs experience varying degrees of success in different schools or classrooms?

In East Vancouver elementary schools, good leaders were described as those who created the kind of atmosphere where innovative programs had a chance of success. Susan Fletcher, social worker, argued: "The tone of the school is set by the people, the administration, the teachers, the support staff. I'm thinking of New Lake Elementary. We've worked very closely with New Lake Elementary, and when I think about why is it that those children have had access to services, it's really about the openness that the school has had, and the recognition that they can't do it all alone. And that community partnerships are actually really in the best interests of the children, and having key people with that kind of mentality."

While some leaders were described as effective collaborators and coalition builders, others were described as more visionary. For many parents, though, just the friendliness and helpfulness of the school principal matters the most. Rochelle Grant, a parent of two children enrolled at Wellington Elementary, felt that Brown was a good principal. "[The old principal] he was nice, but I think Mr. Brown is more active ... He is very active. Every time he tried to keep Wellington Elementary up, up, up in district level or … He's a very good man. Talks to parents. Friendly. Smiling every time. He is happy too."

What kind of leadership would help create success in urban elementary schools?[29] Some emphasized the importance of understanding what is going on in the classroom and building relationships with teachers, parents, and students to go beyond the statistics. Principal Teresa McDonald of Soaring Eagle Elementary explained:

> With the teachers, I want to know from their perspective what's happening in the classroom that's blocking everything that they want to do to see those kids grow academically, what's blocking [them]. We don't always use hard and fast data for that. We also listen to what teachers say. "I struggle every day just to get the kids to school." "I can't talk to the parents." "The kids are hungry." All of these: "I find that the program that I'm using requires home reading, and the home reading isn't getting done." I want to know all those kinds of things. Not just data. And from there, we put together the plan. "Well maybe we need a parent education program at the beginning of the year. We need to get it translated so that the parents see it. We need to keep it simple." So that comes not necessarily from data, but teachers know. They don't need to show me on a test or an FSA [standardized exam]. We use that data for sure, we use it. But it's just one of many things we use to figure out the needs.

Using data in a way that creates positive change is one of the main challenges facing school staff. The effective use of data to improve school performance is crucial for the success. Unfortunately there are also ways of using data such as ranking schools that can harm more than help.

Identifying problems and addressing them is key. In education, this often requires sustained intervention. According to sociologist Karl Alexander and colleagues, "Children at risk of academic failure require early and ongoing interventions."[30] These interventions are "most effective in combination." They pointed out that: "Importantly in the Chicago [Longitudinal] study neither preschool alone nor school year supplementation alone proved sufficient. Rather they are most effective in combination, one building on the other. After strong programmatic support leading up to first grade, "just in time interventions" are needed to catch problems early.[31]" Interventions should build upon each other (admittedly a challenge in dynamic communities with high levels of residential insecurity and instability).

It is particularly important in the early years to prevent at-risk children from falling behind. Programs should aim to build a foundation for future success by ensuring early literacy and numeracy skill mastery in the first few years of elementary school. One-on-one or small group tutoring and multi-age classrooms represent two important innovations. It can be easier to group students at similar skill levels, rather than just physical age, to achieve foundational reading and math milestones. More broadly, other potentially successful structural reforms include extending the school year, perhaps targeting programs at struggling students, or universally for all students. High expectations of all students' capacity to learn is a key factor.[32] Each school must determine what would meet the needs of its students, but the system should provide resources to make these reforms possible.

The School as a Societal Institution

One of the central legacies of modern democracy, with its roots in Enlightenment classic liberal tradition, and most evident in the twentieth century in work as diverse as W.E.B. Du Bois, Raymond Williams, Cornelius Castoriadis, John Dewey and Paulo Freire, among others, is the important recognition that a substantive democracy cannot exist without educated citizens.
    – Henry A. Giroux, "The Politics of Public Pedagogy"[33]

In a globalizing era, the cities of North America and Europe are becoming increasingly diverse, with waves of immigrants arriving from around the world. These cities are the economic, cultural, and political hubs of their regions, and countries. This diversity brings many positive features, as it reshapes community and cultural life in many urban neighbourhoods. It also presents some unique challenges for institutions in these communities, such as schools. No one distinct program, factor, or policy guarantees school success. Instead, multiple routes help achieve positive outcomes in terms of children's early mastery of literacy and math skills. At the same time, certain factors clearly facilitate or inhibit success. For example, schools need to ensure that all students have their basic needs met because hungry children cannot learn. Schools should also engage with neighbourhood and community organizations. While leadership matters, it is the capacity to engage and mobilize individuals and communities around the school, to inspire and innovate, to negotiate and critically reflect, rather than carrying the metaphorical bat through the hallways, that defines effective leadership. Schools need capable, effective, and flexible leadership as well as adequate resources for programming and skills development.[34]

The public school plays a contradictory role as a social institution. My research has been driven by concern over the consequences of growing inequality and the social exclusion of low-income visible minorities living in North American urban centres.[35] Sorting and evaluative processes by schools – from the assignment of grades to tracking students – often translate structural disadvantages into individual deficiencies through labelling and categorization of failing or at-risk students. Simultaneously, public schools act as equalizing institutions, opening up opportunities for some to move up in the socio-economic hierarchy.

Samuel Bowles and Herbert Gintis's book *Schooling in Capitalist Society* and other classic works such as Paul Willis' book *Learning to Labor* still have relevance for understanding educational inequality, even as Canada, the United States and the United Kingdom as well as much of Europe have transformed into largely post-industrial economies dominated by the service sector.[36] While in the past, educational inequality meant that the school system prepared students from privileged backgrounds to become factory owners or CEOs and prepared students from poor backgrounds to work the line, educational inequalities today mean that privileged students are being trained to become symbolic analysts in management consultancies, while the students from poor families are being set up for careers as shelf-stockers in Walmart, or, in the case of all too many First Nation students in Canada and inner-city schools in the United States, for life in and out of the rapidly expanding criminal justice and prison system.

The gap in resources, wealth, and well-being is actually greater in the neoliberal post-industrial economy than in earlier eras. Social welfare programs have been slashed. The minimum wage has stagnated to levels far lower in terms of purchasing power than in earlier decades. The percentage of workers covered by union contracts has declined somewhat in Canada and dramatically in the United States, as new barriers to organizing prevent successful unionization and domestic and international outsourcing threaten secure living wage jobs.[37] The challenge for schools serving students from economically disadvantaged families is even greater.

Cities are becoming more diverse in concert with growing inequality; Canada is currently experiencing among the fastest increasing rate of income inequality among all OECD countries.[38] As inequality increases, Canada's standing in the United Nations Human Development Index has shamefully fallen from first place in the late 1990s to eleventh place in 2013.[39] The failure of the government to live up to its 2000 commitment to end child poverty has resulted in enduring hunger and hardship in Canada; the province of British Columbia currently has the dubious distinction of having the highest child poverty rate in the country. The undermining of hard-fought social and labour protections by increasingly sophisticated campaigns by lobbyists and advocates for powerful corporate interests, the ongoing assault on public sector workers, and demands for across-the-board tax cuts and other reforms that disproportionately benefit the wealthiest, also reduce the resources and political will available to meet the growing needs of the working poor and the disadvantaged. It is too much to ask that public schools solve all of these problems. They can't and they won't. But that does not mean that public schools are and cannot do more to serve as an equalizing force in the face of these disturbing trends.

The Public School: An Equalizing Institution

While society does not stop at the schoolhouse gate, society is, in turn, shaped by the schoolhouse. Schools are one of the most important institutions in the lives of families and for their communities. Schools create hope. They socialize and sometimes reform. They can enable, but they can also limit. They introduce and connect the future generations to their society. My research in East Vancouver elementary schools deconstructs simple stories of causality about student academic achievement and school success. Multiple, interactive and complex factors explain why some students in one school are performing better than others in another school. Different actors provide different narratives about the causes of success or challenges, in part based on their vantage point and past experiences. Extensive social research shows the enormous importance of early childhood education. Indeed what happens in the first few years of a child's life (and even prenatally) creates a solid foundation for the possibility of success, or a lifetime of struggle and challenge.

Schools today continue to rank students, some providing greater opportunities to move up those rankings than others.[40] There are many ways they create equality of opportunity, but also many ways they cement social inequalities.[41] And what they also continue to do – as astutely described by Jay MacLeod in his classic book *Ain't No Makin' It* – is translate a student's personal, social, and cultural resources as well as their initiative and luck into their socio-economic position in society.[42] As in the earlier industrial era, school remains the institution that leads people to accept their social position, or worse, develop a sense of self-loathing and shame for not succeeding. How many people working in terrible service sector jobs lament not having finished school, or gone to college, or completed that last degree? How many hope their children will fare better than themselves?

Part of the connection between inequality in public education and social inequality, more broadly, comes down to the larger questions about what kinds of societies and economies we are constructing in the post-industrial, globalizing era. In this new context, investing in urban education may help create the foundation for more critical engagement, activism, and innovation in the economy, politics and society, more broadly. High quality urban public schools can attract and retain families from different social classes.[43]

One fundamental question remains: how do we define success in this era? That definition depends in part on the equality of educational opportunities. It is impossible to imagine an economy where everyone is "fortunate" to work 80 hours per week to earn high-six- and even seven-figure salaries. In reality, we need greater educational equality in order to reverse the trend towards a shrinking middle-class and greater disparities in the economy, polity and society.

Investing in high quality urban education could perhaps play a contributory role similar to the role of mass unionization in the industrial era in building the middle-class. While increasing unionization is also important, high quality public education is a countervailing force to growing income inequality.[44] According to Carola Suárez-Orozco and colleagues: "Worldwide, schooling has emerged as the surest path to well-being and status mobility. Schooling is now powerfully associated with such beneficial developments as better health, smaller families, and greater economic security. Solving the big problems of the day, whether deep poverty, infectious disease, environmental degradation, global warming, or terrorism, will require the active engagement of well-educated, cognitively flexible, and culturally sophisticated individuals able to work in groups."[45]

Without a large, well-educated middle-class, those with resources will continue to withdraw from the diminished public realm. They will also utilize their greater resources to continue to extract greater wealth off the labour and innovations of others. The early acquisition of basic reading skills is not only a predictor of an individual's educational success and fortunes, it is also fundamental to creating a just, vibrant democratic future. Learning to read is foundational for a citizenry that understand their rights and responsibilities, and are more likely to engage in public life.

Debates around education, unsurprisingly, often mimic broader ideological debates. The politics of the day runs the gamut of right to left, from solutions like "back-to-basics" curriculum, competition, testing and market forces, and greater discipline in schools to policies for increased funding to meet the needs of students and improve self-esteem, the abolishment of standardized testing and streamed classes. In East Vancouver elementary schools, the issue of resources is most important. These schools need more funding to provide the staffing and services required to meet the needs of their students. While the current form of standardized testing and publicized ranking operating in British Columbia is clearly highly problematic and unhelpful, that does not exclude some other form of "standardized" data collection, which could be useful for addressing challenges. The key should be to implement a system that, from the beginning, engages teachers, administrators and the broader community as stakeholders. It is also important that tests are not used to rank schools or assess performance of individual institutions, particularly not to "shame" poor performers.

Given what is known about early and literacy numeracy skill acquisition, going "back to basics" feels like building a bridge to a past that no longer exists. The students are different. The economy has been transformed. Society has changed. The basics that are now required, as ample empirical evidence reveals through extensive evaluation of educational programs, is a mastery of basic level foundations of literacy; this is the key to ensuring steady improvement in learning. In light of this evidence, it is questionable why anyone would advocate going back to rote memorization. Why shouldn't students learn the basics of math, but also learn how to use a calculator and a computer to solve problems?

Despite the negative consequences of educational inequality and the role of the school in social reproduction, the public education system represents one of the most equalizing universal institutions in advanced societies.[46] In Canada, many visible minority groups are performing as well or even better academically as other Canadians, yet children from certain marginalized communities such as Filipino and First Nations children are struggling. Inequalities exist between the educational success of students in wealthier parts of cities and towns as compared to lower-income areas.

Immigrant Children in Urban Schools

There is currently a debate in sociology about a theory called "segmented assimilation." This debate concerns the poor outcomes of particular groups of immigrant children, who often have similar collective experiences, including reasons for migration and contexts of reception. Some of this literature emerged from research in the United States, where sociologists Alejandro Portes and Ruben Rumbaut compared the fortunes of privileged immigrant children and their less privileged counterparts.[47] Much of this debate centres on the values and orientations of the youth themselves.[48] Do they embrace an "oppositional" culture at school like other socially excluded and disadvantaged groups? Do they embrace mainstream values, such as a desire for recognition and importance, and seek them in other arenas, where opportunities for success do not seem as limited as in the classroom or as their parents have experienced? Does the difference in their cultural orientation in turn cause them to do worse than their parents in the labour market? And, at a group level, do these factors lead to a downward migration into the ranks of the intergenerational urban poor, trapped in a cycle of poverty or social exclusion?[49] Yet the evidence suggests that in the United States, most adolescents – from all groups – expect to go to college.[50] Educational differences among groups are smaller in terms of "values" or "expectations" than they are for actual outcomes.

The segmented assimilation research literature has thus far focused heavily on immigrant-specific factors, including both group characteristics and immigration policy. In terms of policy, segmented assimilation scholars tend to focus more on immigration selection policies, such as comparing the warm welcome received in Florida by Cuban refugees who initially fled the Castro regime to the temporary refugee status granted to the Nicaraguans fleeing the Sandinistas.[51] While these kinds of policies – along with the human capital demographics of these groups – are important, the broader context of reception is also critical to shaping the fortunes of immigrant children. Do these children enter a highly unequal society where only a few can make it, or are they part of a society that guarantees them a secure economic future?

Do they attend decrepit urban public schools rife with violence, where basic needs are not met, and they fail to learn? Or do they have the chance to obtain a public education where they master the kinds of skills and learning necessary for them to succeed later in life? These kinds of differences matter enormously for the outcomes of these children's lives. My research in East Vancouver elementary schools highlights the importance of the school as a public institution that shapes the trajectory of future generations of immigrants. As most migrants to advanced industrial countries initially settle in major cities, the role of urban public schools in shaping these future trajectories has been understudied, and merits further research.[52]

Urban public schools need more resources – from all level of governments – to cope with the challenges of educating the next generation. That new funding should be focused heavily on early childhood education as an important investment in the future. As society becomes more unequal economically, the disadvantages of the poor grow relative to the increasing privileges of the elite. Quality public schools with support and resources from the broader community can begin to counteract some of the deleterious consequences of social and economic inequality.[53]

Schooling is becoming more standardized globally, as institutional factors – such as requirements, curriculum, and approaches – continue to shape the training and teaching conditions across different countries.[54] The good news is that, in terms of gender equality, this global standardization of education concurs with declining numbers of countries where male students outperform female students.[55] At the same time, the economy is rapidly globalizing. India and China as well as other large developing countries are graduating engineers and other skilled workers, who represent competition for good jobs at lower cost.[56] Already, corporations are offshoring and relocating work – from call centres to computer programming – whenever feasible. In light of these global economic trends, the importance of an educated citizenry with strong foundational reading and math skills for the economic health of a country's economy is clear.

At the same time, the current neoliberal approach to school reform in Canada, the United States, and the United Kingdom, consists largely of the greater use of standardized testing for accountability, and is based largely on problematic assumptions. This trend is likely to exacerbate educational inequality, rather than improve outcomes. Testing and competition is setting the stage for even greater use of vouchers and even private and corporate control of education.[57] According to education scholar Pauline Lipman, "Opening up public education to competition through privatization and the market is the ultimate neoliberal solution."[58] It would be naive to view the current trend to implement standardized testing as an accountability tool without considering the broader economic context of growing multinational corporations hungrily seeking opportunities to tap public resources for private profit, from water to education to health care.[59]

Changing Economies: New Realities

The changing economy creates new needs that the school system should address. The economy has shifted dramatically since the end of the Second World War. Public schools should be reformed to better match the reality of the economy and the needs of working parents. Increasingly both parents need to work full-time for families to make ends meet, and so the school calendar should evolve to reflect this. It makes sense to move towards universal early childhood education starting as early as age three, as in the province of Ontario. It also makes sense to keep schools open during summer months, not shutter them up. At minimum, schools should be a vibrant hub in the community during summer months, providing extensive programming for children and learning opportunities for the entire community.

Equality of school funding is important. Most middle-class Canadian parents living in cities send their children to the local public school; all too many American families flee city centres to the suburbs because of "the schools" or evade the local public school through private education or magnet programs and other oases in dysfunctional systems. One reason for this trend in the United States is the unfair allocation of education resources – through funding regimes based on local property tax wealth – that disadvantages urban schools vis-à-vis their surrounding suburban counterparts. In an era where suburban sprawl will be ecologically, economically, and socially more expensive and unsustainable, it is increasingly important that urban public schools, particularly in lower-income communities, have the resources to address the challenges facing their students and provide quality education.

Greater equality in education is key to the health and vitality of democratic society. It is a fundamentally important factor for the economic and social well-being of society. Public schools are one of the most important institutions in their communities.[60] Reforms supported with additional resources can help these schools mitigate some of the deleterious consequences of economic change and growing inequality; the key is to intervene early.

Early elementary education must provide the critical basic and foundational skills in reading and math. Investing in programs for preschool-aged children is an investment in the future that is guaranteed to pay rich dividends. It is also one of the few mechanisms available to expand equality of opportunity and to address some of the root causes of growing inequality. The benefits also go well beyond dollars and cents. Educational investments in the early years has been shown to reduce crime victimization, foster a healthier economy, and provide healthier and more competent workforce, thus improving the quality of life for everyone. In some cases, the school can break down some of the barriers condemning some of the urban poor into reproducing cycles of poverty. The stakes are enormous: improving urban education is key to the success of building a just, prosperous and sustainable democracy.

The Public School in Global Cities

With innovations in technology and the near universal expansion of affordable air travel in an era of neoliberal globalization, people as well as goods are increasingly moving from their place of origin to new places, inspired by motivations including hope for a better future and/ or reconnection to family. In cities across North America and Europe, the public school is now one of the most important universal institutions that shape the lives of young people. These schools are training the future workforce and citizens for participation in post-industrial democratic societies. When they succeed, they help advance equality of opportunity and help define a prosperous future. When they fail, they limit opportunities not only for the children they teach, but also for the communities and larger society, who miss out on the potential political, social, and economical contributions of these enthusiastic young people.

Among all societal institutions, public schools have the greatest potential to create equality of opportunity and provide the foundation for future economic equity and vibrant democratic societies. Research from inside the schoolhouse, instead of simply analysing statistics and trends, reveals that a lack of resources and the high proportion of students with recognized and unrecognized special needs present challenges for these schools. Yes, urban schools are struggling with the consequences of growing inequality in a neoliberal era. But it is the failure to provide adequate resources to schools, not the institution itself, that is problematic.

Public schools, generally speaking, are among the few universal and equalizing institutions in every community. They are the most important institution for countering the deleterious consequences of growing economic disparity to improve social cohesion, equality of opportunity and fulfil the democratic promise of advanced countries, and need to be a site of investment and activism to further enhance their equalizing role beyond theory and in reality. Improving public education means opening up the promise of the multicultural democratic society, albeit an imperfect one, but perhaps from a pragmatist perspective, the best of many alternative options. For many countries around the world, improving the quality and effectiveness of urban public schools could potentially prevent and address future social problems, through instilling practical and critical thinking skills, and usher in a new era of active engagement, unprecedented peace and prosperity.

Methodology Appendix
Sitting in the Classroom: Determining School Success

In the middle of the afternoon on May 21, 2007, near the bustling Main Street SkyTrain station at Terminal Avenue, a fight erupted between two groups of youths near Science World, the Vancouver science museum. Each group included 10-to-12 young males between the ages of 13 and 15.[1] One of the boys took out a flick knife and when the brawl ended, four of the boys had been stabbed. One of the stabbing victims, Chrisna (Chris) Poeung – a 13-year-old student at Mt. Pleasant Elementary in East Vancouver – was rushed to St. Paul's Hospital. A friend of his, 14-year-old friend Deanne Tran, was with Chris at the hospital that night when he succumbed to his chest wounds and died. Tran said about the incident, "It was just shocking, so horrifying ... It just happened so sudden, so unexpectedly."[2] A 14 year old from a nearby secondary school was caught fleeing the scene on a bus headed up Kingsway Avenue and was charged with second-degree murder.

The spontaneous memorial at the blood-splattered section of sidewalk where the fight took place included a picture of Chris Poeung, along with flowers, a small teddy bear, and a poem from his devastated sister that said, "Everyone was your friend."[3]

Police spokesman Tim Fanning shared with the public that, based on interviews with 30 witnesses, they believed that the fight was not gang-related and that drugs or alcohol were not factors. One witness, 16-year-old Phillipe Bui, didn't even think that Chris was involved in the argument, but that "he was just helping a friend."[4]

In the aftermath, the community reeled with grief and tension. According to an article in the *Globe and Mail*, while community leaders urged calm, some people threatened revenge using online platforms like Facebook. One such threat was "I'm gonna kill the bitch that did this."[5] Another posting on the Internet stated, "This group is for people who hate [the accused]. He is responsible for the killing of Chris Poeung. If anybody knows where he live[s] please let me know."[6] At Mt. Pleasant Elementary, Principal Steve Agbob brought counsellors to the school to help the students and staff cope, and a student assembly was held to provide both facts and sources of support to grieving students.[7]

Welcome to the world of East Vancouver, and urban education more generally. Elementary school students knifed to death after school: unusual, yes, but tragically, violence in the community does not stop at the schoolhouse gate. In many urban schools in the United States, police officers are deployed for security. In Baltimore, Maryland, some schools have begun using metal detectors to screen students at the school entrance.[8] And, in Toronto, Ontario, police recently began patrolling 27 inner-city schools after a spate of shootings in several high schools.[9] While violence in schools is not exclusive to those in inner cities – as was so painfully highlighted by the recent schoolyard rampages in rural American communities – it is more pervasive at some urban public schools located in lower-income communities as compared to rural, suburban, and wealthy urban public schools.[10] The scope of challenges facing urban public schools in lower-income communities is usually much greater, and the resources to meet these needs much smaller.

The Determinants of School Success Study

"You have to go back to the schools themselves ... You have to sit on the little chairs in the first and second grade, or on the reading rug with the Kindergarten kids, and listen to the things they say and the dialogue between them and their teachers. You have to go down to the basement with the children when it's time for lunch, and to the playground with them, if they have a playground, when it's time for recess, if they still have a recess at their school. You have to walk into the children's bathrooms in these buildings. You have to do what children do and breathe the air the children breathe. I don't think there is any other way to find out what the lives that children lead in school are really like."
                    – Jonathan Kozol, *The Shame of the Nation*[11]

The Determinants of School Success Study began with the following question: Why are some East Vancouver elementary schools with high percentages of students from low-income visible minority families more successful in teaching early childhood literacy and numeracy skills than are other schools in the same area that have similar student demographics? The wealth of statistical data on child development and achievement appeared to create a research opportunity to uncover why certain schools are doing so well, and why other schools with demographically similar student populations have much higher proportions of their students scoring below expectations on standardized exams.

At an initial glance, the statistics on test scores across the city reveal the critical importance of socio-economic factors for explaining differences in test scores between schools: schools with children from middle class and wealthy families generally do much better on standardized exams than do schools with high percentages of children from low-income households.[12] At the same time, when you looked at the Vancouver schools that have similar socio-economic demographic student populations – with relatively high percentages of children from low-income families – some had much higher percentages of students performing much better than expected on the Foundation Skills Assessment (FSA) literacy and numeracy exams administered annually to all fourth grade students in British Columbia. I became interested in what explains the differences in outcomes between the schools. As schooling is so important for children's future, if some elementary schools were doing much better at providing foundational skills in literacy and numeracy, then figuring out why could illuminate ways for struggling schools to improve student outcomes. My initial research design proposed using qualitative research methods to get inside the "black box" of varying school outcomes through a comparative analysis that aimed to explain divergent test score profiles between elementary schools serving statistically similar student populations.

While socio-economic factors are clearly important for explaining standardized test score outcomes, the comparative research design employed in the study aimed to explain differences in performance between elementary schools and to recommend specific policy interventions – beyond reducing socio-economic disparities and child poverty – that could make a difference in the early literacy and numeracy achievement of at-risk children in urban elementary schools.[13] Identifying factors and programs that improve the literacy and numeracy achievement of these urban schools could potentially improve the likelihood of students gaining the skills necessary to fulfil their potential and achieve their dreams.

I used public data from the results of standardized testing in one particular school year (2001–2002) to identify several East Vancouver elementary schools in low-income neighbourhoods where only a very small percentage of students were "failing to meet expectations" on standardized tests given to all fourth graders in the province of British Columbia in the areas of reading, math, and writing. Other schools in East Vancouver – with statistically similar student populations – had much higher percentages of students "failing to meet expectations" on these standardized exams.[14]

In order to select schools to include as case studies for this study, I attempted to categorize each as "successful" or "high challenge" based on a composite of the first few years of test score data available. Unfortunately though, this process turned out to be more difficult than expected. Why? There was a much smaller variation in outcomes between schools for the standardized exams measuring math skills as compared to the variation in outcomes for reading skills. I grappled with how to rank a school that has average passing rates in math but lower-than-average passing rates for reading exams. In the end, the way I categorized the schools relied more heavily on reading test score outcomes than math, because of the emphasis in the research literature on early reading skill mastery as a predictor of future success.

The Determinants of School Success Study Methodology

The research behind this book includes interviews with administrators, teachers, and parents as well as classroom observations at 10 elementary schools in East Vancouver.[15] The idea was to compare schools with similar student populations statistically, but which had different outcomes in terms of standardized test scores.[16] While approximately 50% of the students at these schools speak English as a second language, between one-third and one-half of the children in these schools live in households earning less than the Low Income Cut-Off (LICO) poverty line in Canada. These are not the highest poverty schools in Vancouver, yet they have higher rates of poverty than most schools in the district. At the same time, these elementary schools share similar student demographics to many urban public schools in lower-income communities in the larger cities of Canada and some regions of the United States.[17]

I hoped to reveal replicable factors that promote academic achievement among elementary school students. I also aimed to identify specific programs that are successfully improving literacy and numeracy

Table 1. Design: Determinants of School Success in East Vancouver Elementary Schools (Based on 1999–2000 and 2000–2001 FSA Literacy Data for Grade 4 Students)

Strong Performers	Centennial Elementary	Arthur Lang Elementary	East Harcourt Elementary	
Median Performers	Soaring Eagle Elementary	Pearson Elementary	Wellington Elementary	Great Forest Elementary
Weak Performers	New Lake Elementary	Ashfield Elementary	Lakeview Elementary	

skills in East Vancouver elementary schools. These programs include curricular programs, community literacy programs, school mentoring partnerships, and special resources for ESL students. I felt that while much empirical research has focused on poorly performing urban schools, few have examined successful schools in similar contexts or attempted to compare schools with similar students and divergent outcomes.

I began by assessing the publicly available test score and census data for elementary schools in East Vancouver, particularly those located in the neighbourhoods where many of the low-income immigrant hotel employees I previously studied lived. Out of a total of 18 elementary schools identified, I selected 10 elementary schools as case examples for qualitative field research (see Table 1 for a visual model of the initial research design). Of these schools, based on 1999 to 2000 and 2000 to 2001 school year data (the first years of data available), some were performing at or near the provincial average in fourth grade literacy and math scores, others were performing somewhat below the provincial average (as expected for schools with higher proportions of students from low-income families), and some were performing far below the provincial average.

Qualitative research methods – including interviewing and participant observation – provide valuable data from the perspective of those working "on the ground" in public schools to help improve the quality of public education.[18] Part of the reason for this is that the recommendations generated by qualitative research come from some of the most important stakeholders in the education system: principals, teachers, and parents.

The first person interviewed in each school was the principal, for the purpose of getting invaluable context and also to obtain permission to

access the school as a research site. These interviews were often followed by a guided tour of the school facilities and introductions to
teachers, who were later contacted and asked if they would be willing
to have their classroom observed and to be interviewed for the project.[19] Parents were generally recruited through recommendations from
the principal or through observations at Parental Advisory Council
members.[20] Supplementary fieldwork included school and playground
observation as well as neighbourhood-based observation, including
visits to community institutions such as community centres.[21]

Selecting Schools

So how did my thinking about these issues evolve over the course of
the study? I initially categorized the schools based on the results of standardized test scores in the fourth grade from the 1999 to 2000 and 2000 to
2001 school year.[22] At first, the interviews with principals, teachers, and
parents, as well as the observations in classrooms and school functions
appeared to reveal specific programs and policies that seemed important for understanding variations in test score outcomes. In the beginning, I even felt that the findings illuminated current debates about the
value of standardized testing for improving school performance as well
as other theories that highlighted the importance of choice, role of the
principal, funding, programs, class sizes, and so forth.

   As I began my research, I clung closely to my original design. I thought
I would uncover some clear factors. To help illustrate my thinking at
the outset of the study, following is part of my conversation with one
teacher at Centennial Elementary. At the end of my interview with her,
she asked me to reiterate the purpose of my research (while I was still
recording): "I'm primarily looking at early literacy and early numeracy
success in math and reading. As some background, [researchers] did a
lot of work with these in quantitative data, everything from FSA scores
to kindergarten assessments [of early childhood development], looking at what percentage of students are vulnerable in different schools
and where they see problems in these specific areas, but they've sort
of come to the great conclusion that socio-economic status matters ..."

   The teacher jumped in, commenting "big surprise!" I concurred and
went on: "In a way, what I propose to do is look inside the black box
and get a sense of what's going on [on] the ground and look at some
schools that kind of seem to be explained by that statistic exactly."
When she asked me why I chose her school as a case, I replied: "Well ...
I'm interested in this neighbourhood in general just because it's in the

southeast of Vancouver. A lot of hotel workers [I interviewed for a previous study] live in these areas, and they had their children go to the schools here. So what I did is look at a mix of schools, and in some ways Centennial Elementary was doing much better [than] we expected. Then again, that's going against the census data, so there were things like the [special magnet] program that we didn't know [about]. I found out about [it] when I started studying Centennial Elementary, and that does kind of explain maybe why it's doing better."

At those early stages of the fieldwork, I felt like I was making good progress. I was only basing my categorization of school "success" on the one year of available data. So it was pretty clear that some schools were performing better than others. Of course, this was not necessarily consistent across reading, math, and writing, which are all tested separately. Yet I identified many schools as doing "better or much better than expected" and others as performing "worse than expected" based on the data from one year of test scores.

Initially I received immediate and enthusiastic responses from the principals of the "successful" schools to my letter of contact and/or follow-up, while the same approaches were ignored or explicitly turned down by schools that I had categorized as performing below expectations, even though I hadn't informed them that I had categorized their school that way. Why? I suspect the administrators knew in which category their school belonged.

In explaining their outright rejection of my inquiry, one administrator at a poorly performing school claimed that they were inundated with researchers, which perhaps may have been true, but I was sceptical. I worried that these schools were closing their doors to outside scrutiny. Perhaps as a result of negative publicity based on one year of poor standardized test results, they felt defensive, maybe even attacked. While at the time it made me feel frustrated, I realize now that what happened is one of the deleterious consequences of standardized testing or "ranking" of schools that undermines one of its explicit goals. If schools that do poorly are "shamed," the response is often to close ranks and become more resistant to recommendations for improvement or change. In this case, the stick is far less effective than the carrot.

Fieldwork

I began my fieldwork, promisingly enough, at schools characterized as "successful schools." There I met beaming principals who were eager to throw open the school doors and share with me the secrets of their success. These schools were indeed wonderful. Vibrant. And the people I met there were simply thrilled that someone was interested in trying to understand their secret to success. At the time, I thought, "Wow, so little research is done in schools that are doing well, and so much is focused on the worst schools"; it felt exciting. And I also felt that the reasons these schools were doing better than expected were quickly becoming very apparent.

Their catchment areas, which were affected by the rapid gentrification in parts of East Vancouver and the real estate boom in Vancouver overall, included many affluent and middle class families. These schools quickly distinguished themselves as having a greater number of children from lower middle class families than from working poor families or families living on social assistance. So part of the story was clearly a time lag of data, between the census data I was using to get catchment area poverty statistics and the testing data, which were from the year before I began interviewing. At the same time, one of these schools turned out to have a special magnet program that attracted privileged children with motivated parents from all over the city, including the wealthier neighbourhoods. Another black box mystery uncovered, or so I thought.

Things started to get complicated as we entered the subsequent year of the study, when another round of FSA test scores was published. At this point, I had been fortunate to receive a grant from Social Sciences and Humanities Research Council of Canada (SSHRC), which allowed me, among other things, to hire several graduate students to work as research assistants (RAs) on my study. Two RAs in particular were incredibly helpful: Charlene Warrington and Siobhan Ashe. They were very committed to getting access to schools that I had originally categorized as performing below expectations or well-below expectations. They were very persuasive and their social networks helped a lot; both had personal contacts and connections inside the school system that worked wonders in terms of opening doors.

While the project continued, things also changed with the schools. The new FSA test score results for the elementary schools studied were somewhat different than the previous year. Of course, at a macro-level, schools on the wealthy west side and in the tony suburb of West Vancouver were still at the top of the list with, generally, the highest passing marks. And those schools in the poorest neighbourhoods, like the Downtown Eastside, still ranked among the lowest, with the highest rates of failure. But in between, on the east side, some schools seemed to move up quite a bit, and others down. My research assistants and I felt this provided an amazing research opportunity as we could seek to identify the factors that explained the change.

One school, originally categorized as performing well-below expectations, was now performing above expectations. I began interviewing teachers and administrators at that particular school and indeed found a lot of evidence to explain the reasons for this dramatic improvement. The school had just received Inner City designation, which provided much-needed additional funding and resources as described in chapter 6, as well as a new principal from one of the top-performing schools in the region.

Our team was also now completing interviews and observations in several of what I had initially categorized as poorly performing schools. Although, based on census data, the catchment area of one of these schools appeared to have a similar level of poverty as some of the other more "successful" schools, I soon discovered the presence of a major public housing project near the school. Given the relatively high level of average household income in the catchment area, buried within this statistic was a disproportionate number of extremely poor children, refugees, and recent arrivals, compared to other schools with high numbers of children from working poor families. The children from the housing project had enormous needs, and their school had only recently begun to receive the resources to begin to address them – such as through a free breakfast and hot lunch program.

Initial Findings

My presentations of the preliminary findings at a Vancouver conference on child development were greeted with enthusiasm by members of the Pacific Sociological Association and of the American Sociological Association. A leader in the field who heard the presentation told me that he felt this kind of research was critically important.[23]

It was a stimulating time; our research team held regular reflection meetings at a neighbourhood coffee shop, and my RAs would excitedly describe their field experiences. We began identifying some reasons why certain schools were performing poorly. At the same time, the RAs were amazed at the commitment of the staff and the kinds of exciting programs going on at these supposedly "poorly performing" schools. A lot of these were the same programs as at the "successful" schools.

It was in these meetings that the RAs began pointing out that the neighbourhoods and student populations at the schools initially identified as "highly performing" were qualitatively different than that of the schools initially identified as "poorly performing." They even suggested limiting the comparison to a more closely comparable subsample of schools, taking out two of the successful schools I had initially studied because the areas around these schools had become so middle class. I drove around with one RA for a few hours comparing school sites and was convinced that there were more single-family homes in some of the school areas than in other school neighbourhoods, which had a higher number of rental apartment buildings. At the same time, these schools did share similarities despite differing in the severity of the needs of students enrolled. I began to worry we were comparing apples and oranges.

As time passed, we also got additional rounds of test score data, and the statistics shifted again, while criticism of the FSA standardized testing regime grew and opponents became more vocal. I realized that at the successful schools many of the programs that appeared important were also operating at what I had initially categorized as schools performing below expectations. I had to confront the weakness of the "good" school / "bad" school model implicit in comparative designs, and this led me to look at common challenges and school-based responses.

My next presentation of the preliminary findings was to a group of academics, policy makers, and NGOs sponsored by the BC Attorney General's Office of Multiculturalism and the RIIM (Vancouver's branch of the international Metropolis project). The intense interest and positive feedback from this group re-energized me. Increasingly, it became clear from the analysis of the data that there were fundamental problems with the standardized test score results and the way they were being used to rank or judge schools.

Changing Course

As these data were the basis for the original comparative design, this methodological approach increasingly seemed unworkable in its original form. Most schools were not consistently performing better or worse than expected. Rather, the small sample sizes at each school, resulting from the testing of only fourth grade students, as well as the process, rules, and politics around the way the testing was being completed – including who was included and excluded (or suggested to be absent) – undermined the year-to-year validity of the tests for accurately representing a school's performance. Sure, at one level, schools with nearly 100% passing rates every year are doing better than schools with passing rates consistently below 70%. But the explanation for the difference has much more to do with the demographics of the children – their resources and challenges – than the school itself. And that raises the critically important question: What is a successful school in the context of a highly unequal society? Is a school that has many students with special needs and disadvantages and is meeting those needs, worse than a school that has only a few students with needs but does not bother addressing them?

One simple way to think about the results of my study and the issues raised by it is the following thought experiment: What would happen if all the children at Cassandra Elementary in the extremely low-income Downtown Eastside went to West Castle Elementary in the wealthiest neighbourhood in the west side of Vancouver, and vice versa? While some modest improvements might be expected for the Cassandra Elementary students who would now be attending their new extremely "successful" West Castle Elementary, some students might actually do worse without the kind of supportive programming available at Cassandra Elementary, much of which was created and implemented to meet the unique needs of the students in the community. Eventually a school like West Castle Elementary would find resources to address some of these needs, but the West Castle Elementary teachers may also find that coping with these problems would take time and resources away from learning in the classroom. Some West Castle Elementary teachers might become frustrated and request transfers or quit their jobs in order teach at a private school or a school in wealthy West Vancouver, where they would not have to deal with the problems brought into the classroom by students with difficult home and community circumstances. Of course, 80% of the new students from West Castle Elementary now at Cassandra Elementary would certainly not all suddenly begin failing the FSA exams. These west-side children would bring with them the cultural and social capital of high-resource parents living in wealthy neighbourhoods, who have focused on the concerted cultivation of their children. While some former West Castle Elementary students now at Cassandra Elementary may have challenges and special needs, these would be addressed at home and at school, and parents would advocate strongly and forcefully to make sure the resources were in place to make it happen.

What this thought experiment makes clear is that, in the end, standardized testing results tell us far more about who the students are at these schools than what kind of job these schools are doing educating them.[24] Based on varying sample sizes as small as 20 fourth grade students completing a set of exams in a school, the FSA results provide far too limited data to make assessments about how a school is doing, particularly in terms of distinguishing between those performing in the middle ranges. With sample sizes this small, the decision of one child, who would have failed, to stay home sick on testing day could impact the total school ranking. While using statistical techniques to control for the socio-economic status of the student body, as completed by economist David Johnson for the C.D. Howe Institute in his study of schools in British Columbia and Ontario, provides more interesting rankings, the test score data are just not of sufficient quality to tell us, with any accuracy, much about how one school is actually performing compared to other schools.[25] Cassandra Elementary and West Castle Elementary are apples and oranges, as it turns out, and, in the sense that all schools are unique, so are the schools that appear to serve similar students studied in my research.

Now that the basic foundation of the initial comparative design had become problematic, the analysis was forced to proceed in a new direction. On the one hand, the discovery of the problems with standardized tests for assessing school performance is an important finding in itself, both generally and specifically in the case of East Vancouver. This discovery and its ramifications were instrumental when it came to writing chapters 7 and eight 8 their focus on policy recommendations. Chapter 7 ends with recommendations specific to standardized testing and both chapters include insights into how to utilize multiple methodological approaches to help students in urban public elementary schools master early literacy and numeracy.

On the other hand, if the data collected through my research were not going to be based on a comparison of schools performing above expectations and schools performing below expectations with similar student populations, then how should the analysis of the data proceed? I struggled with this issue for some time. At times, I wanted to hold on to the old design with all its theoretical rigour and empirical appeal, but every time I tried to delve into the data that way, it simply wouldn't work. When I focused on how these schools were different, I came up short, beyond some of the obvious differences, such as the hosting by certain schools of a special magnet program. While I could explain how some of the neighbourhoods were different or had unique characteristics, in many ways the more interesting finding was how similar some of these areas were to each other and the kinds of transformations, usually involving gentrification, they were going through, albeit at different stages. So eventually I decided to approach the analysis from a different angle. Instead of focusing on the differences between these schools, I decided to examine their similarities. What kinds of programs were teachers enthusiastically supporting in every school? What kinds of challenges were administrators and parents talking about at each school?

Lessons Learned

In 2007, the fieldwork wrapped up. The digitally recorded interviews were transcribed. The field notes collected. Articles, reports, and other materials were gathered and scanned where possible. I coded the data based on themes, looking as much for similarities as differences between the schools. Instead of comparing schools and how they were performing, I wanted to understand how most of these schools were reacting, coping with their unique and their similar challenges. Each school used a combination of programs, some alike and others their own, to address these challenges, with varying success. Ultimately, it is the larger story that became more interesting. No magic bullets were uncovered, yet the premise that there are many different routes to "success" for urban elementary schools was confirmed. The kinds of challenges these schools are facing and the similarities in how these challenges were addressed are important findings. The data provided policy lessons and supported and challenged many of the theories in the sociology of education and urban education literature. Elementary schools in East Vancouver provide valuable lessons about and insights into urban education in an increasingly diverse and globalizing urban world.

Methodologically my research reveals insights about the triangulation of quantitative and qualitative research in practice. Qualitative research helps get inside the black box of explanatory analysis. It also provides a dynamic perspective on changing schools and communities. While the results may not be as easily replicated, qualitative research studies raise critical questions, provide new perspectives, and often present additional hypotheses for future empirical analysis and theoretical development. The focus and design of this particular study evolved over the course of the fieldwork. Explicitly describing this process in this methodology discussion, particularly the evolution in the plans for analysis of the data collected, will, I hope, both inspire others who find themselves in situations where easy comparisons turn out not to be so easy, and give readers a better sense of the research process leading to clearer evaluation of the findings and conclusions of this book.

My personal journey in education will continue in my role as a social policy professor at a public university, where I teach courses to inquisitive and inspired students from a diverse range of backgrounds. My hope is that these students will help reshape society to make it more equitable and fair, while always striving to follow their passions and inspire others.

Notes

1. Introduction

1 Internationally, franchise school reform programs, most notably the Success for All program, provide convincing evidence that strong academic achievement, demonstrated on standardized tests, is possible to achieve in elementary schools serving high-poverty urban populations. Slavin and Madden (2001); See Kozol (2005) for some critiques of the Success for All program.

2 Statisticians analysing standardized test score data across North America, and specifically in British Columbia, have found a strong relationship between the percentage of students from low-income families in a school and the percentage of students performing poorly or failing to meet expectations on these exams. Simply put, the greater the proportion of low-income students, the higher the percentage of students who are failing the exams. In the case of British Columbia, the findings of factor analysis regressions point – unsurprisingly – to the role of socio-economic factors in children's developmental vulnerability starting in kindergarten, and in academic achievement as measured by standardized Foundation Skills Assessment exams taken during the fourth grade (Hertzman et al. 2002).

3 We know that some schools with similar student populations have higher passing rates than others; there is still quite a bit of variation between schools serving similar student populations (based on their demographics). In Vancouver, Grandview Elementary provides a well-publicized example of a school serving a largely low-income and vulnerable student population that dramatically increased its students' performance on standardized math and literacy exams over a short period of time, from just over 20% passing to 80% of fourth grade students meeting expectations.

Yet these gains can be short-lived. Recently the passing rates have fluctuated and even dropped somewhat.

4 Beyond neighbourhood and school factors, broader policy and economic
factors have been identified as important for explaining student achievement and educational attainment. In an *American Journal of Sociology*
article, Mayer (2001) finds, based on her analysis of Panel Study of Income
Dynamics (PSID) data and state level data in the United States from
1970 to 1990, that states with higher levels of income inequality had
greater inequality in educational attainment, related primarily to
differences in state spending on education and increasing returns to
education.

5 Of course, the specificity of the case raises obvious limitations to the generalizability of the findings. These include the dynamics of immigrant and
urban settlement in Vancouver, and the broader city, regional, provincial,
and Canadian socio-economic and policy context. Throughout the book
I have attempted to make clear where these contextual factors might be
particularly important for limiting generalizability. At the same time,
I argue that neoliberal globalization in a time of mass migration has created similar challenges and trends as well as policy responses in cities
across the advanced industrialized world.

6 Kozol (1992)

7 Pat Rubio Goldsmith finds that students attending schools with
higher percentages of black or Latino students in the United States are less
likely to have earned a high school diploma and a bachelor's degree by
age 26 than similar students at schools with largely white student populations. (Goldsmith 2009). At the same time, the proportion of black or
Latino people in the zip code did not associate significantly with school
achievement (Goldsmith 2009).

8 Kozol (1992)

9 Orfield and Eaton (1997). Based on ethnographic research at three distinct
southern California elementary schools, sociologist Amanda E. Lewis
(2003) explores how race and racial inequality is enacted daily in schools –
from the curriculum to daily teacher–student interactions.

10 Alexander, Entwisle, and Dauber (2003: 12)

11 For Canadian data on growing urban polarization, see Chen, Myles, and
Picot (2012) and Hulchanski (2010).

12 Wilson and Taub (1996)

13 Donziger (1996: 31). For a devastating analysis of the consequences
of increasing incarceration for minorities in the United States, see
Alexander (2012).

14 Bronfenbrenner (1979)
15 Brooks, Pugh, and Shagen (1996)
16 Reich (1992)
17 Kozol (2005: 185)
18 Although the trends are similar, important country-specific differences are important. For example, Gaskell and Levin (2012: 33) point out that US urban diversity reflects the legacy of slavery and high levels of immigration from Mexico in contrast to Canada, where immigration and settlement patterns have contributed to diversity in Canadian cities.
19 In the United States, Asian immigrants have better educational outcomes than whites overall, but other immigrants, such as Puerto Ricans and Mexicans, fare worse than white students, in large part due to socio-economic status (Harris, Jamison, and Trujillo 2008).
20 Aronowitz (2004: 38)
21 In the United States, a long tail of poor performance on achievement exams by the poorest-performing one-third of students reduced the average test scores on the Trends in International Mathematics and Science Study (TIMMS) and other international achievement comparisons (Elley 1996).
22 Coleman (1990: 22)
23 Jencks (1972)
24 See Bowles and Gintis (1976) book, *Schooling in a Capitalist Society*.
25 The classic book *The Hidden Injuries of Class* – based on Richard Sennett and William Cobb's research on working class men in Boston – examines the role of education in the reproduction of social inequality. Other more recent studies have reached similar conclusions. For example, Patricia Adler and Peter Adler's (1994) study of after-school activities employs a Bourdieu-inspired approach to examine how the increasing institutionalization of after-school activities transmits cultural capital and habitus of achievement to certain students and thus, results in the reproduction of social inequality over generations.
26 Giroux (2005: 75)
27 Noguera (2008: 230)
28 Smith and Noble (1995: 18)
29 Alexander et al. (2003)
30 Hart and Risely (1995: 76) in Alexander et al. (2003:13)
31 Burkam et al. (2004)
32 Entwisle and Alexander (1992). The study is based on the analysis of mathematical test scores.
33 Entwisle and Alexander (1992)

34 For example, research on streaming or tracking based on a case study in Ontario found that the process greatly disadvantaged youth from working class and especially poor families (Curtis, Livingstone, and Smaller 1992).
35 Lareau (2000: 9)
36 Based on analysis of intracohort and intercohort college admissions data in the United States, published in the *American Sociological Review*, Alon (2009) also finds that socio-economic status is an ever-present factor in admissions.
37 Smith (2000)
38 Smith (2000)
39 Igoa (1995: 6)
40 Theories of "segmented assimilation" propose that the second and third generations of immigrants selectively adopt cultures and values of the broader "host" society. Thus, much of the research in this area has focused largely on how immigrant-group–specific factors and immigrant-specific policies shape the context of reception for immigrants (Alba and Nee, 1997). At the same time, other kinds of non–immigrant-specific institutional factors also clearly matter for creating the context. In my book *Differences That Matter*, I describe how the context of reception for the mostly immigrant hotel employees in Seattle and Vancouver differed cross-nationally because of social policy differences between the United States and Canada (Zuberi 2006). During the fieldwork for that book, I also became aware of the important role that public schools in these neighbourhoods had for helping to understand the experiences and trajectories of immigrant youth and groups who migrate to US and Canadian cities.
41 Kozol (1992)
42 Gaskell and Levin (2012:198) argue, "Schools with high levels of disadvantage will need additional resources to compensate – not just for smaller classes, but for individualized support to students, community outreach, or enrichment activities such as music or travel that many other students take for granted."
43 Coleman (1990); Jencks (1972)
44 Hanushek (1981)
45 Baker (1991: 628, 629)
46 Hanushek (1981) concluded that money does not matter for educational quality simply because not *enough* of the studies he reviewed found a significant and positive association between educational expenditure levels and achievement. Yet many of the studies reviewed had serious methodological problems of their own. These problems include relying on cross-sectional data without even controlling for socio-economic status (SES)

variables and comparing school districts with dramatically different levels of need, such as percentage of disabled students, special needs students, infrastructure costs, and so on. Some studies compared urban, suburban, and rural schools together, while others compared schools within the same district, where funding from federal and state resources provided marginally higher resources explicitly targeted to meet these schools' higher needs (Baker 1991: 629). Given these methodological problems, it is not surprising that many of the studies did not show a strong positive association between per-pupil funding and student achievement.

Many researchers question the validity of Hanushek's use of a "vote-counting" method to draw conclusions about expenditure and performance, especially without clear decision rules. Baker (1991: 630) used a different and explicit decision rule to complete a meta-analysis with the same vote counting methodology and study data, and arrived at the opposite conclusion: per-pupil expenditure was positively and significantly correlated with student achievement. These researchers also question the appropriateness of vote counting as an inference tool because of its failure to account for the magnitude of relationships and susceptibility to Type II errors. The weak associations and large sample sizes in typical social science studies paradoxically cause the inclusion of a large number of studies in vote counts to seriously diminish the probability of correct detection, even if the effect exists in every study (Hedges, Laine, and Greenwald (1994: 5–8). Hedges et al. (1994) also used a more sophisticated tool of literature review, known as meta-analysis, and found a significant and positive association between school resources and outcomes.

47 Gaskell and Levin (2012: 198)
48 Slavin (1994: 99)
49 Ferguson (1991) in Kazal-Thrasher (1993)
50 Card and Krueger (1992) in Arum (1996); Slavin (1994: 99) Other researchers who have found a relationship between school resources and student outcomes include Eberts and Stone (1988) and Murnane (1991)
51 Murnane and Olsen (1990) in Slavin (1994: 100)
52 Kozol (1992)
53 Kozol (1992)
54 Rossmiller (1992, 519) For example, multiple studies have demonstrated that educating disabled students costs substantially more than average students – generally twice as much per pupil. (Rossmiller 1992, 519)
55 Bomster (1992, 1A)
56 Bomster (1992: 1A)
57 Harvey (1996: 393)
58 Kozol (1992)

59 For example, see Zuberi (2013) and United Way Toronto (2011).
60 Ungerleider (2003); Weissbourd (1997)
61 For example, when leading education sociologists Karl Alexander, Doris Entwisle, and Carrie Horsey (1997) examined the factors that explained why some students drop out of high school, they found it necessary to adopt a life-course perspective as the students' decisions resulted from long-term academic disengagement. They examined a student's first grade experiences as well as family- and child-specific factors to explain this outcome, and found them to be significant predictors.
62 Lipman (2008: 62)
63 See Hertzman (2000)
64 For an excellent discussion, based on extensive research, see the book *Reaching Higher* by Rhona Weinstein (2002).
65 Suárez-Orozco et al. (2008). They emphasize that the experiences of immigrant children born abroad and the 1.5-, second-, and third-generation youth, while they have some similarities, should be examined distinctly. For example, first-generation immigrant children tend to be more disoriented as compared to second-generation children born in the United States. Their study (the Longitudinal Immigrant Student Adaptation Study) focused exclusively on foreign-born children; unsurprisingly, many were working poor (Suárez-Orozco et al. 2008: 8).

Based on a five-year study of 400 foreign-born children in the United States, their study reveals the challenges that new immigrant children face attending schools in high-poverty urban neighbourhoods. Despite high hopes in their new land, only some – those with especially supportive and resourceful parents or other mentors – overcome the obstacles and succeed. It should be noted that some research suggests that, in some cases, third- or higher-generation immigrants are performing more poorly than first- and second-generation immigrants. Based on their analysis of National Education Longitudinal Study (NELS) data (1998 to 1994), Glick and White (2004) argue that the immigration paradox also holds for post-secondary education, with immigrant and second-generation students in the United States more likely to attend university than third- or higher-generation students, controlling for other factors. Immigrant parents have high expectations that their children will complete post-secondary education (Glick and White 2004).
66 Metro Vancouver (2008): 1
67 Metro Vancouver (2008): 4
68 Suárez-Orozco et al. (2008): 6
69 Vertovec (2007)

70 At the same time, many of these regions are also experiencing growing concentrations of immigrants and immigrant groups clustering in inner-ring suburbs and other parts of the metropolis.

71 See Florida (2004); Sassen (2001)

72 Barnett and Boocock (1998); Knapp and Shields (1991); Stevenson and Stigler (1992); Patchen (2004)

73 Weissbourd 1997

74 I examined East Vancouver elementary schools' standardized test score and census data available to the public. Many of these schools were in neighbourhoods already familiar to me through a previous study on low-income immigrant hotel employees (Zuberi 2006).

75 The Canadian Low Income Cut-Off poverty line is set at a higher level than the US poverty line.

76 All of the names of respondents, schools, and students who participated in the research have been changed to protect confidentiality. Before the field-work commenced, the research received ethical approval after review by the UBC Behavioural and Research Ethics Board and the Vancouver School Board Research Division.

77 Even though these schools shared similar overall levels of poverty, as measured by percentage of families with incomes below the Low Income Cut-Off, Canada's unofficial poverty line.

78 Yet, more recent performance suggests that the dramatic improvements have more recently diminished over time at this school (and many others).

79 See Gordon (2007)

80 A report based on the experiences of nine "successful" high-poverty urban schools in different US cities – from Detroit to Atlanta – also found that each school faced unique demographic and other conditions, and that these schools had utilized very different programs and policies to achieve strong reading and math results. The authors of the report argue that the schools did use similar strategies to become "high-performing" schools. These include leaders who created achievable and measurable goals; leaders who focused on conflict reduction, appropriate behaviour by students, and creating positive learning environments; leaders who maximized teachers' instructional time and provided requested training and classroom resources; and leaders who collaborated with teachers and other stakeholders, including parents, to achieve improvement and academic success (U.S. Department of Education, 1999).

81 These findings support the insights of Anyon (1997).

82 Wilson (1997); Alexander (2012)

2. Diversity in the Classroom

1 McDonald (1996)
2 Vertovec (2007)
3 Older immigrant children in the household must often act as a "language broker," translating for their parents (Orellana 2009). Based on her ethnographic research in schools, she reports

> "Translations were provided mostly for family members, as when children read signs, labels, maps, and directions; often public *para*-phrasing involved the most challenging kind of mediating work in which children spoke to and for authority figures representing educational, legal, medical and financial institutions, negotiating between these people and their families in multiparty interactions." (Orellana 2009: 66)

Orellana (2009) argues that this translation work represents a form of unrecognized labour by the children of immigrant parents.
4 The social exclusion of Aboriginals in Canada has been extensively described by many scholars. For example, Kendall (2001); Dupuis (2001); Campbell (2001); Robertson and Culhane (2005). In Vancouver, Aboriginal students experience disproportionately high levels of failing to meet expectations on standardized exams as well as high school drop-out rates. There are several schools in East Vancouver with over 60% Aboriginal student enrolments. My research did not focus on these schools, despite the fact that many are experiencing challenges. The issues of colonization and oppression of First Nation people and culture in Canada has a long history (Dupuis, 2001; Kendall, 2001). Schools with high proportions of Aboriginal students in Vancouver have been the focus of extensive research, as compared to limited research attention being focused on the more typical, diverse urban elementary schools, with large percentages of visible minority and immigrant students. For example, Richards et al. (2008) utilizes the FSA standardized exam scores in the fourth and seventh grade to compare performance of schools with high percentages of Aboriginal students in British Columbia.
5 Canada's unofficial poverty line, the Low-Income Cut-Off (LICO), is set at a higher dollar amount than the US poverty line, because of differences in the way the two poverty lines are calculated.
6 See Belle (1999).
7 For an excellent description of the vitality of the underground economy in urban poor neighbourhoods in Chicago, see Sudhir Venkatesh's books *Off the Books* (2006) and *Gang Leader for a Day* (2008).

8 See Jane Jacobs' classic book *The Death and Life of an American City* (1963). For an updated discussion of the "eyes on the street" theory applied to today's city, see the book *Sidewalk* by Mitchell Duneier (2000).

9 Claire Winslow, an outreach coordinator who works with New Lake Elementary, explained that:

> There've been issues. A lot of issues around things like break-ins and stealing and muggings, particularly what's been one of our toughest ones has been the Queens SkyTrain station. It's slowly shifting. I think there [is a] huge amount of drug recruitment there, and drug sales. Predominately in marijuana, a lot of crystal meth, and a lot of recruitment there for trying to recruit our younger under-12s to run their drugs for them, because they unfortunately know how to utilize the legal system. Someone under the age of 12 cannot be legally charged, and once they've got someone under their wing and they're giving them a few bucks and they know they don't have a lot of money themselves. They also know how to put the fear in to them about any kind of disclosure of reporting them to police and that sort of thing.

In addition to drug problems, there are also problems with prostitution near New Lake Elementary, including a complex of apartments used for prostitution. Winslow said,

> There was a huge complex of apartments here that were used for prostitution. So ... here one of our ladies of the evening do their hosting in those apartments, and they're known to be rented by pimps, and they live there, and they do their business there as well. So ... this is our area. I think there's definitely been a lot of work to try and improve the area, and try and build up a little bit more in terms of policing and that sort of thing. But it's still happening, and it's still not a safe place to be after four o'clock.

10 Claire Winslow, outreach coordinator at New Lake Elementary:

> Now we have our families that have grow ops in the area. Quite a few, actually, and [they] like to throw their clippings over our fence over here, and they have bags of marijuana clippings. [Why?] Well, it's actually for their benefit to hide, not putting them in to their bins [to avoid] detection of a grow op. So they'll throw it into a schoolyard. Who knows where it's come from, right, 'cause it's not like there's any kind of security cameras. But yeah, we've had that [happen] a few times.

11 The importance of social networks in providing critical support for urban poor families has been described extensively in sociological research, stretching back to Carol B. Stack's research in a housing project she calls "The Flats," published in her classic book *All Our Kin* (1974). In Katherine S. Newman's *No Shame in My Game* (1999) and *Chutes and Ladders* (2006), detailed analysis of extended family trees shows both the extensiveness and resourcefulness of the urban working and non-working poor in Harlem to utilize their networks to survive crises and secure jobs, housing, childcare, and other important essentials.

12 According to Claire Winslow,

> There's a lot of families here that don't want to move out of the area, despite some of the situations that are here, because this is their neighbourhood. This is their network. They have their neighbours that they know and trust, and they have a support network with the school and the community and community agencies that they're used to going to getting resources and support. And so I think it's where you've grown up, where you have your home, [it's] where you are used to.

13 The recent recession has had little impact on Vancouver-area housing prices; they have inflated so rapidly that owning a home remains unaffordable for many families.

14 Small (2004)

15 How are elementary students assessed to see if they are ESL? According to Angela Myers, who works as a literacy consultant for the Vancouver School Board:

> [With] the elementary kids, if you get a child coming in who plays deer in the headlights, you back up to an informal screening conversation. Looking at basic colours and things like that. And [you] kind of start with that beginning conversation. Then if it's clear that they know more, you might actually give them a reading comprehension test so see what they've got from grade 3 and up. The younger ones, they do a little writing sample and draw a picture. You get them to engage in conversation about the picture and you scribe and get some idea of what capacity they have in English, if any. Sometimes the interview is over pretty quick because they have none.

This is the process for both English speakers. She said, "English-speaking or ESL [students]. The ESL kids are then assessed. The English-speaking kids you figure out pretty quickly they don't need assessment ... In elementary, they just go into grade/age appropriate placement. The secondary system, it's a lot more complex ..."

16 Angela Myers argued:

> The practical reality in our schools is that you've got elementary schools where you've got nine part-time support teachers. So they can't even get together to talk because they are on different days and doing different things ... And the danger of that is that kids slip between the cracks.

17 Angela Myers said:

> But you also need the time to collaborate. In terms of teaching and so on, in general, if you ask me what is the cornerstone of good education, it's relationships. And here's another example of where relationships are breaking down because the structure mitigates against it. Some schools have done amazing jobs with this. Other schools they're sort of, "Take them away and fix them."

18 Angela Myers, Vancouver School Board consultant, described a handout she is making for secondary school teachers:

> What is your reaction if they never ask questions? "How do I know they don't understand? They won't ask questions." Well nobody is asking, "'Why is it they never ask questions?" or "What have you done to set up an atmosphere where it's okay to take risks and ask questions?" That's one part. And the other is, "Could it be they don't ask questions because in their culture it's tantamount to saying, you're a schmuck and you don't know what you're talking about?" And [the teachers] look at me like ... "What? Why would anybody think that?" I say, "Well, you're dealing with kids from a dozen different cultures. They've been raised in different ways."

19 Dachyshyn (2006: 256–7)

3. Coping with Challenging Students

 1 Carrier (1983) argues that the very definition of learning-disabled is a socially constructed category (not an objective category) that acts to support hierarchy and reproduce inequality. He highlights the class bias with non-conforming males as being particularly likely to be "underachieving" and thus considered learning-disabled. Behaviour and underachievement – not underlying neurological biology – are at the basis of the classification of learning-disabled, a classification that is socially determined and based, and which contributes to the reproduction of socio-economic inequality (Carrier 1983).

2 Based on the analysis of a restricted-use sample of the Educational Longitudinal Study, Anthony Peguero reports that first-generation immigrant
 students in the United States experience fear in their schools, while third-
 generation Latino students are more likely to be victims of violence in
 school. Educational Longitudinal Study (2002) in Peguero (2009). At the
 same time, Watkins and Melde (2009) found that Asian students reported
 experiencing more disorder at school than Latino students in the Children
 of Immigrants Longitudinal Study (CILS) yet performed better, and question the importance of school "order" for explaining achievement.
3 Follow-up research on the impact of the "bat man" principal, who currently runs a juvenile detention centre, found that most of the 300 students
 who were thrown out of the school for absence, tardiness, or disciplinary
 problems ended up in jail, which is hardly an outcome worth celebrating
 or emulating. (Kozol 2005: 199)
4 Visible minorities and non-native English speakers in the United States
 are disproportionately classified as special education students, including learning-disabled, emotionally disturbed, and mentally challenged.
 While some argue this is unproblematic if they receive extra resources and
 services from this designation, it is highly problematic if biased policies
 and procedures result in inappropriate and disproportionate classification because these students are denied access to the mainstream academic
 curriculum and the negative consequences of stigma and separation from
 other students. Klingner et al. (2005). Klingner et al (2005) also argue that
 improving general education, including the quality of instruction and the
 provision of educational supports, can reduce inappropriate special education classifications and reduce disproportionality. This includes teacher
 training, qualifications, addressing systematic biases against minorities,
 low SES students in assessment tools, and an emphasis on early intervention (as opposed to the "wait to fail" strategy). They propose "culturally
 responsive education systems." Data-driven policy and partnerships with
 community institutions and families are highlighted as important education system factors (Klingner et al. 2005). They recommend studying
 highly effective urban schools. Embracing culturally responsive practices,
 especially in literacy instruction, is also emphasized as important.
5 Szente and Hoot (2006: 232)
6 Dachyshyn (2006: 253)
7 Dachyshyn (2006: 254)
8 In his excellent book *Class and Schools*, Rothstein (2004) shows why
 improving curriculum and teachers won't alone be enough to improve the
 educational achievement of children from low-income families. Rothstein

(2004) documents how social class differences affect learning, from language to health. For example, low-income children are much more likely to have vision problems, dental problems (such as untreated cavities), and asthma. Children distracted by health problems will struggle to learn. Rothstein highlights how school reform cannot solve the problems of poverty and inequality alone or erase the achievement gap between black and white students, and he details specific reforms, such as universal health care in the United States, which would make a big difference in improving the educational attainment of minority youth.

9 Langhout, Rhodes, and Osborne (2004). Sustained mentoring relationships with non-parental adults have also been found to be important. Erickson, McDonald, and Elder (2009) report in a *Sociology of Education* article that mentorship – or the support of non-parental adults – has an important effect on educational success. On the one hand, advantaged students were more likely to enjoy the benefit of mentorship, yet mentorship – especially teachers as mentors – had the strongest positive effect on the educational success of youths with few resources (Erickson et al. 2009). A growing body of research supports the notion that supportive adults in the lives of youth are critically important. Suárez-Orozco, Rhodes, and Milburn (2009), for example, found in their analysis of the adaptation experiences of 408 immigrant youth in the United States from Central America, China, the Dominican Republic, Haiti, and Mexico, that supportive relationships had a mediating role in countering the "immigrant paradox" – where initial educational performance advantages erode over time in the United States – and improving the engagement and outcomes of these youth.

10 Roth et al. (1998); Rhodes (2002); Sánchez et al. (2011)

11 High mobility rates also undermine one of the theoretical premises of standardized testing as a tool to measure "school performance." With many students moving to other schools, as a result in part of gentrification, classrooms have a different set of students at the end of the year than at the beginning. This means that testing – particularly standardized testing completed only with fourth and seventh graders – can provide an inaccurate assessment of educational skills provided by these individual schools. Angela Myers, a literacy consultant for the Vancouver School Board, is convinced that transiency is a big issue for East Vancouver elementary schools. She notes that one cannot follow a student's test results from one grade to the next and assess for improvement. Because of the high turnover, they are not the same students. She says, from one year to the next "you've got a totally different clientele; how can you compare apples and oranges?"

12 See Alinsky (1971); Bobo, Kendall, and Max (2001)
13 Research points to the effectiveness of this approach in Japan (Stevenson and Stigler 1992).
14 While helping to identify these problems, teachers frequently lack the resources to solve them. Ashfield Elementary teacher Amy Peterson said,

> I think that as an educator you identify what those problems are, but that those health issues should be dealt with by the health people, right? It shouldn't be education money used for that. So if [kids] have a speech problem, that should be covered under medical and they should be getting medical services, right? [Health and learning issues] overlap, but it's not really education that's holding them back.

Amy Peterson is forced to deal with some difficult children without the skills, training, and resources needed to address their issues. She explained:

> Behaviour is something that needs to be dealt with, and I can control them. I can work with them in the classroom [and] quite often they're really happy in the classroom, but outside it's just horrendous. These kids are filled with anger. I can't do that. I'm not a psychologist. I'm not a psychiatrist. You need family counselling; that's medical, that's not educational. It affects education. It affects [kids'] ability to learn because they are so angry, but really as a teacher I can't fix that. So that's really out of my control.

15 Despite many teachers' reservations about standardized testing, many would be more likely to support it if it helped demonstrate positive educational gains. Ironically, more regular testing could be a more useful learning tool than the current fourth and seventh grade regime currently in place in British Columbia per year standardized testing regime.
16 Alexander et al. (2003)
17 Based on his analysis of market-based experiments in education, such as the Edison project, Smith concludes that, "Private education companies have consistently run into problems with teachers' unions, often failed to deliver on their high promises, and raised questions about their worthiness and credibility as worthy investments of public trust by providing their executives lavish salaries while seeking to cut instructional labor costs." (Smith 2003: 139).
   It also helps explain why superficial cross-sectional studies of the role of money in education fail to show that funding is clearly connected to learning outcomes. As described in chapter 1, urban schools with high-needs

student populations and crumbling infrastructure are compared with other schools receiving similar per-pupil funding, such as in rural areas, with much lower levels of need and more qualified teachers. The results are used to support spurious claims that per-pupil funding levels do not matter for educational outcomes. See, for example, Hanushek (1981)

18 Peterson and Howell (2002)

19 And that does not even take into account the Hawthorne effect: when a subject knows he or she is being evaluated as part of a study, he or she tends to improve performance to show the desired effect (Mayo 1949).

20 Kozol (2005). Superficial statistical similarities or controls for social class, such as the percentage receiving subsidized or free school lunches, do not address this serious evaluation issue.

21 Wood (2008)

22 According to Angela Myers, other research suggests similar results. She related a recent study that had tracked student outcomes:

> Well, the levels based on the Ministry guidelines of level one, two, three, four are put in to our computers. In [Lee Gunderson, Dennis Murphy Odo, and Reginald D'Silva's] book [*ESL (ELL) Literacy Instruction: A Guidebook to Theory and Practice*, 3rd ed.] that came out recently, they tracked secondary kids for 10 years by using the database system to see what happened to our immigrant learners. And it [caused] a lot of controversy in the news when the book first came out in the beginning of August because some huge percentage of kids seemed to "disappear" because they did not show up in the academic courses at secondary. And the question is, why not? Is it because they haven't had enough time to learn the language? Is it because the programs aren't meeting their needs? Is it because they moved somewhere else? So is it a variety of factors, and how do we figure this out?
>
> One of [Gunderson's] PhD students has actually tracked a bunch of those kids to find out how many ended up in the end completing high school. So what I'm saying is, there is data available to look longitudinally at how kids are doing and how they've progressed.

Myers noted that the findings of Lee Gunderson's research revealed that whether or not a kid was from a working poor family emerged as a key factor. She went on to describe one kind of outside support for ESL students:

> SSWs are student support workers and they're not teachers. They have been given strategies for working with kids like focusing on adolescence

or focusing on whatever age. And some of them have been specifically trained to work with [certain kinds of kids] like special needs learners. Some of them have been specifically trained to deal with adolescence and behaviour issues and so on. And they're assigned based on specific needs ... There's one group called urgent intervention workers, [who are used when] a crisis has happened. A kid is ricocheting off the walls and an urgent intervention worker goes in for six weeks to try to calm the situation down, and then they're gone and the school has to cope.

23 Szente and Hoot (2006).
24 Susan Fletcher continued,

Now we want that connectedness to extend to the school so that [the kids] feel better connected to school, so the program we run is always in collaboration with a school-based staff. All the groups [have a] family services counsellor and school-based staff because we know that we are leaving [and] we'll be gone after 10 weeks, but we want those kids to feel connected once we go, and so that's happening. We're hearing that even after the group ends those kids are going to see the area counsellor and the Youth and Family Worker and they're touching base and they're building relationships.

4. Engaging Parents and the Community

1 How important are parents for children's academic achievement? Kaufman (2004) argues that close-knit immigrant communities can facilitate educational success, but that the failure of other students to succeed in urban schools remains unexplained. Pong, Hao, and Gardner (2005) find, based on an analysis of Adolescent Health Survey data on the relationship between parenting style and social capital and school grade-point averages (GPAs) of three generations of Asian and Hispanic students in the United States, that while these factors are important for explaining aggregate performance differences between subgroups, they operate independently of other factors, such as socio-economic status, for explaining group and generational differences. At the same time, Chang and Le (2005) argue that parental factors fail to explain GPA differences for 329 Chinese, Cambodian, Laotian or Mien, and Vietnamese youth in the United States surveyed; instead they found that their attitudes towards school and how they mediated peer relationships were more important. Based on a four-year critical ethnographic study of Hong Kong–born immigrant students

in a Canadian high school, Goldstein (2003: 247), in a *Sociology of Education* article, documents how these students utilized "ethnic-sociolinguistic resources and channels, despite being de-legitimized by the school, to achieve educational and professional success." (See also Abada and Tenkorang 2009.)

2 For an excellent guide for administrators who want to actively set up partnerships between schools, families, and communities, see Epstein et al. (2008), who provides extensive support for the benefits of these partnerships based on research and detailed instructions on how to make them happen. The guide is based on working with thousands of schools across many US states, part of Johns Hopkins University's National Network of Partnership Schools (NNPS).

3 Angela Myers, a consultant to the Vancouver School Board, explained that in East Vancouver elementary schools,

> ... the parent-teacher communication issue is a complicated one. We have multicultural liaison workers, and they help often with parent-teacher interviews, but there's more to it than that because how [kids] do school is so different around the world. We make a lot of assumptions about what parents will or won't do and how they will or won't participate. In fact, we get a little annoyed if they don't participate the way we think they should. But there hasn't been any effort made to understand where they are coming from. When you come from a culture where your child is your most precious possession, and you're handing [him or her] over to this expert to deal with, and that's it – "Hands off, it's not your area of expertise" and then [you] get accused of not supporting your kids, not helping them with their homework, and so on. It's kind of like a slap in the face [to the parents, who are like] "Hey, I'm doing what I'm supposed to be doing, aren't I?"

4 Evans (2004: 187)

5 Parent Advisory Councils (PACs) are the Canadian equivalent of the Parent Teacher Association (PTA) in US schools.

6 Based on their analysis of National Longitudinal Survey of Youth (NLSY) data on US parents, Barbara Schneider and James S. Coleman found that parental involvement in children's education is shaped by three important factors: first, the parents' orientation towards education; second, their financial and social resources; and third, the opportunities provided by the schools and the community where they live (1993).

7 Lareau (2003). In her first book, *Home Advantage* (2000), Lareau found that there was no difference in the value placed on education between poor

parents and their wealthier counterparts per se, but that they did not have the same kinds of resources to engage with teachers in school.

8 Dachyshyn (2006): 259

9 Lareau (2003)

10 In her global research, Heymann (2006) captures how working parents struggle when their children get sick, for example, in the absence of family-friendly policies and programs.

11 This supports Lareau (2003)'s findings about the middle class bias of many teachers in schools with low-income and working class students.

12 Lareau (2003)

13 Susan Fletcher has had to rely on other school staff to address language challenges in some cases:

> It's really hard, because we try to recruit staff who are multilingual. But, on the other hand, they also need to have the educational background to do the job. So half of our staff has a second language. We really draw on the schools for [support]. In the school system, they have multicultural workers with a broad range of language abilities, so if there's a family referred to our program [for whom] we're not going to be able to do an intake meeting in English, we'll reach out to [school staff] to see if they'll accompany the family and provide that support. So really, the onus is on the agencies and the schools to put in those services to ensure that the families can come for that appointment.

14 Claire Winslow explained,

> There've been so many parents and, interestingly enough, we've had parents attending from other schools – three other elementary schools for sure. Some are coming from the Ashfield Elementary area, Wellington Elementary area, and someone who would actually be in the High Point Elementary catchment area. And interestingly enough, they've heard [about the club] through their connections, and so they've come here. And because Julie Rogers has a mom and tots program, they've coupled up with their friends to come over.

15 Claire Winslow explained that in terms of her coffee club,

> ... that was one of the big things we really wanted to make sure parents understood: who [the other people] are [who] spend time with their children [in their school] lives. [So that, for example], [it's not taken as such a big deal] if [those people] come and ask [the parents] to sign a consent form for education assessment. Now, that's huge – huge in terms of the

amount of interpretation that goes in to what [the form] means. I know [right] off the bat [that] if anybody [had given the form] to my [own] parents, [they] would have been like, "My kid is not crazy." [But] that's not what it means at all. So [parents who aren't engaged with school staff or familiar with school practices] make the assumption that you're trying to [assess their kids because] you think there's something wrong with them or that they're crazy. And the wall goes up. And [the] same [things happens] when you look at things like getting resources for the mental health team or counselling.

The [parents'] interpretation is, "You think there's something seriously wrong with my kid. You think [he or she] is crazy." And that's where I come back to having that relationship with that parent. [Being] able to say to the parent, "Seriously, it doesn't," [and having them believe you]. I had a parent come up and say I'm so glad you're at the high school because my daughter said she feels okay now going [to school], 'cause she knows you're going to be there.

16 At the same time as attempting to secure funding for this program, Claire Winslow said they are also trying to "better expand that [group] to be inclusive of all parents and cultures in our schools and have it be parent theme–driven. A lot of us will say, 'Well, here's a parent program, so let's put this on for the parents.' But who's asked the parents?"

17 In order to get funding to maintain and expand her school's coffee club program, Claire Winslow had to demonstrate the program's success:

It's hard because some of your main funders, they want numbers – statistics and numbers. And we deal with that as a team having to do that reporting right. But what [those reports don't] show, and [what] you strain your brain trying to figure out, [is] how to show ... [certain nuances] ... in a flow chart.

And in that measure of success, it's skewed as to what people think, but at the same time, to me, when you have an expanding or growing program, or you're getting more and more parents hearing about it [and] showing up to be a part of something, then to me that's success. Just in the sheer fact that parents are coming ... So already the parents are feeling a connection to being there, being able to have staff to connect with.

And that's the other thing: we're trying to build a connection not just to ourselves but also to the other staff around the schools. The schools are trying to invite other staff who can attend at different times to come on over and be a part of it. I've got five, four other schools other than this one, and I'm one of the connections, but to have connections with the staff who are here daily, you want those relationships to start to grow and build as well.

The coffee club meets every Wednesday from 10 a.m. to 11 a.m., although Winslow says, "I find that by the time we do things, you know, we're usually here 'til noon." On the agenda, she said "this Wednesday, we're doing a bit of … family dinner cooking, and the parents have been really eager to get involved in this and do something that's … well, a bit maybe more North American than … what for [them] would not be the norm in terms of their style of cooking, sort of thing."

18 These findings support the research by sociologist Min Zhou, who, based on ethnographic research in three immigrant neighbourhoods in Los Angeles, found that local history and context of reception helps explain differences between immigrant resources in Chinatown, Koreatown, and Pico Union (a Mexican/Central American neighbourhood). She emphasizes the importance of ethnic-based community organizing and the ethnic-specific and exclusionary access to neighbourhood-based local resources (Zhou 2009a).

19 Kerry Reynolds said she plans to build on this successful program and create a similar program for children in higher grades. She said, "We're going to have UBC [University of British Columbia] students parallel that program where they'll come with a book [and] read to the class." In this new program, the UBC students will also work one-on-one with students who failed to meet expectations on the grades 4 and 7 standardized exams.

20 Research has demonstrated the importance of these institutions for low-income families and communities (Zuberi 2006). For example, the role of these community institutions in facilitating the settlement and integration of new immigrants in to the community has begun to be recognized by researchers. In her book *Becoming a Citizen,* sociologist Irene Bloemraad examines the critical role that community institutions play in the political incorporation of immigrants in Canada and the United States (Bloemraad 2006) Likewise, the 2006 documentary *When Strangers Become Neighbours* by Giovanni Attili and University of British Columbia geography professor Leonie Sandercock, explores the important role played by programs at the Collingwood Neighbourhood House in East Vancouver in the settlement and integration of new immigrants in this community (Attili and Sandercock (2006); See also Sandercock (2004)) My previous research comparing the experiences of Vancouver and Seattle hotel workers who work as room attendants and other lower-tier positions for the same multinational chains, highlighted the important role of Vancouver's stronger public neighbourhood institutions, such as community centres, for improved the quality of life (Zuberi 2006).

21 Noguera (2003) highlights the important social welfare role played by urban schools in their communities as one of the only institutions with steady funding and resources in many high-poverty communities, going as far to call them, "the last and most enduring remnant of the social safety net for poor children in the United States." (Noguera 2003: 7). He concurs with Anyon's (1997) insights that school reform will not work unless something is done about the serious urban social dislocations that plague many high-poverty, segregated communities.

22 Additional information and the pamphlet *Ready, Set, Learn: Helping Your Preschooler Get Ready for School* can be found at: http://www.bced.gov. bc.ca/early_learning/rsl/ Accessed June 24, 2013.

23 Amy Peterson, a teacher at Ashfield Elementary, describes preschool programs as helping children begin school ready to learn:

> The challenges here are learning English. That's the major challenge. And learning how to get along with each other. A lot of these children haven't had preschool, so a lot of them were in their homes until they came to kindergarten. Now that's starting to change because the Grant Williams Neighbourhood House offers a pre-kindergarten program. So we're getting a few more kids now who do that kind of thing, and there's a few other parents who have more money now, and they're putting their kids in to daycare or putting them in to preschool. So they've had a little bit of experience with working as a group. But a lot of kids used to come to us and still do come [without preparation], that's their first experience away from home. So kindergarten [for them] is a startling experience.

24 Reynolds et al. (2001)

25 Schweinhart and Weikart (1990); Barnett and Boocock (1998); Barnett (2000)

26 For wonderful examples of these kinds of partnerships, see the collection edited by Johnson et al. (2005), which profiles urban schools and initiatives that partner with local community organizations, parents, and other organizations to improve the education of children.

27 As described by Dryfoos (1994) in her book *Full-Service Schools*.

5. Addressing Needs and Supporting Resiliency

1 Kozol (2005: 199)

2 Education can be viewed as embodying competing ideological values: democratic vs. market values (Smith 2003).

3 For an excellent critique of the introduction of corporate influence in schools in the United States, see Kenneth J. Saltman's (2000) book *Collateral Damage*.

4 Of particular interest and concern were what kinds of programs and reforms aided in the early mastery of basic literacy and numeracy skills. As supported by findings elsewhere, this study demonstrated that resources matter and that the funding of programs to meet the special needs of at-risk students at diverse urban schools is crucial for ensuring that all children master literacy and numeracy skills in their early elementary school years.

5 As well as children from low-income families coming to school hungry, as found by Annette Lareau (2003), students from low-income families in the United States often have difficulty affording even basic school supplies and minimal fees for field trips.

6 According to Angela Myers, a consultant for East Vancouver schools, different kinds of specialists, supported by the Inner City Schools Project, including support teachers for ESL, LAC [Learning Assistance Centre) teachers, and special needs teachers, are now known by the catch-all term "resource teachers."

7 Resource teachers also liaise with the community, with the goal of mobilizing resources and other kinds of supports for at-risk students. As described in chapter 5, the Inner City designation attracts offers from the community and other organizations to get involved and help children at the school.

8 Kershaw and Anderson (2009)

9 Alexander et al. (2003: 260)

10 The Canadian Press (2008)

11 The economic crisis has stalled, if not permanently derailed, the implementation of the full-day kindergarten proposals in British Columbia. This is a clear example of the short-sightedness on the part of some policy makers, who should understand the positive future impact that this investment will have for many vulnerable children in the province. The policy barriers here are familiar but worth noting. First, the costs of spending on early childhood education are immediate, while many of the benefits won't be realized until some point in the future. Second, expanding kindergarten to full-day is expensive, like many other universal programs, yet it is precisely the universal nature of the policy that makes it most likely to continue to generate popular political support and be implemented in a way that will actually benefit poor children. For example, a quick look at the underfunding of Head Start preschool programs in the United States, which are targeted towards low-income children, compared to universal

early childhood education programs in France or Scandinavian countries illustrates this phenomenon.

12 According to Angela Myers, one school in East Vancouver has dramatically improved through the strategic deployment of its skilled teaching and resource staff. She described the school as, "One of the east-side schools that [has] Inner City status, [a] fairly small school. They have a high transiency rate." She said,

> They have the benefit of having had a stable staff for a long time and they have had, by sheer luck, support people who have specialist training in two of the three areas. So they have done what I think needs to be done. They've said "Okay, what's this school about? It's about the kids. It's not about your class or my class or your schedule or my schedule. We're going to plot the kids for the whole school that have the [special] needs first, and group them in appropriate ways to meet their needs. Then we'll build classes around that and then we'll assign teachers to those classes."

This is in contrast to the traditional way that schools tend to organize classrooms, as Angela Myers explained,

> So [the administrators] have turned the whole thing upside down because usually what happens is the teachers are assigned their classes and we try to balance it. Not too many of this and not too many of that, which has value and they do that too. But they do it the other way around. "Okay, we need a critical group of six kids who have these kinds of needs." Ideally they'd be together so we can pull them off together. Okay, what if we put them two groups of three? So it's not too tough on one teacher in adjacent classrooms. So it's easier to assemble the group for specific work or there's a joining door between the two rooms so we can actually do it as a double ... I've actually gotten them to document how they set this up.

Angela Myers would like to see more schools follow a similar model in East Vancouver. She said,

> And it's good. I would love to have more schools begin to do that. But why does it work for them? Because these are the people who are well-grounded. They know their stuff. They've been there for years. They know the kids and they say, "Okay, excuse me Mrs. or Ms. Administrator, this is all about kids, [would] you agree?" "Yes. Okay. This is how we think it should be set up. We will talk to the staff. We will sell them on this idea and they did."

Angela Myers particularly credits the support teachers. She said,

> The support teachers. The ones who, because they've been there a good,
> long time, they feel very passionate about their particular areas of exper-
> tise and you've got people who have solid training and they know what
> they're about. They've been doing it for a while. They know what works
> and what doesn't. And they're saying, "We're doing kids a disservice
> fragmenting ourselves. Let's turn the whole thing upside down and start
> over." And I'd love to see that catch on.

Again there is a challenge of measuring success based on this reform.
A more qualitative approach rather than hard data is telling teachers that the
new focus on meeting students' needs is working. Angela Myers explained,

> They haven't particularly been documenting the outcomes of the
> approach. They know anecdotally that this is working for them. It's just
> the way they have set up the whole process of dividing up kids into
> classes and assigning teacher and so on. They basically said, "Okay, let's
> start with the kids. Here [are] the kids. Here are their needs. Here's the
> chart on the wall of the whole staff, of all the kids, and now let's sort
> them into reasonable groupings." So that we can support them opti-
> mally. And then we'll worry about who's going to teach what later.

One result of this non-traditional arrangement of students is that the first
week of school can be a little more chaotic. She said, "Well, I'm sure there's
a lot of negotiating going on in the back rooms and so on, but they've
made it work for the last several years so."

13 I speculate that the success of this visual approach at East Harcourt Elementary might relate in part to the school having a higher number of students with middle class backgrounds as compared to other East Vancouver
elementary schools.

14 Other kinds of school-based programs were described as being important
for the schools. Teacher Amy Peterson said this about the programs offered
at Ashfield Elementary: "Well, we've had things like chess clubs. We've
had a girls club. We've had sports activities, things that happen in the gym
after school. One of the teachers does a floor hockey program after school.
So there are tons of different things going on."

15 The challenge of accurately assessing the success of programs is discussed
in greater depth in chapter 7.

16 According to Principal Katherine Drucker of Ashfield Elementary,

> Going back to social/emotional [development], I don't know if the other
> administrators mentioned the programs in this school. One is called

Second Step. Everyone in the Vancouver School Board can be trained. Our school board offers training for that and it's a kit that is about anger management, and how to deal with [it] ... and problem solving. And then also the school board offers programs [about] personal safety. So we have one at kindergarten talk about touching, and Feeling Yes, Feeling No. I don't know if you're familiar with those programs, but right through the grade levels, there are those programs and teachers are encouraged to do [them] every year.

17 Another reason to adopt peer mediation and other programs to improve empathy and conflict resolution early in the education curriculum is that, "... the more severely students were harassed, the greater the likelihood that they suffered from psychological problems or academic difficulties ..." (Boocock and Scott 2005: 139) Harassed students are also more likely to report harassing students.

18 See Gordon (2007)

19 One person felt the program should be modified so that the babies adopted in the classroom were from similar ethno-cultural minority groups as the students in East Vancouver classrooms. Angela Myers has attempted to improve the Roots of Empathy program by getting more ethnic minority parents and babies "adopted" by Vancouver classrooms:

> Roots of Empathy is an interesting one. I heard about [the [program] years ago, but when I was in the classroom I didn't get the opportunity [to use it]. I wasn't teaching the right grade or something. And when I got into this position I had the opportunity to take the Roots of Empathy training because I didn't have to worry about a sub and so I could just take the time to do that, and just catch up on my own. And I thought, "Okay ... what I'm seeing with Roots of Empathy is all these white kids and white moms and white dads in schools, where there's hardly a white face. This is not right." So I took the training. I took the video explaining what it's all about to the multicultural liaison workers' monthly meeting and said "I have an idea here. I need your help." And [I] showed them what it was, told them about it. And I said, "You know me. You know I teach ESL. You know I will help an immigrant adult woman who is interested make sure that she's understood and lead [her] through it and hold [her] hand and whatever. Find me some moms who would like to do Roots of Empathy," and I've been doing it ever since.

20 A formal evaluation of the Roots of Empathy program is headed by Professor Kimberly Schonert-Reichl at the University of British Columbia's

School of Education, with the support of the Human Early Learning
Partnership (HELP).

21 Coleman (1990)

22 MacLeod (2009)

23 Some East Vancouver elementary schools lost their Inner City designation
and its associated funding support as a result of the way gentrification
changed the demographics of their student populations. In these cases,
some staff argued that as their schools still had many needy students, losing these vital resources had deleterious consequences. Principal Katherine
Drucker described losing Inner City status as devastating for Ashfield
Elementary. "Unfortunately they lost it the year I came, so they lost staffing, they lost money ... All the staff [were asking], 'But where's the money
for [this]? Where's the money for that?' [only to be continually told] 'There
isn't any, it's gone.' We lost a full-time Youth and Family Worker. So we felt
the impact," she explained.

24 The BC government distributes gaming revenues to support non-profit
organizations and to benefit extracurricular activities in schools.

25 According to Angela Myers, consultant to the Vancouver School Board,
before that time, the ESL pilot project had impressive results, even attracting international attention. "We had people from all over North America
and England and Australia coming to see what we were doing," Myers
said. Yet, as in the case of many successful experimental programs in
education, many are simply not replicated due to a lack of funding. She
explained,

> And then very soon after the money ran out [the program] started to
> peter away. And then there [were] cutbacks from the government level
> and basically the positions were cut one by one, and it got to the point
> where in the middle of the 1990s, there wasn't even a single ESL consul-
> tant anymore, even though our ESL numbers continued to grow.

26 Angela Myers feels confident they now recognize the value of ESL support
at a district level, and that these positions will continue to be funded. "Our
understanding is, the writing on the wall appears to be that they are not
going to cut back to one [ESL support teacher] again," she said. "So that's
really good news."

27 According to Angela Myers, she must often work with teachers to help
them understand why they are experiencing a particular challenge teaching literacy to ESL students. For example, she has trained teachers to
understand how grammatical differences across languages can affect
children's sentence structure in English. According to Myers, the teachers

often reply, "Oh, I wish I had known that!" or "I've been beating my head against the wall because this kid [is] having this particular grammar problem."

28 Angela Myers said,

> And we used to have a very strong district pro-d[evelopment] program ... You could do cooperative learning and have two or three full days with release time to really focus in on those ideas. Well, all that got cut. And in fact, we're having a very unfriendly discussion at the moment about that because we all want to do in-service [training] with our very limited budget, just as district staff people and the union [are] saying you can't ask people to make internal arrangements and not give them a sub. Which means we can just cut most of what we want to do because we can't afford to have the subs. Or we can say, "Okay, I'm sorry, we can only pay for 10 people. The rest of you are out of luck." I mean, that doesn't make sense. It's a discussion that we need to continue. I understand the issues on both sides of it, but we're caught between a rock and a hard place. And so are the teachers who want the training.

29 Alexander et al. (2003: 260)
30 As Boocock and Scott (2005: 260) point out, "... after three decades and generally positive reviews, Head Start programs [in the United States] are still available to only a fraction of the children who are eligible and rarely deliver all the services as designed. Universal programs also reach children from middle-income families who do not qualify for targeted programs but who tend to lag behind wealthier children in social and cognitive skills ... The highly regarded *ecolles maternelles* attended by virtually all French children ... are a strong case in point."

6. Standardized Testing

1 Kozol (2005: 122)
2 Noguera and Wing (2006: 7)
3 Even upgrading and maintaining the aging infrastructure of older schools in North American inner cities generally requires more resources to heat and repair than newer suburban schools (Kozol 1992).
4 For many poignant examples of how high-stakes testing is manipulated and corrupts as well as directly causes harm to children and the education system, see Nichols and Berliner's (2007) book *Collateral Damage*. These problems go well beyond "teaching to the test," and include cheating.

Those interested in reforming standards and accountability need to keep in mind Campbell's Law, which posits that the greater emphasis put on a measure, the more it will become distorted, twisted, and invalid (Nichols and Berliner 2007). Nichols and Berliner also argue for using more holistic measures for accountability.

5 Greene (2008: 3)
6 Downey, von Hippel, and Hughes (2008)
7 Johnson (2008)
8 Wagner (2008) argues that the problem with No Child Left Behind high-stakes testing, despite the intention, is that it reinforces the reliance on memorization as learning in the classroom, and it further moves public education in the United States away from teaching critical thinking skills and other higher-order thinking skills, which are highly desired by and considered essential to corporate employers. The rapid advancements in education and skills in other countries threaten the future economic well-being of the United States, unless the public education system improves. In line with Robert Reich, and inspired by the insights of *The World is Flat* by Thomas Friedman (2006), Wagner states:

> "It is no longer enough to teach most kids the Three R's and have them memorize the parts of speech, all of the state capitols, and the dates and generals of famous battles. And we can no longer tolerate large numbers of kids dropping out of school or only graduating with minimal skills. The days of well-paid unskilled or semiskilled work are over in this country, due to the forces of global competition. As we know, any job that can be routinized is being automated or offshored. Increasingly, the only decent jobs that will remain in this country will go to those who know how to continuously improve products or services or create entirely new ones – the knowledge workers of the twenty-first century." (Wagner 2008: 256).

He focuses on high schools, and finds that in elementary schools, "we at least agree on the skills that all students must learn: basic reading, writing, and computational skills." Zhou (2009b) argues, from a global perspective, that one of the most negative consequences of the standardized testing regime brought in by No Child Left Behind, is the expansion of standardization and increasing homogeneity in education, which works against the current diversity provided by the American education system – a great strength that he argues many countries, like China, are trying to emulate.

9 Assaf (2006: 158)
10 Horn (2005: 337)

11 For a discussion of the empirical evidence demonstrating this shocking practice in US schools, see the popular book *Freakonomics* (Levitt and Dubner, 2005). Also see Nichols and Berliner (2007) and Kozol (2005).

12 Giese and Alphonso (2013) See also the *International Human Development Report, Canada* (2014); Sahlberg (2011); Després et al. (2013); and Hargreaves and Shirley (2012).

13 Kohn (1999); Kozol (2005)

14 Smith (1996); Kelly (1995)

15 Proponents of publishing test score data at the school level argue that parents' have a right to know the data. They believe that if parents can use the data to make choices about school enrolment within the public system or private alternative, then that will pressure schools to improve their performance and scores in the hopes of maintaining enrolment. (At the same time, school choice also results in cream-skimming that hurts some schools). While this regime does cause stress, it does not appear to actually improve performance.

16 The BC Teachers' Federation – the provincial teacher's union – recommended that parents keep their children home on testing day as a tactic to fight the implementation of the FSA testing regime.

17 While interesting evidence, it is also a fairly well-known and established phenomenon.

18 Economist David Johnson (2008) completed this reanalysis for the standardized test score data in the provinces of Ontario and British Columbia.

19 Assaf (2006)

20 Kozol (2005: 207)

21 As the data would be collected from a random sample of schools in the province, then it would only provide "data" for province-wide achievement in literacy, numeracy, and math overall, and it could not be extrapolated to the school level (with the exception of the schools randomly tested).

22 Hillocks (2002) in Lofty (2006: 235)

23 Noguera (2008: 228)

24 For more detail, see Hertzman (2002).

25 Unfortunately this program was cancelled after the election of a minority Conservative government and replaced with $100 monthly rebates for parents of young children.

26 Giese and Alphonso (2013)

27 As Suárez-Orozco et al. (2008: 92) argue, "Many newcomer immigrants enter poor and segregated schools, and are consequently at a significant disadvantage as they strive to adapt to a new culture, learn a new

language, master the necessary skills to pass high-stakes tests, accrue graduation credits, get into college, and attain the skills needed to compete in workplaces shaped by the new global economy."

28 Delpit (1995: xiii)

7. Conclusion

1 Giese (2011)
2 Adamuti-Trache, Bluman, and Tiedje (2012)
3 Vancouver Foundation (2013).
4 My research also contributes to a debate in the sociological literature. Determinists who posit that schools simply act as a "trading post," where privileged children trade their advantages in cultural capital in order to be tracked into elite and professional job positions, approach schools as institutions in an overly simplistic and functional manner (MacLeod 2009).

In the United States, what is needed is massive public investment, particularly by states and the federal government, to improve urban public schools. Indeed, the only faint praise for the mostly standardized testing focus of the No Child Left Behind policy in the United States is that it has resulted in the much needed injection of additional federal resources into public education and urban public schools. Yet this extra support has come at a high cost in terms of the emphasis on "accountability" based on standardized test results.

One of the most challenging questions I have been asked during this project – from friends, colleagues, and new acquaintances – is simply, "So what did you find? What are your solutions for improving urban education?" Initially, I'd hoped that perhaps I would arrive at this neat list or sound bite sometime later in the process of analysing the data. Eventually though, I concluded that there is no easy takeaway lesson or answer from the results of my research. Indeed, the question itself is problematic because of the underlying assumptions of causality and the simplicity of viewing "school performance" through the lens of standardized test score results.

Yes, early literacy matters. Yes, all children can learn. Yes, meeting basic needs is important. Yes, one-on-one tutoring and other supports help address the needs of challenging students. Yes, principals and teachers have different styles and strengths, as well as leadership styles; some are even better at their jobs than others. Yes, standardized tests are helpful at diagnosing associations between socio-economic factors and educational equality, but they are a lot less helpful at improving education or identifying what factors make a school "successful." Certainly, qualitative methods and diagnostic ethnography can help get inside the "black box" to understand dynamics within schools, but sometimes what is found inside the school is so wondrously and beautifully complex that it does not reveal previously unspecified reified variables.

The diagnostic ethnography approach exposes a system, with institutions and organizations, operating in synchronized and discordant ways, and it exposes stories about challenges and the ways these challenges have or have not been met. It reveals differences in programs and differences in the ways programs are implemented. In this case, though, it revealed more similarities than differences. It revealed common challenges and a set of common approaches, which appeared to be working with varying degrees of success, more often related to the scope of the challenge and resources available to meet these challenges than anything as straightforward as just leadership.

5 Peterson and Howell (2002)
6 Coleman (1990)
7 For a dynamic debate on the evidence around the impact of class size on learning between Alan B. Krueger and Eric A. Hanushek, see Mishel and Rothstein (2002).
8 One of the leading proponents of the small schools movement is Deborah Meier (1995).
9 Tyack and Cuban (1997). They also importantly argue that reformers should remind themselves of the democratic purposes of the public education system.
10 Stevenson and Stigler (1992)
11 Slavin and Madden (2001)
12 Angela Myers began an online course to help provide some of this training. She explained,

> One of the reasons I created my online course was to try to help with some of that. So I did ... I do that sort of thing and then I basically give all those students my e-mail and if you are running into trouble ... Well, one teacher actually felt so guilty when I said "Two hours, you want me to tell them everything about ESL?" She said, "We'll do it so sessions are one two hour, one three hour." So that's the best. And there's an ESL component in their pre-service training, but that component is one week, which means two classes. So it's five hours. It's just not good enough because some changes need to happen there big time.

Teachers and teachers-in-training are clamouring for increased training in this area in particular. Angela Myers said,

> Well, we actually had an interesting meeting, where we had this forum where we had the teacher training people, people from language and literacy, people from the district, and teachers in training who had got to go on their practicum do a little discussion forum about how should teacher ed[ucation] be changed? And I was very pleased when one of the ones that was in my online course stood up and said, "You are not preparing us for what the reality is out there, especially if we are going to the Lower Mainland schools, which most people do, if they are training here. And this is just not good enough!" And she was very articulate. And she said it better than it coming from anybody else who were stakeholders and had their own axes to grind. So it was quite interesting to listen to her because she was a more mature teacher. She wasn't brand new out of high school. She had some life experience under her belt and kids of her own.

13 Angela Myers said,

> The other piece is in service. The reality is we've got all these teachers here with the best will in the world [who] haven't got the appropriate training to do the best job they can and we need to have the time and the money to train them during school time. Not afternoons, evenings, and weekends; that's not fair.

14 Smith and Noble (1995)
15 Policies in British Columbia and other Canadian provinces are more equitable than school funding policies in the United States that link the property tax base to per-pupil school funding, which is then only partly mitigated by supplemental state and federal funding. This calculated inequality is extremely unfair to economically disadvantaged school districts, and underfunding has devastating consequences for the quality of public education at segregated urban schools that largely serve visible minority pupils in the United States. These fiscal inequities create an almost apartheid-like system of public education, where many visible minorities from low-income families attend urban public schools that fail to give them the critical basic skills they need if they are to have a chance of succeeding in American society.
16 Slavin and Madden (1989: 4–12)
17 Slavin et al. (1994: 639–47); Of course, someone like Jonathan Kozol would retort that while the wealthy get wonderful public schools with excited,

engaged, and fabulously trained teachers, the poor get SFA (Success for All). (Kozol 2005).

18 Along with labour economist Philip Oreopoulos, I am working with the Regent Park Community Health Centre and the Regent Park Pathways to Education staff to complete a mixed-methods study of the program and its impact on youth and the community.

19 The City of Toronto just took a major step in the wrong direction with a decision to cut funding and eliminate subsidized and free student lunches to needy students.

20 Alexander et al. (2003: 13)

21 In the United States, these policies would include state and federal programs that provide health insurance, greater income support and tax credits for working poor families, and full funding for the Head Start program for young children. One of the critical foundational reforms for the United States to be able to achieve this level of social policy reform is the passage and implementation of the *Employee Free Choice Act*, which would dramatically reduce the barriers for workplace unionization that currently exist under National Labor Relations Board regulations.

22 Berliner (2006) argues that poverty is the most important challenge facing poorly performing schools; reducing poverty is linked to strong increases in school performance by children.

23 Anyon (2005)

24 Ungerleider (2003)

25 Anyon (2005: 2)

26 Sizer (2004: 32)

27 As in the highly publicized case of Vancouver's Grandview Elementary, which experienced dramatic gains in passing rates in standardized test scores in the second year of testing, followed by subsequent declines, although the outcome was still far above the dismal performance in the first year.

28 One important way principals lead is in the building of linkages between schools, parents, and the community: "A successful principal reaches out to parents and makes links with community organizations, creating strategic alliances with local businesses to invest needed resources in their schools." (Suárez-Orozco et al. 2008: 89)

29 Suárez-Orozco et al. (2008: 88) argue that, "Ample research demonstrates that effective schools have high expectations for all students regardless of their backgrounds; respect for students' heritage cultures and languages; and a safe, orderly school climate." They find that too many immigrant

students in the United States attend schools that are highly segregated by race, poverty, and linguistic segregation.

30 Alexander et al. (2003: 259)

31 Alexander et al. (2003: 260)

32 Corbett et al. (2002) focus intensively on teacher practices and their adoption of a "no excuses" approach to helping children from low-income and disadvantaged backgrounds excel in school, based on fieldwork in schools in a Midwestern US city and a second city on the Eastern seaboard. Based on interviews with students at six Philadelphia schools, Wilson and Dickenson Corbett (2001) conclude that what's missing from too many reforms is, "an underlying belief that all children can succeed and that it is the schools' responsibility to ensure that this happens." (Wilson and Dickenson Corbett, 2001: 117) While important, their emphasis on teacher attitude – and bias against professional development in best practices, programs, and policies – ignores the structural changes and support required to achieve desired attitude changes. High expectations must be structurally supported through resources at all levels.

33 Giroux (2004)

34 Based on their longitudinal study of 400 foreign-born immigrant youth in the United States, (Suárez-Orozco et al. (2008: 89) found that, "… most of the newcomer children in our sample attended schools that fell far short of these ideals. In fact, most of these children attended schools that not only obstructed learning and engagement but also were, in many ways, toxic to healthy learning and development."

35 As argued by Karl Alexander and colleagues: "It is important to recognize that most 'school problems' do not originate there. Low achievement, underachievement, and other problems reach public attention in schools, but these problems trace mainly back to resource shortfall in children's home and community environments." (Alexander et al. 2003: 259)

36 Bowles and Gintis (1976); Willis (1981)

37 See Zuberi (2006, 2013).

38 Grant (2011)

39 International Human Development Indicators Country Profile: Canada. (2013).

40 Based on analysis of the National Survey of Youth 1979 using HLM and propensity scores and published in the *American Sociological Review*, Brand and Xie (2010) found that individuals in the United States who were the least likely to graduate from university are also those who benefit the most. This "negative selection hypothesis" – in contrast to the perspective that those who are already privileged benefit the most from graduating

from college – highlights the critical importance of improving the successful transition of visible minority youth from low-income families to postsecondary education and graduation.

41 In this domain, Canada appears to be better off than the United States. The Pew Charitable Trusts Economic Mobility Project recently published a report by economics professor Miles Corak titled *Chasing the Same Dream, Climbing a Different Ladder: Economic Mobility in Canada and the United States*, which presented empirical evidence that intergenerational economic mobility is much higher in Canada – indeed as much as three times higher – than in the United States. The report suggests that levels of intergenerational father-son mobility (a traditional measure) in Canada are greater than even in Sweden, with its social democratic welfare state, and more similar to the other highest-mobility Scandinavian countries than the United States, which has much lower levels of social mobility. Particularly noteworthy is the finding that children in families of the lowest- and highest-income quintiles in Canada were more likely to move up or down in the socio-economic hierarchy than those in the United States (Corak 2009).

42 Bowles and Gintis (1976)

43 It may also attract innovative, "job creators," such as the symbolic analysts as defined by Robert Reich in the book *Work of Nations* or the creative class gurus as extolled by Richard Florida in his book *The Creative Class* (Reich 1992; Florida 2004). These bright stars help create new kinds of jobs for others – perhaps even good jobs – particularly for those with skills.

44 McLaran (1980, 1995, 2003)

45 Suárez-Orozco et al. (2008: 2)

46 Evidence for this can be seen in the closing gap between racialized minorities and whites. The good news is that according to Fry (2007) in an *International Migration Review* article, immigrant students' school performance in the United States has been improving, even beyond what would be expected based on the increasing educational background and lower poverty rates among immigrants; this includes a 43% decline in drop-out rates among Mexican youths during the 1990s.

According to a review article by Grace Koa and Jennifer S. Thompson published in the *Annual Review of Sociology*, racial and ethnic minority children in the United States have been closing the gap in academic achievement with non-minority children by every available measure. Of course, serious gaps remain, particularly in the achievement of African-American, Hispanic, and Native American children compared to white and Asian-American children (Kao and Thompson 2003).

Despite progress and some positive trends, according to Pedro Noguera in *The Trouble with Black Boys*, "urban schools in the United States are the backwater of public education, and their continued failure blends easily with the panorama of pathologies afflicting the inner-city and its residents." (Noguera 2008: 229)

Indeed, the substandard public schools in US inner cities should be viewed as an example of what sociologist Eduardo Bonilla-Silva (2006) would characterize as "racism without racists"; the poor quality of education offered by these schools for urban poor minorities drastically curtails economic opportunities and life chances for minority youth, even when individuals do not generally explicitly use Jim Crow–era language. The No Child Left Behind Act in the United States purportedly aims to address these issues; yet its effects so far have been to label and further stigmatize urban schools with large numbers of visible minority and low income students, without providing the financial resources required for these schools to meet the needs of their students. It also shifts blame onto the schools and their leaders, and away from the central issue of racial and class segregation as well as the racial inequalities and discrimination that lie at the root of these disparities.

47 Portes and Rumbaut (1996, 2001)
48 Based on an analysis of data from the Children of Immigrants Longitudinal Study (CILS), Kroneberg (2008) argues that traditional dichotomies proposed by segmented assimilation theorists of supportive immigrant communities and racialized minority oppositional cultures are incorrect. Instead, his findings suggest that ethnic community social capital with regard to education varies between groups, in line with socio-economic resources and aspirations.
49 Based on interviews with 68 low-income youth in Yonkers, NY, Carter (2005) challenges the conception of an oppositional culture and its focus on delinquency and poor performance in school (as argued by education anthropologist John Ogbu and others). Instead Carter posits that youth embrace a much more varied, and complex, set of outlooks, values, and practices, in response to their perception of opportunities. She also brings in the overlooked aspect of gender as an important and understudied factor, in light of the "feminization" of academic achievement. She challenges the simplistic way that "oppositional culture" is deployed as an explanatory variable to explain the educational achievement gap, in part because students can possess different kinds of cultural capital. She also highlights the survey evidence that shows that minority youth place a similar value on education as do other youth. (Carter 2005: 12) Researchers also focus

heavily on the negative or maladaptive features of minority youth culture, without examining the "positive functions" played by these "styles and tastes."

50 Kao and Thompson (2003)

51 Fernández-Kelly and Konzcal (2005)

52 Indeed, some empirical evidence presented by Boyd (2002) in an article published in the *International Migration Review* suggests that segmented assimilation does not appear to be an issue in Canada, as compared to the United States, based on analysis of statistics that suggest children of visible minority immigrants in Canada have greater educational attainment than other groups. In terms of explaining the difference, she points to differences in immigrant demographics and the lack of what she calls a large racially identifiable "underclass" in Canadian cities. While these explanations likely explain some of the differences, she ignores other potentially important factors, including greater equality of public education funding in Canada and social policies differences that I discuss extensively in my book *Differences That Matter* (Zuberi 2006).

53 The findings support the conclusion of Adam Gamoran (2001) on educational inequality in the United States in terms of race and class. Like Gamoran, the findings of the *Determinants of School Success* study suggests the importance of maintaining current programs as well as implementing new initiatives that reduce educational inequality.

54 Baker and LeTendre (2005)

55 Baker and LeTendre (2005)

56 See Wagner (2008) and Hira and Hira (2008).

57 While some argue that private schools offer more superior education than public schools, the research evidence casts doubt on these claims. Based on case studies of 16 schools in California, Benveniste et al. (2003) found that public and private schools teaching similar student populations are not systematically different in the ways assumed, providing support to those who argue that selection effects help explain better test score performance, for example (Benveniste et al. 2003). The socio-economic background of the students was the most important factor: "Inner-city private schools shared more characteristics with public schools in low-income communities than with affluent suburban private schools." (Benveniste et al. 2003: xiii).

58 Lipman (2008: 46)

59 Segregated schools in the United States are failing children of colour (Fruchter 2007). Fruchter (2007) argues that talk of a "broken" public education system is really a guise for introducing market interests and forces into education. While much of public education is performing well, urban

public schools are clearly a major problem. He argues that only grassroots organizing and non-profit groups can hold urban school systems accountable for reducing the achievement gap will help improve the educational achievement of minority youth (Fruchter 2007).

60 Although the findings of my research support the conclusions of the effective schools research literature, and many of the same characteristics emerged as important factors for success, the findings fall in the middle of the overly deterministic perspective put forward by James Coleman and Christopher Jencks that students' background characteristics alone determine their own academic achievement and schools don't matter and that of the effective schools researchers that act as if school characteristics alone can overcome the deleterious consequences of poverty, segregation, and social exclusion.

From these two extreme poles, with passionate actors on both sides (from diverse ideological perspectives) – used to support policies ranging from vouchers to maintaining the status quo – clearly student achievement is linked to personal, family, school, community, policy, and broader contextual factors (not to mention luck).

Methodology Appendix

1 Saltman (2007)
2 Saltman (2007)
3 CBC News (2007)
4 Saltman (2007)
5 Ligaya (2007)
6 Saltman (2007)
7 Saltman (2007)
8 Alonso and Goodwin (2008). "Lock-down: Metal Detectors, surveillance cameras, uniformed inmates, uniformed armed guards, chain-link buzz-in security systems – countless urban schools resemble prisons." (Saltman 2000: 86)
9 CBC News (2008)
10 Based on three years of fieldwork in a west coast school in the United States, Ferguson (2001) traces how 11- and 12-year-old black boys are socialized by schools into institutionalized incarceration, by visits to the "punishing room" and by being singled out as being at risk and told a cell awaits them with their name on it.
11 Kozol (2005: 163)

12 This finding is in line with the research literature, such as Ma and Klinger (2000), who employed Hierarchical Linear Modelling (HLM) to test the role of individual and school-level socio-economic factors on sixth grade academic achievement in math, reading, and writing.

13 By comparing statistical outliers, the project aims to get inside the empirical "black box" of school-level differences to explain why these cases are deviating from predicted outcomes based on regression analysis. In other words, this project proposes to use qualitative methods to go beyond the numbers and explore differences in achievement test outcomes from an "on the ground" perspective.

14 The Human Early Learning Partnership's (HELP) Early Development Community Asset Mapping Project (CAMP) at the University of British Columbia (UBC) (Hertzman et al. 2002)

15 Interviews with administrators, principals, and parents at these schools were supplemented with interviews with literacy consultants and others who work at a district level or in programs that span several elementary schools.

16 Although I didn't realize it at the time, my research reflected a classic tradition in education literature that emerged in response to the *Coleman Report* and Christopher Jencks' arguments about the predominant effect of student family background for explaining student achievement, and claims that "schools don't matter." In response, an "effective schools" research movement emerged, led by Ronald R. Edmonds as well as Larry Lezotte and Wilbur Brookover, that emphasized school-level factors such as effective leadership, high expectations, an emphasis on teaching basic skills, and safe school environment, that were argued to be important for student achievement (Marzano 2003; see http://www.effectiveschools. com/). This research often looked at exemplary or outlier schools in terms of achievement for insights about which school-level factors made a difference. For example, Levine and Lezotte (1990) compared case studies of outlier schools – top 25% vs. bottom 25% – and pointed to similar school-level factors, but also included staff development, parent involvement, and monitoring student progress.

17 Although differences exist cross-nationally as a result of policy differences in the health care, labour, and social welfare policy regimes, which result in greater hardships for the US urban poor as compared to their Canadian counterparts (Zuberi 2006).

18 Zou (2002). The qualitative approach has some inherent weaknesses, which are important to acknowledge, as they are important for the reader

to reflect on when reading and assessing the findings. Although the relatively small sample size, compared to survey research, prevents generalizing the findings of this research with statistical significance, the data clearly reveal patterns in responses that would most likely also emerge in any potential replication of the study. What is gained by the qualitative methodological approach over a larger survey sample is depth. The insights in to the black box of the school go beyond what we can identify simply as variables in a regression analysis. Yet this does not mean that some of the findings cannot be triangulated and tested utilizing available quantitative data. That is why I view both research approaches as largely compatible and believe the combination of approaches yields the most nuanced, rich, and valid findings.

19 This was a snowball sampling approach, in that it led to recommendations from the people interviewed, who suggested others who they felt would add important information for the study.

20 Parents who participated in the interviews received $20 to compensate them for their time and any expenses related to completing the interview, such as parking or childcare.

21 The interview transcripts and reflection notes for fieldwork were compiled and the thousands of pages of data analysed with the help of Qualitative Social Research's *NVivo8* software. The analysis focused on identifying emergent patterns and themes in the interviews. Occasionally, dissonant views and opinions emerged, providing unique insights. When I present these here, they are clearly described as such.

22 Despite the enthusiasm and support of the research branch of the Vancouver School Board for my research, I faced initial challenges when it came to accessing certain schools. One of my first dilemmas was: What do you do when the principals of schools that are classified as successful quickly open their doors, while the administration at schools classified as experiencing challenges simply don't respond? When I followed up, many of the principals' support staff in the schools experiencing challenges replied that they were over-researched and flooded by well-meaning academics with their investigative lenses. Eventually, other channels (such as in one case, the personal connections of my graduate research assistant) opened the door at some of the schools that initially ignored or turned down my invitation to participate in the study. My second dilemma was: What do you do when successful schools turn out to look very different in terms of student composition than the other schools in the study, as was the case with one of the first schools I studied? Another dilemma: What happens when a school goes from being successful to average and back again in

a short time period? In this case, the challenges that emerged from trying to achieve the proposed research design ultimately drove some of the
major findings about the adequacy of using standardized testing to explain
school "performance."

23 He also gave me a good tip: to look at the differences in the *implementation* of programs at different schools rather than just the presence of
them; however, in the fieldwork this did not emerge as a major difference
between the schools studied.

24 This supports an insight by author Alfie Kohn in his book *The Schools Our
Children Deserve* (1999).

25 Johnson (2008)

References

Abada, Teresa, and Eric Y. Tenkorang. 2009. "Pursuit of University Education among the Children of Immigrants in Canada: The Roles of Parental Human Capital and Social Capital." *Journal of Youth Studies* 12 (2): 185–207. http://dx.doi.org/10.1080/13676260802558870.

Adamuti-Trache, Maria, George Bluman, and Ian Tiedje. 2012. "Student Success in First-Year University Physics and Mathematics Courses: Does the High-school Attended Make a Difference?" *International Journal of Science Education.* http://dx.doi.org/10.1080/09500693.2012.667168.

Adler, Patricia A., and Peter Adler. 1994. "Social Reproduction and the Corporate Other: The Institutionalization of Afterschool Activities." *Sociological Quarterly* 35 (2): 309–28. http://dx.doi.org/10.1111/j.1533-8525.1994. tb00412.x.

Alba, Richard, and Victor Nee. 1997. "Rethinking Assimilation Theory for a New Era of Immigration." *International Migration Review* 31 (4): 826–74. http://dx.doi.org/10.2307/2547416.

Alexander, Karl L., Doris R. Entwisle, and Susan L. Dauber. 2003. *On the Success of Failure: A Reassessment of the Effects of Retention in the Primary School Grades.* 2nd ed. Cambridge: Cambridge University Press.

Alexander, Karl L., Doris R. Entwisle, and Carrie S. Horsey. 1997. "From First Grade Forward: Early Foundations of High School Dropout." *Sociology of Education* 70 (2): 87–107. http://dx.doi.org/10.2307/2673158.

Alexander, Michelle. 2012. *The New Jim Crow: Mass Incarceration in the Age of Colorblindness.* New York: The New Press.

Alinsky, Saul D. 1971. *Rules for Radicals.* New York: Random House.

Alon, Sigal. 2009. "The Evolution of Class Inequity in Higher Education: Competition, Exclusion, and Adaptation." *American Sociological Review* 74 (5): 731–55. http://dx.doi.org/10.1177/000312240907400503.

Alonso, Andrés A., and Marshall T. Goodwin. 2008. "Baltimore City Public School System School Police Force Protocol for School Searches." Baltimore: Baltimore City School System. http://www.pcab.baltimorecityschools.org/Departments/School_Police/PDF/BCPSSMetalDetectors.pdf Accessed December 10, 2014.

Anyon, Jean. 1997. *Ghetto Schooling: A Political Economy of Urban Educational Reform*. New York: Teachers College Press.

Anyon, Jean. 2005. *Radical Possibilities: Public Policy, Urban Education, and a New Social Movement*. New York: Routledge.

Aronowitz, Stanley. 2004. "Education, Social Class, the Sites of Pedagogy." In *If Classrooms Matter: Progressive Visions of Educational Environments*, ed. Jeffrey R. Di Leo and Walter R. Jacobs, 27–44. New York: Routledge.

Arum, Richard. 1996. "Do Private Schools Force Public Schools to Compete?" *American Sociological Review* 61 (1): 29–46. http://dx.doi.org/10.2307/2096405.

Assaf, Lori. 2006. "One Reading Specialist's Response to High-Stakes Testing Pressures." *Reading Teacher* 60 (2): 158–67. http://dx.doi.org/10.1598/RT.60.2.6.

Attili, Giovanni, director, and Leonie Sandercock, producer. 2006. *Where Strangers Become Neighbours: The Story of the Collingwood Neighbourhood House and the Integration of Immigrants in Vancouver*. Vancouver: Vancouver Cosmopolis Lab.

Baker, David, and Gerald LeTendre. 2005. *National Differences, Global Similarities: World Culture and the Future of Schooling*. Palo Alto, CA: Stanford University Press.

Baker, Keith. 1991. "Yes, Throw Monday at Schools." *Phi Delta Kappan* 72 (8): 628.

Barnett, W. Steven. 2000. "Economics of Early Childhood Intervention." In *Handbook of Early Childhood Intervention*, 2nd ed., ed Jack P. Shonkoff and Samuel J. Meisels, 589–610. New York: Cambridge University Press. http://dx.doi.org/10.1017/CBO9780511529320.027.

Barnett, W. Steven, and Sarane Spence Boocock, eds. 1998. *Early Care and Education for Children in Poverty: Promises, Programs, and Long-Term Results*. Albany, NY: State University of New York Press.

Belle, Deborah. 1999. *The After-School Lives of Children: Alone and with Others While Parents Work*. Mahwah, NJ: Lawrence Erlbaum & Associates.

Benveniste, Luis, Martin Carnoy, and Richard Rothstein. 2003. *All Else Equal: Are Public and Private Schools Different?* New York, London: RoutledgeFalmer.

Berliner, David. C. 2006. "Our Impoverished View of Educational Reform." *Teachers College Record* 108 (6): 949–95.

Bloemraad, Irene. 2006. *Becoming a Citizen: Incorporating Immigrants and Refugees in the United States and Canada*. Berkeley: University of California Press.

Bobo, Kim A., Jackie Kendall, and Steve Max. 2001. *Organizing for Social Change: Midwest Academy Manual for Activists*. Santa Ana, CA: Seven Locks Press.

Bomster, Mark. 1992. "Mommy, I Can't Read" *Baltimore Sun*, June 11: 1A.

Bonilla-Silva, Eduardo. 2006. *Racism Without Racism: Color-Blind Racism and the Persistence of Racial Inequality in the United States*. 2nd ed. Lanham, MD: Rowman and Littlefield.

Boocock, Sarane Spence, and Kimberly Ann Scott. 2005. *Kids in Context: The Sociological Study of Children and Childhoods*. Lanham, MD: Rowman and Littlefield.

Bowles, Samuel, and Herbert Gintis. 1976. *Schooling in Capitalist America*. New York: Basic Books.

Boyd, Monica. 2002. "Educational Attainments of Immigrant Offspring: Success or Segmented Assimilation?" *International Migration Review* 36 (4): 1037–60. http://dx.doi.org/10.1111/j.1747-7379.2002.tb00117.x.

Brand, Jennie, and Yu. Xie. 2010. "Who Benefits Most from College? Evidence for Negative Selection in Heterogeneous Economic Returns to Higher Education." *American Sociological Review* 75 (2): 273–302. http://dx.doi.org/10.1177/0003122410363567.

Bronfenbrenner, Urie. 1979. *The Ecology of Human Development: Experiments by Nature and by Design*. Cambridge: Harvard University Press.

Brooks, Greg. A.K. Pugh, and Ian Shagen. 1996. *Reading Performance at Nine*. Slough: National Foundation for Educational Research.

Durham, David T., Douglas D. Ready, Valerie E. Lee, and Laura LoGerfo. 2004. "Social Class Differences in Summer Learning between Kindergarten and First Grade: Model Specification and Estimation." *Sociology of Education* 77 (1): 1–31. http://dx.doi.org/10.1177/003804070407700101.

Campbell, Bart. 2001. *The Door Is Open: Memoirs of a Soup Kitchen Volunteer*. Vancouver: Anvil Press.

Canadian Press. 2008. "B.C. studies all-day kindergarten for 2009." http://www.cbc.ca/canada/british-columbia/story/2008/08/14/bc-all-day-kindergarten.html. Accessed January 1, 2009.

Card, David, and Alan Krueger. 1992. "Does School Quality Matter? Returns to Education and the Characteristics of Public Schools in the United States." *Journal of Political Economy* 100: 1–40. http://dx.doi.org/10.1086/261805.

Carrier, James G. 1983. "Masking the Social in Educational Knowledge: The Case of Learning Disability Theory." *American Journal of Sociology* 88 (5): 948–74. http://dx.doi.org/10.1086/227765.

Carter, Prudence L. 2005. *Keepin' It Real: School Success beyond Black and White*. New York: Oxford University Press.

CBC News. 2007. "Teen faces murder charge after weekend stabbing." http://www.cbc.ca/news/canada/british-columbia/teen-faces-murder-charge-after-weekend-stabbing-1.662133 Accessed December 10, 2014.

CBC News. 2008. "School shooting 1 of 3 on deadly day in Toronto." http://www.cbc.ca/news/canada/toronto/school-shooting-1-of-3-on-deadly-day-in-toronto-1.726800 Accessed December 12, 2014.

Chang, Janet, and Thao N. Le. 2005. "The Influence of Parents, Peer Delinquency, and School Attitudes on Academic Achievement in Chinese, Cambodian, Laotian or Mien, and Vietnamese Youth." *Crime and Delinquency* 51 (2): 238–64. http://dx.doi.org/10.1177/0011128704273469.

Chen, Wen-Hao, John Myles, and Garnett Picot. 2012. "Why Have Poorer Neighbourhoods Stagnated Economically While the Richer Have Flourished? Neighbourhood Income Inequality in Canadian Cities." *Urban Studies (Edinburgh, Scotland)* 49 (4): 877–96. http://dx.doi.org/10.1177/0042098011408142.

Coleman, James S. 1990. *Equality and Achievement in Education*. Boulder, CO: Westview Press.

Corak, Miles. 2009. "Chasing the Same Dream, Climbing Different Ladders: Economic Mobility in the United States and Canada." Washington, DC: Economic Mobility Project: An Initiative of the Pew Charitable Trusts.

Corbett, Dick, Bruce Wilson, and Belinda Williams. 2002. *Effort and Excellence in Urban Classrooms: Expecting – and Getting – Success with All Students*. New York: Teachers College Press.

Curtis, Bruce. D.W. Livingstone, and Harry Smaller. 1992. *Stacking the Deck: The Streaming of Working-Class Kids in Ontario Schools*. Toronto: Our Schools / Our Selves Education Foundation.

Dachyshyn, Darcey M. 2006. "Refugee Families with Preschool Children: Adjustment to Life in Canada." In *Global Migration and Education: Schools, Children, and Families*, ed. Leah D. Adams and Anna Kirova, 251–62. Mahwah, NJ: Lawrence Erlbaum & Associates.

Delpit, Lisa. 1995. *Other People's Children: Cultural Conflict in the Classroom*. New York: The New Press.

Després, Sébastien, Steven Kohn, Pauline Ngirumpatse, and Marie-Josée Parent. 2013. *Real Accountability or an Illusion of Success? A Call to Review Standardized Testing in Ontario*. Action Canada. http://testingillusion.ca/wp-content/uploads/2013/01/illusion_of_success_EN.pdf Accessed June 25, 2013.

Donziger, Steven R., ed. 1996. *The Real War on Crime: The Report of the National Criminal Justice System*. New York: The National Center on Institutions and Harper Collins.

Downey, Douglas B., Paul T. von Hippel, and Melanie Hughes. 2008. "Are "Failing" Schools Really Failing? Using Seasonal Comparison to Evaluate School Effectiveness." *Sociology of Education* 81 (3): 242–70. http://dx.doi.org/10.1177/003804070808100302.

Dryfoos, Joy G. 1994. *Full Service Schools: A Revolution in Health and Social Services for Children, Youth and Families*. San Francisco: Jossey-Bass.

Duneier, Mitchell. 2000. *Sidewalk*. New York: Farrer Strauss, Giroux.

Dupuis, Renée. 2001. *Justice for Canada's Aboriginal People*. Trans. Robert Chodos and Susan Joanis. Toronto: Lorimer.

Eberts, Randall W., and Joe A. Stone. 1988. "Student Achievement in Public Schools: Do Principals Make a Difference?" *Economics of Education Review* 7 (3): 291–9. http://dx.doi.org/10.1016/0272-7757(88)90002-7.

Elley, Warwick B. 1996. *The IEA Study of Reading Literacy: Achievement and Instruction in Thirty-Two School Systems*. Pergamon for IEA.

Entwisle, Doris R., and Karl L. Alexander. 1992. "Summer Setback: Race, Poverty, School Composition, and Mathematics Achievement in the First Two Years of School Source." *American Sociological Review* 57 (1): 72–84. http://dx.doi.org/10.2307/2096145.

Epstein, Joyce, and Associates. 2008. *School, Family, and Community Partnerships: A Handbook for Action*. 3rd ed. Thousand Oaks, CA: Corwin Press.

Erickson, Lance D., Steve McDonald, and Glen H. Elder. 2009. "Informal Mentors and Education: Complementary or Compensatory Resources?" *Sociology of Education* 82 (4): 344–67. http://dx.doi.org/10.1177/003804070908200403.

Evans, Robert. 2004. *Family Matters: How Schools Can Cope with the Crisis in Childrearing*. San Francisco: Jossey-Bass.

Ferguson, Ann Arnett. 2001. *Bad Boys: Public Schools in the Making of Black Masculinity*. Ann Arbor: University of Michigan Press.

Ferguson, Ronald F. 1991. "Paying for Public Education: New Evidence on How and Why Monday Matters." *Harvard Journal on Legislation* 28 (2): 465–98.

Fernández-Kelly, Patricia, and Lisa Konzcal. 2005. "Murdering the Alphabet: Identity and Entrepreneurship among Second-Generation Cubans, West Indians, and Central Americans." *Ethnic and Racial Studies* 28 (6): 1153–81. http://dx.doi.org/10.1080/01419870500224513.

Florida, Richard. 2004. *The Rise of the Creative Class: And How It's Transforming Work, Leisure, Community and Everyday Life*. New York: Basic Books.

Friedman, Thomas. 2006. *The World Is Flat: A Brief History of the Twenty-First Century*. New York: Farrar, Straus and Giroux.

Fruchter, Norm. 2007. *Urban Schools, Public Will: Making Education Work for All Our Children*. New York: Teachers College Press.

Fry, Richard. 2007. "Are Immigrant Youth Faring Better in U.S. Schools?" *International Migration Review* 41 (3): 579–601. http://dx.doi.org/10.1111/j.1747-7379.2007.00086.x.

Gamoran, Adam. 2001. "American Schooling and Educational Inequality: A Forecast for the 21st Century." *Sociology of Education* 74:135–53. http://dx.doi.org/10.2307/2673258.

Gaskell, Jane, and Ben Levin. 2012. *Making a Difference in Urban Schools: Ideas, Politics, and Pedagogy*. Toronto: University of Toronto Press.

Giese, Rachel. 2011. "Arrival of the Fittest: Canada's Crime Rate Is Dropping as Immigration Increases: Is There a Connection?" *The Walrus*. Toronto, ON. http://thewalrus.ca/arrival-of-the-fittest/ Accessed December 10, 2014.

Giese, Rachel, and Caroline Alphonso. 2013. "The Debate over Standardized Testing in Schools Is as Divisive as Ever." *The Globe and Mail*. http://www.theglobeandmail.com/news/national/education/the-debate-over-standardized-testing-in-schools-is-as-divisive-as-ever/article12299369/?page=all Accessed June 25, 2013.

Giroux, Henry A. 2004. "The Politics of Public Pedagogy."In *If Classrooms Matter: Progressive Visions of Educational Environments*, ed. Jeffrey R. Di Leo and Walter R. Jacobs, 15–36. New York: Routledge.

Giroux, Henry A. 2005. *Schooling and the Struggle for Public Life: Democracy's Promise and Education's Challenge*. 2nd ed. Boulder, CO: Paradigm Publishers.

Glick, Jennifer E., and Michael J. White. 2004. "Post-Secondary School Participation of Immigrant and Native Youth: The Role of Familial Resources and Educational Expectations." *Social Science Research* 33 (2): 272–99. http://dx.doi.org/10.1016/j.ssresearch.2003.06.001.

Goldsmith, Pat Rubio. 2009. "Schools or Neighborhoods or Both? Race and Ethnic Segregation and Educational Attainment." *Social Forces* 87 (4): 1913–41. http://dx.doi.org/10.1353/sof.0.0193.

Goldstein, Tara. 2003. "Contemporary Bilingual Life at a Canadian High School: Choices, Risks, Tensions, and Dilemmas." *Sociology of Education* 76 (3): 247–64. http://dx.doi.org/10.2307/3108468.

Gordon, Mar. 2007. *Roots of Empathy: Changing the World Child by Child*. Markham, ON: Thomas Allen Publishing.

Grant, Tavia. 2011. "Canada's Wage Gap at Record High: OECD." *The Globe and Mail*. Toronto, ON. http://www.theglobeandmail.com/report-on-business/economy/canadas-wage-gap-at-record-high-oecd/article4099041/ Accessed June 25, 2013.

Greene, Stuart. 2008. "Introduction: Teaching for Social Justice." In *Literacy as a Civil Right: Reclaiming Social Justice in Literacy Teaching and Learning*, ed. Stuart Greene, 1–25. New York: Peter Lang.

Hanushek, Eric A. 1981. "Throwing Money at Schools." *Journal of Policy Analysis and Management* 1 (1): 19–41. http://dx.doi.org/10.2307/3324107.

Hargreaves, Andy, and Dennis Shirley. 2012. *The Global Fourth Way: The Quest for Educational Excellence*. Thousand Oaks, CA: Corwin Press.

Harris, Angel L., Kenneth M. Jamison, and Monica H. Trujillo. 2008. "Disparities in the Educational Success of Immigrants: An Assessment of the Immigrant Effect for Asians and Latinos." *Annals of the American Academy of Political and Social Science* 620 (1): 90–114. http://dx.doi.org/10.1177/00027 16208322765.

Hart, B., and T.R. Risely. 1995. *Meaningful Differences in the Everyday Experience of Young American Children*. Baltimore: Paul H. Brookes.

Harvey, David. 1996. *Justice, Nature, and the Geography of Difference*. Oxford. Blackwell.

Hedges, Larry V., Richard D. Laine, and Ron Greenwald. 1994. "Does Money Matter? A Meta-Analysis of Studies of the Effects of Differential School Inputs on Student Outcomes." *Educational Researcher* 23 (3): 5–14. http://dx.doi.org/10.3102/0013189X023003005.

Hertzman, Clyde. 2000. "The Case for an Early Development Strategy." *Isuma: Canadian Journal of Policy Research* 1 (2): 11–8.

Hertzman, Clyde. 2002. *Leave No Child Behind!: Social Exclusion and Child Development*. Toronto: The Laidlaw Foundation.

Hertzman, Clyde, Sidney A. McLean, Dafna E. Kohen, Jim Dunn, and Terry Evans. 2002. *Early Development in Vancouver: Report of the Community Asset Mapping Project (CAMP)*. Vancouver, BC: Human Early Learning Partnership.

Heymann, Jody. 2006. *Forgotten Families: Ending the Growing Crisis Confronting Children and Working Parents in the Global Economy*. New York: Oxford University Press.

Hillocks, George Jr. 2002. *The Testing Trap: How State Writing Assessments Control Learning*. New York: Teachers College Press.

Hira, Ron, and Anil Hira. 2009. *Outsourcing America: The True Cost of Shipping Jobs Overseas and What Can Be Done about It*. New York: AMACOM.

Horn, Catherine. 2005. "Standardized Assessments and the Flow of Students into the College Admission Pool." *Educational Policy* 19 (2): 331–48. http://dx.doi.org/10.1177/0895904804274057.

Hulchanski, David. 2010. *The Three Cities within Toronto: Income Polarization among Toronto's Neighbourhoods, 1970–2005*. Toronto: University of Toronto Cities Centre.

Igoa, Cristina. 1995. *The Inner World of the Immigrant Child*. Mahwah, NJ: Lawrence Erlbaum Associates.

International Human Development Indicators Country Profile. Canada. 2014. Hdr.undp.org/en/countries/profiles/CAN Accessed December 10, 2014.

Jacobs, Jane. 1963. *The Death and Life of Great American Cities*. New York: Vintage.

Jencks, Christopher. 1972. *Inequality: A Reassessment of the Effect of Family and Schooling in America*. New York: Basic Books.

Johnson, David. 2008. "School Grades: Identifying British Columbia's Best Schools." Toronto: C.D. Howe Institute No. 258.

Johnson, Lauri, Mary E. Finn, and Rebecca Lewis, eds. 2005. *Urban Education with an Attitude*. Albany: SUNY Press.

Kao, Grace, and Jennifer S. Thompson. 2003. "Racial and Ethnic Stratification in Educational Achievement and Attainment." *Annual Review of Sociology* 29 (1): 417–42. http://dx.doi.org/10.1146/annurev.soc.29.010202.100019.

Kaufman, Julia. 2004. "The Interplay Between Social and Cultural Determinants of School Effort and Success: An Investigation of Chinese-Immigrant and Second-Generation Chinese Students' Perceptions toward School." *Social Science Quarterly* 85 (5): 1275–98. http://dx.doi.org/10.1111/j.0038-4941.2004.00276.x.

Kazal-Thrasher, Deborah. 1993. "Educational Expenditures and School Achievement: When and How Money Can Make a Difference." *Educational Researcher* 22 (2): 30–2.

Kelly, Erin E. 1995. "All Students Are Not Created Equal: The Inequitable Combination of Property-Tax Based School Finance Systems and Local Control." *Duke Law Journal* 45 (2): 397–435. http://dx.doi.org/10.2307/1372907.

Kendall, Joan. 2001. "Circles of Disadvantage: Aboriginal Poverty and Underdevelopment in Canada." *American Review of Canadian Studies* 31 (1–2): 43–59. http://dx.doi.org/10.1080/02722010109481581.

Kershaw, Paul, and Lynell Anderson. 2009. *15 by 15: A Comprehensive Policy Framework for Early Human Capital Investment in BC*. Vancouver, BC: Human Early Learning Partnership; http://earlylearning.ubc.ca/documents/27/, Accessed June 24, 2013.

Klingner, Janette K., Alfredo J. Artiles, Elizabeth Kozleski, Beth Harry, Shelly Zion, William Tate, Grace Z. Durán, and David Riley. 2005. "Addressing the Disproportionate Representation of Culturally and Linguistically Diverse Students in Special Education through Culturally Responsive Educational Systems." *Education Policy Analysis Archives* 13 (38). http://epaa.asu.edu/epaa/v13n38/ Retrieved August 8, 2010.

Knapp, Michael S., and Patrick M. Shields, eds. 1991. *Better Schooling for the Children of Poverty: Alternatives to Conventional Wisdom*. Berkeley: McCutchan Publishing Corporation.

Kohn, Alfie. 1999. *The Schools Our Children Deserve: Moving beyond Traditional Classrooms and "Tougher Standards."* New York: Houghton-Mifflin.

Kozol, Jonathan. 1992. *Savage Inequalities: Children in America's Schools*. New York: Harper Perennial.

Kozol, Jonathan. 2005. *The Shame of the Nation: The Restoration of Apartheid Schooling*. New York: Crown Publishers.

Kroneberg, Clemens. 2008. "Ethnic Communities and School Performance among the New Second Generation in the United States: Testing the Theory of Segmented Assimilation." *Annals of the American Academy of Political and Social Science* 620 (1): 138–60. http://dx.doi.org/10.1177/0002716208322714.

Langhout, Regina D., Jean E. Rhodes, and Lori N. Osborne. 2004. "An Exploratory Study of Youth Mentoring in an Urban Context: Adolescents' Perception of Relationship Styles." *Journal of Youth and Adolescence* 33 (4): 293–306. http://dx.doi.org/10.1023/B:JOYO.0000032638.85483.44.

Lareau, Annette. 2000. *Home Advantage: Social Class and Parental Intervention in Elementary Education*. Lanham, MD: Rowman & Littlefield.

Lareau, Annette. 2003. *Unequal Childhoods: Class, Race, and Family Life*. Berkeley: University of California Press.

Levine, Daniel U., and Lawrence W. Lezotte. 1990. *Unusually Effective Schools: A Review and Analysis of Research and Practice*. Madison, WI: National Center for Effective Schools Research and Development.

Levitt, Steven D., and Stephen J. Dubner. 2005. *Freakonomics: A Rogue Economist Explores the Hidden Side of Everything*. New York: William Morrow.

Lewis, Amanda E. 2003. *Race in the Schoolyard: Negotiating the Color Line in Classrooms and Communities*. Piscataway, NJ: Rutgers University Press.

Ligaya, Armina. 2007. "Police make plea for video, photos of stabbing." *The Globe and Mail*. www.globeandmail.com/technology/police-make-plea-for-video-photos-of-stabbling/article1076809 Accessed December 10, 2014.

Lipman, Pauline. 2008. "Education Policy, Race, and Neoliberal Urbanism." In *Literacy as a Civil Right: Reclaiming Social Justice in Literacy Teaching and Learning*, ed. Stuart Greene, 45–66. New York: Peter Lang.

Lofty, John S. 2006. *Quiet Wisdom: Teachers in the United States and England Talk about Standards, Practice, and Professionalism*. New York: Peter Lang.

Ma, Xin, and Don A. Klinger. 2000. "Klinger Hierarchical Linear Modelling of Student and School Effects on Academic Achievement." *Canadian Journal of Education* 25 (1): 41–55. http://dx.doi.org/10.2307/1585867.

MacLeod, Jay. 2009. *Ain't No Makin' It: Aspirations and Attainment in a Low-Income Neighborhood*. 3rd ed. Boulder, CO: Westview Press.

Marzano, Robert J. 2003. *What Works in Schools: Translating Research into Action*. Alexandria, VA: Association for Supervision & Curriculum Development (ASCD).

Mayer, Susan E. 2001. "How Did the Increase in Economic Inequality between 1970 and 1990 Affect Children's Educational Attainment?" *American Journal of Sociology* 107 (1): 1–32. http://dx.doi.org/10.1086/323149.

Mayo, Elton. 1949. *Hawthorne and the Western Electric Company: The Social Problems of an Industrial Civilisation*. London: Routledge.

McDonald, Robert A. J. 1996. *Making Vancouver: Class, Status, and Social Boundaries, 1863–1913*. Vancouver: UBC Press.

McLaran, Peter. 1980. *Cries from the Corridor: The New Suburban Ghetto*. Agincourt, ON: Methuen Publications.

McLaran, Peter. 1995. *Critical Pedagogy and Predatory Culture: Oppositional Politics in a Postmodern Era*. London, New York: Routledge.

McLaran, Peter. 2003. *Life in Schools: An Introduction to Critical Pedagogy in the Foundations of Education*. 4th ed. Boston: Pearson Education, Inc.

Meier, Deborah. 1995. *The Power of Their Ideas: Lessons from a Small School in Harlem*. Boston: Beacon Press.

Mishel, Lawrence, and Richard Rothstein, eds. 2002. *The Class Size Debate*. Washington, DC: Economic Policy Institute.

Murnane, Richard. 1991. "Interpreting the Evidence on 'Does Money Matter?'." *Harvard Journal on Legislation* 28 (2): 457–64.

Murnane, Richard J., and Randall J. Olsen. 1990. "The Impacts of Salaries and Opportunity Costs on Length of Stay in Teaching: Evidence from North Carolina." *Journal of Human Resources* 25 (1): 106–24. http://dx.doi.org/10.2307/145729.

Newman, Katherine S. 1999. *No Shame in My Game: The Working Poor in the Inner City*. New York: Russell Sage Foundation and Vintage Books.

Newman, Katherine S. 2006. *Chutes and Ladders: Navigating the Low-Wage Labor Market*. New York: Russell Sage Foundation, and Cambridge, MA: Harvard University Press.

Nichols, Sharon Lynn, and David C. Berliner. 2007. *Collateral Damage: How High-Stakes Testing Corrupts America's Schools*. Cambridge, MA: Harvard Education Press.

Noguera, Pedro. 2003. *City School and the American Dream: Reclaiming the Promise of Public Education*. New York: Teachers College Press.

Noguera, Pedro A. 2008. *The Trouble with Black Boys … and Other Reflections on Race, Equity and the Future of Public Education*. San Francisco: Jossey-Bass.

Noguera, Pedro A., and Jean Yonemura Wing. 2006. "Closing the Achievement Gap at Berkeley High School." In *Unfinished Business: Closing the Racial Achievement Gap in Our Schools*, ed. Pedro A. Noguera and Jean Yonemura Wing, 3–28. San Francisco: Jossey-Bass.

Orellana, Marjorie Faulstitch. 2009. *Translating Childhoods: Immigrant Youth, Language, and Culture*. New Brunswick, NJ: Rutgers University Press.

Orfield, Gary and Susan E. Eaton.1997. *Dismantling Desegregation: The Quiet Reversal of Brown v. Board of Education*. New York: The New Press.

Paris, Scott G., Fred J. Morrison, and Kevin F. Miller. 2006. "Academic Pathways from Preschool through Elementary School." In *Handbook of Educational Psychology*, 2nd ed., ed. Patricia A. Alexander and Phillipe H. Winne, 61–85. New York: Routledge.

Patchen, Martin. 2004. *Making Our Schools More Effective: What Matters and What Works*. Springfield, Ill: Charles C. Thomas Publisher Ltd.

Peguero, Anthony. 2009. "Victimizing the Children of Immigrants: Latino and Asian American Student Victimization." *Youth & Society* 41 (2): 186–208. http://dx.doi.org/10.1177/0044118X09333646.

Peterson, Paul E., and William G. Howell. 2002. *The Education Gap: Vouchers and Urban Schools*. Washington, DC: Brookings Institute Press.

Pong, Suet-Ling, Lingxin Hao, and Erica Gardner. 2005. "The Roles of Parenting Styles and Social Capital in the School Performance of Immigrant Asian and Hispanic Adolescents." *Social Science Quarterly* 86 (4): 928–50. http://dx.doi.org/10.1111/j.0038-4941.2005.00364.x.

Portes, Alejandro, and Rubén G. Rumbaut. 1996. *Immigrant America: A Portrait*. Berkeley: University of California Press.

Portes, Alejandro, and Rubén G. Rumbaut. 2001. *Legacies: The Stories of the Immigrant Second Generation. Berkeley: University of California Press*. New York: Russell Sage Foundation.

Reich, Robert. 1992. *The Work of Nations: Preparing Ourselves for 21st Century Capitalism*. New York: Vintage.

Reynolds, Arthur J., Judy A. Temple, Dylan L. Robertson, and Emily A. Mann. 2001. "Long-Term Effects of an Early Childhood Intervention on Educational Achievement and Juvenile Arrest." *Journal of the American Medical Association* 285 (18): 2339–46. http://dx.doi.org/10.1001/jama.285.18.2339.

Rhodes, Jean E. 2002. *Stand by Me: The Risks and Rewards of Mentoring Today's Youth*. Cambridge, MA: Harvard University Press.

Richards, John, Jennifer Hove, and Kemi Afolabi. 2008. *Understanding the Aboriginal/Non-Aboriginal Gap in Student Performance: Lessons from British Columbia*. Toronto: C.D. Howe Institute; http://www.cdhowe.org/pdf/commentary_276.pdf, Accessed February 20, 2009.

Robertson, Leslie, and Dara Culhane, eds. 2005. *In Plain Sight: Reflections on Life in Downtown Eastside Vancouver*. Vancouver: Talonbooks.

Rossmiller, Richard. 1992. "Financing Schools." In *Encyclopedia of Education Research*, 6th edition, ed. Marvin C. Alkin, vol. 2. New York: Macmillan.

Roth, Judie, Jeanne Brooks-Gunn, Lawrence Murray, and William Foster. 1998. "Promoting Healthy Adolescents: Synthesis of Youth Development Program Evaluation." *Journal of Research on Adolescence* 8 (4): 423–59. http://dx.doi.org/10.1207/s15327795jra0804_2.

Rothstein, Richard. 2004. *Class and Schools: Using Social, Economic, and Educational Reform to Close the Black-White Achievement Gap*. New York: Teachers College Press.

Sahlberg, Pasi. 2011. *Finnish Lessons: What the World Can Learn from Educational Change in Finland*. New York: Teachers College Press.

Saltman, Jennifer. 2007. "Web Threats Trouble Police: Police Urge Calm after Facebook Threats of Retribution" *The Province*. http://www.canada.com/theprovince/news/story.html?id=a70758ec-03d5-42bb-be87-d49941be7340 Accessed June 29, 2008.

Saltman, Kenneth J. 2000. *Collateral Damage: Corporatizing Public Schools – A Threat to Democracy*. Lanham, MD: Rowman & Littlefield Publishers, Inc.

Sánchez, Bernadette, Patricia Esparza, Luciano Berardi, and Julia Pryce. 2011. "Mentoring in the Context of Latino Youth's Broader Village during Their Transition from High School." *Youth & Society* 43 (1): 225–52. http://dx.doi.org/10.1177/0044118X10363774.

Sandercock, Leonie. 2004. *Cosmopolis II: Mongrel Cities in the 21st Century*. London: Continuum.

Sassen, Saskia. 2001. *The Global City: New York, London, Tokyo*. Princeton: Princeton University Press.

Schweinhart, Lawrence J., and David P. Weikart. 1990. "The High/Scope Perry Preschool Study Implications for Early Childhood Care and Education." In *Protecting the Children*. ed. Raymond P. Lorion, 109–32. Philadelphia: Haworth Press. http://dx.doi.org/10.1300/J293v07n01_06.

Sennett, Richard, and Jonathan Cobb. 1973. *The Hidden Injuries of Class*. New York: Vintage Books.

Sizer, Theodore R. 2004. *The Red Pencil: Convictions from Experience in Education*. New Haven: Yale University Press.

Slavin, Robert E. 1994. "After the Victory: Making Funding Equity Make a Difference." *Theory into Practice* 33 (2): 98–103. http://dx.doi.org/10.1080/00405849409543624.

Slavin, Robert E., and Nancy A. Madden. 1989. "What Works for Children at Risk: A Research Synthesis." *Educational Leadership* (Spring): 4–13.

Slavin, Robert E., and Nancy A. Madden, eds. 2001. *Success for All: Research and Reform in Elementary Education*. Mahwah, NJ: Lawrence Erlbaum Associates, Inc.

Slavin, Robert E., Nancy A. Madden, Lawrence J. Dolan, Barbara A. Wasik, Steven M. Ross, and Lana J. Smith. 1994. "'Whatever and Wherever We Choose': The Replication of 'Success for All'." *Phi Delta Kappan* (April): 639–47.

Small, Mario Luis. 2004. *Villa Victoria: The Transformation of Social Capital in a Boston Barrio*. Chicago: University of Chicago Press. http://dx.doi.org/10.7208/chicago/9780226762937.001.0001.

Smith, Dorothy E. 2000. "Schooling for Inequality." *Signs (Chicago, Ill.)* 25 (4): 1147–51. http://dx.doi.org/10.1086/495535.

Smith, George. 1996. "Urban Education: Current Position and Future Possibilities." In *Raising Educational Standards in the Inner Cities*, ed. Michael Barber and Ruth Dann. London: Cassell.

Smith, Kevin B. 2003. *The Ideology of Education: The Commonwealth, the Market, and America's Schools*. Albany: SUNY Press.

Smith, Teresa, and Michael Noble. 1995. *Education Divides: Poverty and Schooling in the 1990s*. London: Child Poverty Action Group (CPAG).

Stack, Carol. 1974. *All Our Kin: Strategies for Survival in a Black Community*. New York: Harper and Row.

Stevenson, Harold W., and James W. Stigler. 1992. *The Learning Gap: Why Our Schools Are Failing and What We Can Learn from Japanese and Chinese Education*. New York: Summit Books.

Suárez-Orozco, Carola, Jean Rhodes, and Michael Milburn. 2009. "Unraveling the Immigrant Paradox Academic Engagement and Disengagement among Recently Arrived Immigrant Youth." *Youth & Society* 41 (2): 151–85. http://dx.doi.org/10.1177/0044118X09333647.

Suárez-Orozco, Carola, Marcelo M. Suárez-Orozco, and Irina Todorova. 2008. *Learning a New Land: Immigrant Students in American Society*. Cambridge, MA: Harvard University Press.

Szente, Judit, and James Hoot. 2006. "Exploring the Needs of Refugee Children in Our Schools." In *Global Migration and Education: Schools, Children, and Families*, ed. Leah D. Adams and Anna Kirova, 219–36. Mahwah, NJ: Lawrence Erlbaum & Associates.

Tyack, David, and Larry Cuban. 1997. *Tinkering toward Utopia: A Century of Public School Reform*. Cambridge, MA: Harvard University Press.

Ungerleider, Charles. 2003. *Failing Our Kids: How We Are Ruining Our Public Schools*. Toronto: McClelland & Stewart Ltd.

United Way Toronto. 2011. *Poverty by Postal Code 2 Vertical Poverty: Declining Income, Housing Quality and Community Life in Toronto's Inner Suburban High-Rise Apartments*. Toronto: United Way.

U.S. Department of Education, Office of the Under Secretary. 1999. *Hope for Urban Education: A Study of Nine High-Performing, High-Poverty Urban Elementary Schools*. Washington, DC.

Vancouver, Metro. *Metro Vancouver Census Bulletin #6: Immigration and Cultural Diversity*. 2008. http://public.metrovancouver.org/about/publications/Publications/Census2006_Immigration_Bulletin_6.pdf Accessed September 26, 2008.

Vancouver Foundation. 2013. "Vital Signs for Metro Vancouver: Addressing Inequities in Our Education System Is Vital for the Future." Vancouver, BC. http://www.vancouverfoundationvitalsigns.ca/society/learning/ Accessed June 25, 2013.

Venkatesh, Sudhir. 2006. *Off the Books: The Underground Economy of the Urban Poor*. Cambridge, MA: Harvard University Press.

Venkatesh, Sudhir. 2008. *Gang Leader for a Day*. New York: Penguin.

Vertovec, Steven. 2007. "Super-diversity and Its Implications." *Ethnic and Racial Studies* 30 (6): 1024–54. http://dx.doi.org/10.1080/01419870701599465.

Wagner, Tony. 2008. *The Global Achievement Gap: Why Even Our Best Schools Don't Teach the New Survival Skills Our Children Need – and What We Can Do about It*. New York: Basic Books.

Watkins, Adam M., and Chris Melde. 2009. "Immigrants, Assimilation, and Perceived School Disorder: An Examination of the 'Other' Ethnicities." *Journal of Criminal Justice* 37 (6): 627–35. http://dx.doi.org/10.1016/j.jcrimjus.2009.09.011.

Weinstein, Rhona S. 2002. *Reaching Higher: The Power of Expectations in Schooling*. Cambridge, MA: Harvard University Press.

Weissbourd, Richard. 1997. *The Vulnerable Child: What Really Hurts America's Children and What Can We Do about It*. Boston: Addison-Wesley Publishing.

Willis, Paul. 1981. *Learning to Labor: How Working Class Kids Get Working Class Jobs*. New York: Columbia University Press.

Wilson, Bruce L., and H. Dickenson Corbett. 2001. *Listening to Urban Kids: School Reform and the Teachers They Want*. Albany: SUNY Press.

Wilson, William J. 1997. *When Work Disappears: The World of the New Urban Poor*. New York: Alfred A Knopf.

Wilson, William Julius, and Richard A. Taub. 2006. *There Goes the Neighborhood: Racial, Ethnic and Class Tensions in Four Chicago Neighborhoods and Their Meaning for America*. New York: Vintage.

Wood, Daniel. 2008. "Nanny Diaries." *Vancouver Magazine* http://www.vanmag.com/articles/08jan/Nanny.shtml. Accessed May 2, 2009.

Zhou, Min. 2009a. "How Neighbourhoods Matter for Immigrant Children: The Formation of Educational Resources in Chinatown, Koreatown and Pico Union, Los Angeles." *Journal of Ethnic and Migration Studies* 35 (7): 1153–79. http://dx.doi.org/10.1080/13691830903006168.

Zhou, Yong. 2009b. *Catching Up or Leading the Way: American Education in the Age of Globalization.* Alexandria, VA: Association for Supervision & Curriculum Development (ASCD).

Zou, Yali. 2002. "Adaptive Strategies of a Chinese Immigrant." In *Ethnography and Schools: Qualitative Approaches to the Study of Education*, ed. Yali Zou and Enrique (Henry) T. Trueba, 195–221. Lanham, MD: Rowman & Littlefield Publishers, Inc.

Zuberi, Dan. 2006. *Differences That Matter: Social Policy and the Working Poor in the United States and Canada.* Ithaca and London: Cornell University Press.

Zuberi, Dan. 2013. *Cleaning Up: How Hospital Outsourcing Is Hurting Workers and Endangering Patients.* Ithaca, London: Cornell University Press.

Index

ability grouping, 34
Aboriginal students, 27
absenteeism, 132
abuse and neglect, 59, 65–6, 72–4, 84, 169
Action Schools program, 119
Ain't No Makin' It (MacLeod), 185
Alberta, Canada, 167
alcohol abuse, 39, 41–3
Alexander, Karl, 5, 9, 121, 148, 178, 181, 240n35
American Sociological Association, 201
Anyon, Jean, 178, 179
Aronowitz, Stanley, 7
artist-in-residence, 113–14, 131
Ashe, Siobhan, 200
Assaf, Lori, 153
assessments of students' reading, 124–5, 175
Australia, 164

Baltimore, Maryland, 12, 13, 194
Baltimore Sun, 12
basic needs programs, 18, 29–30, 50, 63, 65, 67, 69–70, 108, 118, 145,
173, 176–7, 182, 188, 201, 227n21, 228n5, 239n19
BC Lions, 113
BC Teachers' Federation, 161, 163, 235n15
Bennett, William, 11
Bill and Melinda Gates Foundation, 167
Books for Breakfast, 111
Boston, 46
Bowles, Samuel, 183
Bronfenbrenner, Uric, 5
Brown v. Board of Education, 4
Buffalo, New York, 63
bullying, 134–5, 231n17

Canada, Geoffrey, 87, 162
Card, David, 12
C.D. Howe Institute, 152, 204
charter or experimental schools, 87, 117–18, 162, 174
Chicago, 12
childcare, 108, 110, 112, 166, 178–9, 184, 189, 233n30
Clark, Joe, 63

classrooms, learning environment, 4, 12, 52, 66, 80, 122–3, 137–9, 194, 240n34

class sizes. *See* teacher-student ratio

Coleman, James, 7, 8, 140

Coleman Report, 8, 11

collective efficacy, 42

community centres, 40–41, 108–11, 131

Community of Schools program, 119–21, 148

community programs, 107–9, 112, 148, 226n20

counselling services, 88, 142

cream skimming, 86, 140–1, 162, 174, 243n57

Cuban, Larry, 174

cultural differences, 20, 56–60, 73, 76, 90, 92, 94–5, 104–5

curriculum, and innovation, 79–80, 186

cuts to programs and resources, 21, 78, 141–7, 173, 176–7, 191, 232n23, 232n25, 239n19

Dachyshyn, Darcy, 59, 95

Delpit, Lisa, 170

democracy, 6–7, 8

Developmental Reading Assessment (DRA) testing, 125

discipline, school-based, 179–80, 218n3

diversity, urban populations, 14, 19, 25, 26, 48

Downey, Douglas B., 152

drugs: addicts, 35–43, 69; dealing, 37–9, 42, 45

Dubner, Stephen, 161

early academic achievement, importance of, 13, 15, 18, 33, 121, 129, 148, 181

early childhood education, 189–90, 233n30

Early Childhood Longitudinal Study, 152

Early Development Instrument (EDI), 164–7

Early Intervention Program, 129

Early Literacy program, 126–7, 129–30

East St. Louis, 4

ecological model of human development, 5

economic productivity, 6

Edmonton, Alberta, 59, 95

Entwisle, Doris, 9

environment, role of home, 8–9, 240n35

Equality and Achievement in Education (Coleman), 7

equalizing institution, school as, 9, 183–4, 186, 189, 191

expulsion rates, 161

Europe, 183

Failing Our Kids (Ungerleider), 178–9

fees, for supplies, fieldtrips, and extracurricular activities, 8, 9, 67, 145

Ferguson, Ronald, 12

Florida, 187

foster children, 72

Foundation Skills Assessment (FSA). *See* standardized testing

Fraser Institute, 152, 158

Freakonomics (Levitt and Dubner), 161

French immersion, 140
full-day kindergarten, 121–2, 148,
    166, 176, 189, 228n11
funding regimes, 10–12, 238n15
fundraising: parents, 102–3, 112–13,
    115; community institutions, 106–
    7, 112, 115, 228n7

gangs, 37, 45, 193
gender, 86, 188
gentrification, 21, 23, 31, 43–7, 60, 71,
    173, 200
Gintis, Herbert, 183
Giroux, Henry, 8, 182
Globe and Mail, 193
Gordon, Mary, 139
graduation rates, 8
graffiti, 43
Grandview Elementary, 124, 154,
    169, 232n27
Green, Stuart, 151–2
grey-area students, 85–6
grow ops, 37, 40–1, 43, 58, 215n10

halfway houses, 38–9
Hanushek, Eric, 11–12
Harlem Children's Zone, 87, 162
Helping Children Thrive, 132–3
Hertzman, Clyde, 164
Hillocks Jr., George, 164
home environment, 33–4, 73, 98–9,
    142
homelessness, 35, 39, 42, 63, 71–2
Hoot, James, 63
hot lunch and breakfast programs,
    18, 67–8
housing: affordability, 32, 58;
    crowded and/or substandard, 13,
    30

Houston, Texas, 161
Hughes, Melanie, 152
Human Early Learning Partnership
    (HELP), 164–7
hunger, 67

Igoa, Cristina, 10
incarceration: cost of, 5; rates of, 23;
    pipeline, 63, 183, 244n10
inequality, 6–7, 184
Inequality (Jencks), 7, 11
"Inner City" Schools Project, des-
    ignation, 16–17, 21, 34, 44, 73,
    106, 113, 118–19, 148, 176–7, 201,
    229n12, 232n23
integration, of special needs stu-
    dents into classrooms, 64, 83,
    174–5, 229n12

Jencks, Christopher, 7, 11
Johnson, David, 152, 204

Kozol, Jonathan, 4, 6, 12, 117, 150,
    161, 194, 238n17
Kentucky, 164
Kreuger, Alan, 12

language fluency: students, 24–7, 30,
    32, 50, 52–5, 58-59, 76–9, 128, 130,
    140, 146, 167, 172, 173, 175, 177,
    232n25, 232n26, 232n27, 237–8n12;
    parents, 56, 59, 76–9, 93, 101, 104,
    109, 214n3, 216n15, 224n13
language translation, 56, 77, 101
Lareau, Annette, 9, 93
latchkey children, 28, 35
lead, exposure to, 13
leaders, 180, 183, 213n80
Learning Assistance Centre (LAC)
    Teachers, 32, 130

Learning to Labor (Willis), 183
Levitt, Steven, 161
libraries, school, 21, 143–4, 176
Life Skills program, 135, 139
Lions Club, 49
Lipman, Pauline, 13, 189
Literacy Innovation Project, 119
literacy programs, 124–9, 177
Live-In Caregiver Program, 87
Lofty, John S., 163
London, England, 14, 25

MacLeod, Jay, 185
magnet programs, 16, 22, 140–1, 162, 174, 200
manufacturing, decline of, 4, 6
market-based reforms, 86, 151, 154, 161, 171, 173, 174, 184, 189, 220n17
Meier, Deborah, 70
mentoring, 69–71, 88, 107, 115, 182, 219n9, 226n19
methodological issues, 8, 15, 23, 196–9, 202, 204–6, 208n5, 221n19, 236–7n4, 245n13, 245nn15–16, 245–6nn18–22
middle class, 185
minimum wage: increase, 178–9; stagnation, 183
Ministry Designation, 84–5
Ministry of Children and Family Development, 44
mixed groups, 80–1
MOSAIC (Multilingual Orientation Service Association for Immigrant Communities), 45, 109
Mother Goose program, Parent-Child, 18, 22, 92, 130, 148
multi-age classrooms, 81, 122–3, 131, 175, 182
multiculturalism, 57–58

Munsch, Robert, 122
Murnane, Richard, 12

National Geographic, 66
Neighbourhood Houses, 31
Neighbourhood Integrated Service Teams (NISTs), 37, 40
neoliberalism, 7
New York City, 14, 154
Newark, New Jersey, 178
No Child Left Behind (NCLB) legislation, 150–1, 232n8, 241–242n46
Noguera, Pedro, 8, 151, 164, 172
numeracy programs, 129

Olsen, Randall, 12
Ontario, 121, 152, 166, 204, 210n34
On the Success of Failure (Alexander, Entwisle, and Dauber), 5
oppositional culture, 187, 242n49
Orfield, Gary, 4–5
Organisation of Economic Co-operation and Development (OECD), 153, 184
Other People's Children (Delpit), 170
outsourcing, 183, 188

Pacific Sociological Association, 201
Pathways to Education, 177–8, 239n18
Parent Advisory Councils, 20, 47, 91, 93, 96–7, 99–103, 106, 146, 198
Parent Coffee Club, 104–6, 224–5nn15–17
parental leave, paid, 179
parents: engagement, 74–5, 88, 90–7, 101, 103–6, 108, 111, 181, 223n3, 223n6; mobilization of, 45, 114, 115; positive descriptions of

school, 48–50; volunteers, 20, 56, 98, 102; support, 179
parks, 37, 39, 42
partnerships, with community institutions, 21, 49, 110–16, 180, 182–3, 223n2, 239n28
police: community, 39, 45; liaisons, 40; officers in school, 63, 194
policy reforms, 22
Portes, Alejandro, 187
poverty: family and lack of resources, 20, 58, 68–70, 72, 84, 90–2, 99, 104, 158, 172, 178, 181, 184, 196, 239n22, 240n35; neighbourhood, 13, 35–42, 46–7, 60, 62, 68–9, 72, 99, 114–15, 158, 162, 215n9, 226n18, 240n35; working, 28–9, 51, 84, 94, 96
Pratt, Geraldine, 87
pride, in schools, 49–51
professional development for teachers, 21–2, 54–5, 119, 123–4, 147, 175–6, 183, 232n28, 237–8nn12–13
property taxes, 4, 10, 176, 189
prostitution. See sex workers

Quebec, 179
Quiet Wisdom (Lofty), 163

racism, 38, 58
ranking schools, 17, 51
Rays of Hope, 131
Reading Powers program, 119
Read Well program, 131
Ready, Set, Learn program, 18, 111–12, 131, 148
Reagan, Ronald, 11
real estate trends, 26, 30–1
refugees, trauma, 26, 59, 63–4, 72, 168–9

Reich, Robert, 6
Regent Park, Toronto, 177
resiliency, 6, 61, 86
resource teachers, 18, 21, 32–3, 54–5, 65, 82, 118–19, 137, 145, 146, 174–5, 228n6, 229n12
Roots of Empathy, 18, 135–9, 231n19, 231n20
Rumbaut, Ruben, 187

Safe Arrivals program, 102
safety concerns, 37–8
Savage Inequalities (Kozol), 4
Schooling and the Struggle for Public Life (Giroux), 8
Schooling in a Capitalist Society (Bowles and Gintis), 183
school reform, 117, 160–1, 170–1, 174, 244n60, 245n16
segmented assimilation, 22, 187, 210n40, 242n48, 243n52
segregation, 11, 46, 178, 239–40n29, 241–2n46, 243–4n59
sex workers, 36–8, 41, 43, 45, 115, 215n9
Shame of the Nation, The (Kozol), 117, 150, 194
Sizer, Theodore R., 180
Small, Mario, 46
Smith, Dorothy, 9–10
social assistance, 28–9, 200
social capital, 8
social-emotional competence development, 18–19, 22, 80, 85, 131, 133–9, 173, 231n17
social housing, 16, 46–7, 62
social isolation, 13, 59, 68–9, 76, 88, 98–9
social networks, 43, 216n11

social reproduction, 8, 69, 183–5, 209n25, 241n41
Social Sciences and Humanities Research Council of Canada (SSHRC), 200
Sociology of Education, 152
South Bronx, 12
Special Education Assistants, 83
special needs, students with, 12–13, 20, 55, 60, 62–7, 77–8, 82–9, 120, 131, 142, 147, 151, 168, 172, 177, 179, 190, 217n1, 218n4, 220n14, 229n12
standardized testing: scores, 8, 17, 76–7, 118, 127, 128, 151–2, 154–60, 169–70, 181, 195, 207n2, 234n8; use of, 22, 51, 150, 152–3, 160–5, 170–1, 173, 175, 179, 181, 186, 188, 220n15, 233–4n4, 235n15, 235n21
Suárez-Oroco, Carola, 185
SUCCESS (United Chinese Community Enrichment Services Society), 45
Success for All, 175, 207n1
summer setback, 9
super-diversity, 14, 60
Support Service Assistants, 144
supplies, 146, 176
Szente, Judit, 63

teacher-student ratio, 147, 174
Texas, 12, 152–3, 161
Tinkering toward Utopia (Tyack and Cuban), 174
Toronto, Ontario, 177–8, 194, 239n19
tracking, 174, 183, 209n34
Trouble with Black Boys, The (Noguera) 164, 172

turnover, student population, 31, 44, 63, 71–2, 141, 168, 182, 219n11, 229n12
Tyack, David, 174

underfunding, 5
Unequal Childhoods (Lareau), 93
Ungerleider, Charles, 178–179
unionization decline, 183
United Kingdom, 11, 14, 163–4, 183, 188
United Nations Human Development Index, 184
United States, 4–14, 63, 93, 140, 150–1, 152–3, 161, 162, 163–4, 174, 178, 179, 183, 187, 188, 189, 194, 209nn18–19, 209n21, 212n65, 218n4, 233n30, 234n8, 236n4, 238n15, 239n21, 240n32, 240nn34–5, 240n40, 241n41, 241n46, 242n48, 242n49, 243n53, 243n57, 243–4n59, 244n8, 244n10, 245n17
urban disorder, 38, 114–15

Vancouver Art Gallery, 114
Vancouver School Board, 46, 141
Vancouver Sun, 152, 158
Vertovec, Steven, 14
Villa Victoria (Small), 46
violence, 38–9, 45, 58, 62, 67, 69, 73, 135, 188, 193–4
von Hippel, Paul T., 152

Warrington, Charlene, 200
Willis, Paul, 183
Work of Nations, The (Reich), 6

Youth and Family Worker, 84, 107, 120, 141, 147, 222n24, 232n23